1994

W9-CMP-122

THE POLITICS OF SOCIAL CLASS IN SECONDARY SCHOOL

Views of Affluent and Impoverished Youth

THE POLITICS OF SOCIAL CLASS
IN SECONDARY SCHOOL

Views of Affluent and Impoverished Youth

Ellen A. Brantlinger

Teachers College, Columbia University
New York and London

Acknowledgment of Previously Published Material:

Chapter 2: Adapted from Brantlinger, E. A. (in press). Adolescents' reactions to social class disparities in schooling. *Journal of Classroom Interaction*.

Chapter 3: Adapted from Brantlinger, E. A. (1991). Low-income adolescents' perceptions of social class related peer affiliations in schools. *Interchange, 22/23*, 9–27.

Chapters 4 and 5: Adapted by permission of Blackwell Publishers from Brantlinger, E. A. (1990). Low-income adolescents' perceptions of school, intelligence, and themselves as students. *Curriculum Inquiry, 20*, 305–324.

Chapter 6: Adapted from Brantlinger, E. A. (1991). Social class distinctions in adolescents' reports of problems and punishment in school. *Behavioral Disorders, 17*, 36–46.

Chapter 8: Adapted from Brantlinger, E. A. (1992). Unmentionable futures: Postschool planning for low-income teenagers. *The School Counselor, 39*, 281–291.

Published by Teachers College Press, 1234 Amsterdam Avenue,
New York, NY 10027

Library of Congress Cataloging-in-Publication Data

Brantlinger, Ellen A.
    The politics of social class in secondary school : views of
affluent and impoverished youth / Ellen A. Brantlinger.
        p.   cm.
    Includes bibliographical references (p.   ) and index.
    ISBN 0–8077–3270–2 (alk. paper). — ISBN 0–8077–3269–9 (alk. paper: pbk.)
    1. High school students—United States—Social conditions.
2. Social classes—United States. 3. Education, Secondary—Social
aspects—United States.   I. Title.
LC208.4.B73   1993
370.19'341'0973—dc20   93–10134

ISBN 0–8077–3270–2
ISBN 0–8077–3269–9 (pbk.)

Printed on acid-free paper
Manufactured in the United States of America

99 98 97 96 95 94 93   7 6 5 4 3 2 1

To family:

Rose Nott Anderson and the memory of Arnold Anderson

Patrick, Andrew, and Jeremy Brantlinger

Susan, Leroy, and Leroy, Jr., Robinson

Contents

Preface   xi

Acknowledgments   xv

1. Introduction: Social Class and Social Cognition   1

A Social Cognition Approach to Studying Social Class
    Influences on Schooling   2
Understanding Social Cognitions   4
Adolescents' Social Cognitions   5
Understanding Perspectives   9
The Context   12
The Design of the Comprehensive Study   13
Adolescent Interviews   15
Presentation of Results   21

2. Poverty and Segregation   23

The Community   23
The Nature of High- and Low-Income Schools   26
Attitudes Toward the Social Class Composition of Schools   29
School Composition Preferences   33
Perceptions of Wealth and Poverty   35
Social Class Self-Identification   37
Opinions About Social Mobility   38
Conclusion   39

**3. Social Sorting: Student Identifications and Affiliations
in School**   43

Group Classifications and Differentiation   45
Classes, Cliques, and Special-Interest Groups   52
Origin and Stability of Groups   53
Intergroup Perceptions   54
Group Relations   55
Social Class Self-Identification   59
Intragroup Divisions   62
Intergroup Mobility   63

Group Power 64
Conclusion 66

4. School, Tracking, and Teachers **69**

School 70
Stratified Classroom Arrangements 80
Teachers 91
Conclusion 101

5. Self as Student **109**

Strengths and Weaknesses as Students 110
The Impact of School 111
School Evaluation 114
Perceptions of Intelligence 117
Being Part of School 124
Conclusion 125

6. Trouble and Punishment **128**

The Nature and Extent of Trouble-Making 129
The Angry Image of Low-Income Youth 132
Attendance Problems 134
Interpretations of Conduct Problems 135
The Extent and Nature of Punishment 137
Parental Reaction to Trouble in School 141
Conclusion 144

7. Family and Friends **147**

Family 147
Friends 157
Conclusion 166

8. Futures **168**

Aspirations and Expectations for High School Completion 170
Aspirations and Expectations for College 175
Perceptions of the Requirements for College Attendance 176
Post-High School Plans 178
Opinions About Equal Opportunity 180
Personal Chances to Get Ahead 182
Adult Support for Postschool Plans 185
Conclusion 186

9. Problematizing Meritocracies **190**

Limitations of Study *190*
Summary *192*
Conclusion *199*

References **203**

Index **221**

About the Author **231**

Preface

Although I have long been interested in how social class influences the dynamics of intergroup perceptions and relationships, the immediate impetus for this study was a flourish of activities by high-income parents surrounding the closing of certain schools in my community. Before I describe that particular situation, it may be wise to start with a short autobiographical sketch, which may help to clarify the reference point from which I perceived it.

I grew up in the 1940s and 1950s in a small town in Minnesota, where I went to school in the same building with mostly the same classmates for 12 years. My graduating class had a bumper enrollment of 42, in contrast to my sister's class 4 years earlier, which had peaked at 17. Only a few of my classmates went on to college. Certain students never did very well in school and were sometimes retained, but classmates were thought of as peers and aside from some ability grouping for reading, we were rarely separated. Perhaps because the school was so small, most students were recruited for extracurricular activities. The most prestigious role for females was that of cheerleader, the selection criteria for which were beauty and petite size. Most of the cheerleaders in my class were from less affluent families. Participation in school activities, and to a lesser extent friendship patterns, cut across social class lines, and social class distinctions among my classmates were somewhat blurred.

I went to a college renowned for its deliberate structuring of community. There were no fraternities or sororities, and although one could test into advanced-level classes, there were no honors sections, nor was recognition given to the most competent scholars. A few years after I graduated, the college even did away with letter grades. Social concern, social responsibility, and cooperation were the major themes at the college; competition and materialism were definitely frowned upon.

After a few years of teaching secondary social studies and special education in the East while my husband was in graduate school, we moved back to the Midwest to the town where this study took place. I began graduate school and motherhood, bearing one and adopting two children. We bought a house in an older part of town, but in spite of the social class mixture in the area, we socialized mainly with university people. Through the years, I observed that many of our neighbors and friends were extremely forward in demanding privileged circumstances for their own children. They were selective about their children's playmates and schools. For the most part, these people had grown up in suburban areas, often on the East or West Coasts. They talked about the local people with suspicion and disdain, conveying that they were considerably different from themselves.

When my youngest child was in third grade, the small neighborhood elementary school closed. One plan suggested by the school board was to zone neighborhood children to one of two nearby low-income schools. At that point, the previously latent feelings about social class surfaced—affluent parents in the neighborhood vociferously opposed any suggestion of social class desegregation. These were the same people who, from ringside television seats, had been outraged by the negative reactions of whites to racial desegregation a few years earlier.

In my professional roles of teacher educator and field experience supervisor, I visited schools in the community as well as in nearby inner-city and rural areas. During these visits, I was continuously disheartened by the blatancy of social class inequities in schooling. In earlier years, as a teacher, I had noted that, aside from a minimum of literacy skills, certain students did not benefit much from schooling. In fact, the net worth of schooling—both in the short run and in terms of the overall circumstances of their lives— seemed negative. Poor students, in particular, left school with low self-esteem and without much hope for the future. The extreme discrepancies in the material circumstances of children's lives and the schism between people of different social classes bothered me.

Through daily exposure I was in on how my high-income neighbors felt about various policies and practices of local schools, but I had no idea about the perceptions and opinions of low-income people in the community. A compulsion to find out how people from the "other side of the tracks" felt about school circumstances resulted in a study of low-income adults (E. A. Brantlinger, 1985a, 1985b, 1985c, 1986, 1987), which led to a study of low- and, eventually, high-income adolescents. Having taught at the junior and senior high school levels, I had a keen interest in the adolescent age-span, with its burden of transcending childhood to face the responsibilities and possibilities of adult life. Adolescents were also selected as informants because I believed that they would be more likely to be articulate and knowledgeable about the topics of interest than younger children. Additionally, since the elementary schools in the community are typically homogeneous in social class makeup—that is, their enrollments are predominantly high- or low-income following neighborhood residential patterns—it was necessary to go to the secondary level to find students who had been exposed to those of another social class.

In reviewing the literature, I found substantial documentation of social class discrepancies in schooling and considerable conjecture about students' behaviors in subordinate situations, but little about their actual awareness of and reactions to second-class status. Similarly, I found a dearth of research about high-income students' perceptions of their advantaged position in school. I was intrigued at the absence of such information and was determined to find ways to study students' perceptions of the social class influences on schooling as well as to distinguish the views about school of members of different classes.

Acknowledgments

I must first acknowledge the 74 teenagers who trusted me with their thoughts and feelings. I hope that I have been true to them in writing this book.

Next I must recognize the contributions of three fine teachers, April Allen, Bee Miller, and Beth Naulty, who, while students in Indiana University's Teacher Education Program, worked with me on this project. Their sensitive and supportive listening assured that the study was immediately beneficial to adolescent participants.

My thanks always go to Samuel Guskin, my colleague, who as a true mentor encourages me in all my undertakings. Frank Wood of the University of Minnesota saw potential in my project. Russell Gerston of the University of Oregon, a reviewer, pointed out what was important and helped me strengthen my report. Brian Ellerbeck, Cathy McClure, Karl Nyberg, and Karen Osborne at Teachers College Press gave support and practical advice at various stages of my writing.

My husband, Patrick Brantlinger, stocked his shelves with Bourdieu and Bakhtin, leading me to read and relate their work to my own. Our discussions have been helpful to my thinking about social class. Our children, Andrew, Susan, and Jeremy, pulled me into their adolescent worlds literally and figuratively, allowing me to be a part of their coming-of-age. Rose Nott Anderson, my mother, was a teacher who found the best in all children. She and my late father, Arnold Anderson, taught me to be caring and open to new ideas.

THE POLITICS OF SOCIAL CLASS
IN SECONDARY SCHOOL

Views of Affluent and Impoverished Youth

CHAPTER 1

Introduction: Social Class and Social Cognition

American schools distribute rewards based on the merits of children; thus they have been called "meritocracies." Students who conform and achieve according to official standards thrive in meritocracies; they earn good grades, which allows them access to advantaged positions in school, and, ultimately, they get the credentials they need to advance to lucrative and prestigious positions in society. Meritocracies, however, create contests between their constituencies. For there to be winners (high achievers), there must also be losers (low achievers). Winners in American schools have been predominantly white and middle class. Losers are often poor and/or of color. Moreover, because of mandatory school-attendance policies, the losers are compelled to be part of the contest regardless of their chances of winning or the strains of losing. The liberal tradition idealistically presents schools as politically neutral, but schools can also be seen as biased and divisive—as having a dark side. Rather than being a common ground where all groups meet on an equal footing, American schooling, in reality, is essentially stratifying.

In assuming that schools are inherently political and that social class friction is ubiquitous, I take a critical (or conflict) theory stand. Like other educational theorists (e.g., Aronowitz, 1980; Carlson, 1987; Dale, Esland, & MacDonald, 1976; Fay, 1987; Giroux, 1992; Hall & Jefferson, 1976; Kumar, 1989; Lather, 1986; Ogbu, 1978; Shapiro, 1983; Zeichner, 1983), I believe that culture reflects a world ordered through structures that express power and struggle and that tension in class-based societies permeates all events and situations, as well as human thinking, in a variety of ways. And, rather than being exempt from class friction, relations in schools exemplify that friction. Although often accused of holding negative views—for example, by observing that powerful classes pressure schools to serve their own self-interests—conflict theorists are typically drawn to positive, perhaps utopian (democratic), visions of schools, and they critically examine the reality of each historical situation as a distortion of those visions (Ewert, 1991).

In their book *Schooling in Capitalist America*, Bowles and Gintis (1976) introduce "correspondence theory" (i.e., the idea that the structures of schools mimic the structures of society) to explain the social class reproductive function of schools; that is, how schools condition students for the stratified roles they assume as adults. Speculating about the modalities of its transmission, many (e.g., Anyon, 1980; Kohn, 1977; Ogbu, 1986; E. P. Thompson, 1978; Walker & Barton, 1983; Williams, 1982) concur that social class reproduction is a consensual process that involves both dominant and subordinate classes. Class distinctions cannot simply be imposed by dominant groups—subordinate classes must seem willingly to participate in distinguishing practices. This assertion leads to questions about how and why people tolerate, even endorse, practices that do not serve their own interests. I will address this question later in the chapter as I review theories about social cognitions. But, first, I will provide the rationale for my study.

A SOCIAL COGNITION APPROACH TO STUDYING
SOCIAL CLASS INFLUENCES ON SCHOOLING

There are several reasons that social class dynamics should be central to research on schools. In his book *Becoming Somebody*, Wexler (1992) states that he "was not prepared to discover how deeply the differences of class run in the lives of high school students" (p. 8). He chides educators for assuming family influences in socialization while ignoring social institutions, and he notes that textured studies of the psychodynamics of institutional life are underdeveloped. Similarly, Palonsky (1987) claims that little is known about students' understanding of such political aspects of their lives as power, justice, and fairness. In spite of the wealth of evidence of inequalities in schooling, we have not examined students' awareness of disparities, nor have suggestions for school reform and restructuring come from students. Educators call certain children "high risk," "disadvantaged," and "underprivileged," but virtually nothing is known about how students classify themselves. Finally, there is little empirical evidence distinguishing the views of affluent (dominant) and impoverished (subordinate) students.

There is also strong support for a social cognition approach to understanding school life. Such an approach directs attention to people's views of themselves and others in social settings. Humans are social beings, and their social relations are of great importance to them. Furthermore, they are aware and knowing as they actively think about their relations with others. Critical social science is, in fact, based on a belief in the power of human reason. As self-proclaimed critical theorist Fay (1987) maintains: "Through rational analysis and reflection people can come to an understanding of themselves and can re-order their collective existences on the basis of this understanding" (p. 143).

School ethnographers have traditionally observed students' behaviors. But the anthropologist Clifford Geertz (1973) suggests that people's epistemologies (i.e., cognitive models of social reality) be examined in order to connect action to its meaning rather than behavior to its determinants. For example, Payne (1989) cites the fact that individual high school students' behaviors vary from setting to setting and teacher to teacher as an indication that perceptions affect behaviors. Prominent educational researchers (e.g., Dodge, 1980; Good & Brophy, 1991; Gordon, 1981; Hartup, 1979; Rohrkemper, 1984) underscore the importance of a social cognition framework for understanding classroom life. Nevertheless, Hartup (1979) contends: "Our knowledge of children's understanding of classroom phenomena is shockingly incomplete" (p. 944).

Although Weinstein (1983) believes that students actively interpret classroom reality, she goes on to warn that their views are not always rational. On the contrary, Cooper and Good (1983) find that, at least in specific incidents simultaneously observed by researchers, teachers, and students, perceptions are quite similar. Perhaps because of a lingering suspicion about taking students' views at face value, even recent ethnography typically depends more on researchers' observations of actions than on subjects' interpretations of situations. At the same time, researchers have been reluctant to bring up controversial issues with juveniles, and hence they do not directly deal with topics such as social class disparities in schooling. Yet questions about sensitive issues are the most important ones to ask.

Since the cognitions of students about social class, student position, juvenile status, and so on are largely missing in the literature, my work was undertaken to explore the influences of social class on adolescents' thinking about school and society. My study took its shape in recognition of four interrelated beliefs:

1. The cognitive and affective underpinnings of students' actions are as important as their observable behaviors.
2. The social class standing of pupils has a pervasive influence on their schooling.
3. Students' perceptions of social class, as well as of members of different classes, affect the dynamics of schools and classrooms.
4. Unraveling the distinctions between the thinking of students from high- and low-income families is essential to understanding achievement outcomes.

Because of my conviction that school structure is of utmost importance in the socialization of future citizens in a democratic society, I take a close look at what happens in school from the perspectives of both dominant and subordinate participants in the system. By turning a critical eye to the social class influences on local schooling, I hope to enhance understanding of the system by educators, as well as by the general public, and to lay the groundwork for radical school reform. Educators committed to a democratic society must have their ideals clearly in mind and be cognizant of the policies and practices that run countergrain to them. Before I detail the methods used in my research, I will turn to theories about the nature of social cognitions and the effects of social class on cognitions and, particularly, to research directed at adolescents' cognitions. Then I will briefly review the studies of teachers' and parents' cognitions that are directly related to class distinctions in schooling.

UNDERSTANDING SOCIAL COGNITIONS

Recent theories focus on the links between context and cognition. Bourdieu (1977, 1984) maintains that human thought is a form of socialized knowledge conditioned in specific habitats; thus individuals' epistemologies reflect their cultural histories and social class origins. According to this theory, students do not go to school neutral—their views of school and of one another are filtered through the images, dispositions, and myths that accrue from such sources as families, peers, and the media.

Language plays a key role in cognition—learning a language is learning to think and believe like others in that culture (Bakhtin, 1984). Willis (1977) observes the preeminence of language in his study of adolescents and concludes that, just as geographical maps have legends that constitute their meaning, certain key words in students' vocabularies, such as their names for types of students, organize their cognitive maps of social relationships in school.

Self-cognition (i.e., identity formation) is central to social cognition and is frequently singled out as the foremost task of adolescence. Several writers address the connections between social class and self-definition. Wexler (1988, 1992) stresses the importance of cultural signs and social class symbols (e.g., styles, dialects) in what he calls the "self dynamics" (i.e., the construction of identity) of high school students. Aronowitz (1992) also situates the social processes of identity formation within class politics, even as he discusses displacements by race, gender, and sexual orientation. Although not specifically casting his study in a political mold, Nicholls (1989) alludes to power relations when he notes that children are likely to define their success in school in terms of superiority over others. Both Tajfel (1982) and Varenne (1986) contend that feelings of social class identity influence affiliation with groups and perceptions of group alignments in school.

Social cognitions come into being through socialization. Although a common social construct puts families in the position of being the prime, if not sole, socializer, schools—as well as peers within the context of school—play pivotal socializing roles in the lives of children. Children go to school with a knowledge of the social world, and, to some extent, the meanings they attach to events in school are molded to fit their "home" views (Alvarado & Ferguson, 1983; Bourdieu, 1977; Young, 1990).

But cognitions are never static. Once in school, students' cognitions are shaped through the social communication (i.e., discourse) in that setting (Foucault, 1980; J. B. Thompson, 1987). Messages about self and society are contained within the overt formal curriculum, but school rituals are also forms of discourse that transmit ideologies (Eckert, 1989; McLaren, 1986). For example, the ritual of tracking informs students of their comparative worth and of the stratified nature of society. Fay (1987) points to the transcendence of somatic learning that is embodied in structured time and space. Social interactions within the context of school, then, are important not only in developing views of school, but also in socializing more generalized conceptualizations of self and of the nature of the world.

ADOLESCENTS' SOCIAL COGNITIONS

Studies of students' social cognitions are embedded in ethnographic studies of school, but rarely have their thoughts and feelings been the focal point of research. Nevertheless, knowledge of the nature of adolescents' cognitions has gradually evolved as researchers hone in on increasingly finer details of both thought processes and school context.

School Rejection and Resistance

In his book *Learning to Labor*, Willis (1977) integrates theories of correspondence with analyses of the cultural and subjective levels of social relations in writing about working-class youths attending a comprehensive high school in Birmingham, England. Skeptical about their chances for upward mobility, his "lads" scorn the individual achievement ideology (i.e., basically the notion that people can get ahead if they work hard). Willis theorizes that the youths' school-rejecting behaviors (i.e., value inversions) ultimately relegated them to subservient positions in society, a status that could be blamed on their own counterschool actions.

Regarding West Indian youths in Canada, Solomon (1988) claims that "double talk" (e.g., bad becomes good) is a form of dominant value inversion and "doing steps" (i.e., walking in a way that school personnel see as lewd and disrespectful) is a form of resistance; that is, an oppositional stance to school authority. Similarly, in the United States, Apple and Beyer (1983) conclude that certain students actively reject school and legitimate their own right to control their time and space by, for instance, constant truancy. Livingstone (1983) suggests that when established ideologies are inconsistent with reality they become open to ideological reconstruction. Thus, if students find school situations to be problematic, there is the likelihood of resistance, such as delinquency (E. E. Cashmore, 1984; Ray & Mickelson, 1990) or dropping out of school (Fine, 1991; Fine & Rosenberg, 1983).

In a similar vein, Hodge and Kress (1988) detail how adolescent subcultures invert meanings to negate dominant ideology, language, and practice. McLaren (1986) calls youth subgroups' refusal, defiance, and contempt "symbolic rituals of resistance" (p. 80), and Baron (1989) writes that punks' stylistic "displays of masculinity" represent "symbolic violations of the social order that provoke censure from the dominant culture" (p. 208). Hebdige (1979) maintains that youths' rituals are attempts to purify contaminants through what he calls "ceremonial destructurings." Shimahara (1983) also notes the ceremonial and ritualistic nature of class relations in an urban high school, describing them as stereotyped and symbolic, making use of the "expressive domain of experience," which he defines as involving meaning and social function without explicit purpose or reason.

Within-Class Variations in Cognitions

Some of these studies portray the effects of social class as constant, direct, and uncomplicated; that is, they fail to address within-class variations among adolescents. MacLeod's (1987) work illustrates the importance of subgroup perspectives in adolescent cognitions. Like Willis, MacLeod observes a pattern of physical toughness, street wisdom, and inverted values among low-income males who live in a housing project in a northeastern city in the United States. But MacLeod finds differences in the outlooks of European-American and African-American youths. The former reject school as an arena in which they can achieve, while the latter espouse dominant values and have faith in the system in spite of their unsuccessful school careers. Jackson and Marsden (1986) acknowledge different kinds of reactions among their informants, stating that some are "puzzled and resentful" as they recall the shock of school incidents. But the "less assertive" among them passively suffer "permanent loss of confidence" (p. 269). Also addressing subgroup variations, Weis, Farrar, and Petrie (1989) distinguish several kinds of school-leavers (i.e., push-outs, the disaffected, educational mortalities, capable dropouts, stop-outs), all of whom have unique attitudes toward school.

Others have found race, ethnic origin, and gender to be salient in students' cognitions. Holland and Eisenhart (1988) propose what they call a "culturally constructed model of collective knowledge of the social world" (p. 269) in which gender is influential. Similarly, Weis (1988, 1990) looks at the influence of gender in the home and workplace, but she still recognizes the importance of social class in her conclusion that "gendered subjectivities take their shape and form historically in an economic context" (1990, p. 86). Grant and Sleeter (1988) situate their arguments within the camp of conflict theory, contending that social class friction is ubiquitously influential in class societies, but they feel that social tension results from gender, race, and achievement factors as well as social class. Based on his study of youths in Belfast, Ireland, Jenkins (1983) suggests an "ideological refraction" of potential social class solidarity or unity in perceptions due to such "prisms" as sexism, racism, and localism (p. 7).

These writers expand recognition of the complexities of social class analyses by illustrating how human thinking is subject to a variety of social influences and by documenting distinct subgroup reactions to similar circumstances. But even these within-class analyses may artificially polarize groups by pointing out their distinguishing rather than uniting features. It is easy to oversimplify the nature of the thought processes of individuals by ignoring the various levels of reactions and the fluctuations or inconsistencies in reactions within individuals. Willis, for example, describes his participants as being driven by a stance toward school authority and school-conforming youths that is purely and consistently oppositional.

Within-Subject Complexities in Cognitions

Theorists have recently begun to recognize within-subject complexities in cognition, claiming that just as cultural scenes are multilayered and dynamic, so is human thought. Alexander, Schallert, and Hare (1991) separate explicit knowledge, which is easily available to consciousness, from implicit knowledge (i.e., tacit, sociocultural knowledge). Explicit knowledge represents a small, explicated fragment of an individual's knowledge base, whereas implicit knowledge is a pervasive filter through which all experiences and understandings pass. Although implicit knowledge is deeply embedded in individual consciousness, it can surface and become part of conscious, studied thought at any time. According to Alexander and colleagues, knowledge is fluid and dynamic and interactivity between the forms of knowledge is constant.

Bakhtin (1984) describes the power of shared meanings in language and thought, but he also stresses that they are fundamentally "multivocal" and "heteroglossic" sites of conflict as well as agreement. Furnham and Gunter (1989) observe simultaneous idealism and pessimism in teenagers, while Fine and Zane (1989) find "split subjectivities" and "contradictory consciousness" (i.e., sharing dreams and values of affluent classes while resisting domination by such classes) and Lesko (1988) sees "internally conflicted" cognitions among youths in a Catholic high school. Mickelson (1990) distinguishes between two sets of attitudes toward school among students—the abstract, found in dominant ideology, and the concrete, reflecting more pessimistic empirical realities. Those who study high-income people conclude that democratic ideals are present simultaneously with self-interest in their approach to school and society (Bowers, 1987; Bullough, 1987; Livingstone, 1983; Mickelson, 1990; Olson, 1983; Packer, 1992; Sieber, 1982). So, too, in Gramsci's (1971) concept of hegemony, ideologies are portrayed as complex and evolving, with elements of conflict as well as conformity.

Distorted Knowledge and Critical Insight

Early correspondence theory framed values as rigidly set by social class. For example, Kohn (1977, 1983; Kohn & Schooler, 1983) examined the relationship between social stratification and value orientations and concluded that, whereas middle-class parents valued self-direction, working-class parents emphasized conformity to externally imposed rules. These unique values programmed students for stratified school roles. Although such theory was helpful in taking sociological analysis to the psychological level, its social determinism was subsequently shown to be oversimplified, perhaps based more on theory than on reality. Furthermore, it was elitist in implying that low-income people lacked astuteness in perceiving their world and was pessimistic in not offering the possibility of individual control of actions.

Breaking away from a value orientation, Ogbu (1981) looks at belief systems. Consistent with Gramsci's (1971) concept of hegemony, Ogbu explains how ideologies more suitable to dominant classes are also held to some extent by subordinate classes, and he shows how deeply ingrained beliefs in progress and social mobility facilitate the social class reproductive function of American schools. Ogbu argues that such myths as unbiased judgments of student merit (i.e., that school personnel are impartial and disregard students' social class status in evaluating them) result in unsuccessful youths taking the legitimacy of school practices and outcomes for granted. He does, however, credit such students with having a certain degree of insight into their circumstances. Hall and Jefferson (1976) use the term *embourgeoisement* (i.e., working-class people thinking of themselves as middle class) to explain why the struggle between classes became less clear-cut after World War II, due to such factors as widespread affluence and working-class identification with elites.

In contrast to the social determinism of early correspondence theory, recent critical theorists emphasize the importance of human agency by declaring that people are capable of demystifying oppressive circumstances (Fine, 1991; Giroux, 1992). In other words, people can engage in what McLaren (1989) calls "critical self-reflexivity." Habermas (1984) talks about distorted insights, or knowledge that is historically rooted and interest bound, but he also contends that individuals can become self-consciously aware of such knowledge distortions. Becoming "enlightened" is a necessary precondition for individual freedom and self-determination. "Emancipated" individuals take "freeing actions" to change the social system to realize their human potential (Ewert, 1991). And Lather (1992) asserts that the purpose of critical inquiry is to empower change in those whose lives are mediated by systems of inequity.

Giroux (1983) theorizes that, to varying degrees, students' cognitions penetrate myths about the social class neutrality of schooling; that is, they show some critical insight into the stratified character of school. In comparing youths in six communities, Schwartz (1987) observes a "continuum between unyielding resistance and compliant acquiescence to authority" as youths "work their way through the tensions in the environing cultures" (p. 16), concluding that class relations, and cognitions of class relations, are more fluid and ambiguous than suggested in either the radical or the conservative literature. Nevertheless, few researchers have devoted efforts to a detailed examination of students' thinking about the social class dynamics that occur in school settings.

A few ethnographers do allude to students' perceptions of the social class influences on schooling. Jenkins (1983) claims that people act in a context that they constantly interpret; thus he refers to an "individualist theme" in reactions to power relations (p. 40). But in his study of adolescents, Jenkins notes that their insight into circumstances "rarely goes so far as to challenge the wage relationship itself" (p. 8). Grant and Sleeter (1988) conclude that only 2 of their 24 low-income participants attempt to define institutional discrimination and many do not even admit to lower-class status, defining themselves instead as middle class. MacLeod (1987) maintains that class consciousness is evident in his youth but that it is not empowering because the teenagers are cynical and pessimistic about their status in society. Based on her study of the politics of urban public high school life, Fine (1991) concludes that students are aware of social class discrimination—in fact, many quit school because of it—but she asserts that "silencing phenomena" stifle students' voices.

UNDERSTANDING PERSPECTIVES

The design I employ might best be described as hermeneutic/interpretive (Young, 1990). It is hermeneutic in its effort to see things through adolescents' eyes and to examine their interpretations of events in school. But I also apply theoretical positions (e.g., about adolescents, social class, school-

ing) to the analysis of narratives. My approach acknowledges the recommendations of Florio-Ruane (1987):

> Go to the people, pay attention to what is said and done, plan your record-
> ing carefully, proceed inductively (look for local meaning), be alert to inter-
> pretation, find locally meaningful units of analysis, balance explanation with
> narration and verbatim examples, look for disconfirming evidence and dis-
> crepant cases, think about your informants. (p. 193)

In studying adolescents' social cognitions, I attempt to match the characteristics of certain students with their ways of thinking about themselves
and schooling; that is, with their perspectives. A group perspective is a synthesis of views constructed from the commonalities or repeating themes of
individual members. In reporting the results of my study, I will continually
identify and clarify coherent perspectives of high- and low-income respondents. But I will also include the idiosyncratic perspectives of individuals who
vary from the norm. In other words, the nonconformists, or exceptions, are
also important. In order to provide a context in which to better understand
adolescent perspectives, I will briefly review studies of teachers' and parents'
perspectives, particularly those that address social class influences on schooling.

Teachers' perceptions of students have been extensively explored, and
findings reveal that teachers expect inferior academic performance from students from low-income families and from students of color (Cooper & Good,
1983; Fuchs, 1973; Proctor, 1984; Rist, 1970; Rosenthal & Jacobson, 1968;
Seginer, 1983). They subsequently reduce their teaching efforts for such students (Eder, 1981; Oakes, 1985, 1988) and less actively engage them in the
teaching–learning process (e.g., Clark & Peterson, 1985; Good & Brophy, 1991;
Good, Slavings, Harel, & Emerson, 1987; Rist, 1978). Teachers have more
positive feelings about students perceived as brighter (Salvia & Munson, 1985)
and prefer teaching those in higher academic tracks (Goodlad, 1983; Oakes,
1985). Apparently, part of new teacher induction involves learning from
experienced teachers that the blame for the failure of low-income children
resides in the children or their families (Bullough, 1989; Fuchs, 1973).
Recent studies of teacher expectancies have been broadened to include more
comprehensive aspects of teachers' cognitions by making use of interviews,
teacher-written journals, ongoing conferences, and seminar-like sessions
between teachers and researchers (e.g., Fenstermacher, 1988; Goodman, 1988;
Kagan, 1990; McNamara, 1990; Morine-Dershimer, 1989; Rosenberg,
Harris, & Reifler, 1988; Tochon, 1990). Many of these studies report teachers' sincere efforts to break mental bonds in an attempt to meet the needs of
poor children and children of color.

There is no short supply of conjecture about parents' values related to schooling. In fact, because the correlation between social standing and school achievement is so well documented (e.g., Bastian, Fruchter, Gittell, Greer, & Haskins, 1986; Jencks, 1972), there have been a multitude of attempts to attribute school outcomes to differences in parents' values and aspirations (e.g., Harkness & Super, 1985; Hess, 1981; Kohn, 1983). A few studies widen the window of their explorations of parents' thinking about their children and school and document low-income parents' discontent about school conditions (Beckman, 1976; Lightfoot, 1981; Vernberg & Medway, 1981).

In my own interviews with low-income parents (E. A. Brantlinger, 1985a, 1985b, 1985c, 1986, 1987), I discovered strong feelings and well-formulated opinions about a number of school-related issues. Although asked to discuss their children's school experiences, these parents inevitably launched into lengthy and emotional accounts of their own school careers, detailing a profusion of humiliating and painful experiences. Even elderly parents recalled conversations and events that had happened many years earlier. It was clear that school had been a setting of great significance and that the parents carried the mental baggage of their own problematic school careers into parenting.

In evaluating the importance of school knowledge, achievement, and attainment, these low-income parents vacillated. On one level, they felt education was the vehicle for social mobility. But they were so discouraged by their own school experiences that they did not believe that positive school careers were likely for their children. They wanted their children to be successful, but they were not surprised when they failed. Moreover, although they valued literacy and the stamp of approval of the diploma, they were not convinced that school knowledge was relevant to other aspects of their present and future lives.

The low-income parents in my studies also wavered between attributing school failure to inadequacies in their children—ultimately to deficiencies in their own parenting—and to social class discrimination. Their narratives revealed the belief that children of "respectable" (i.e., affluent) people were inherently smarter than those of "ordinary" people. Because of asymmetrical relationships with school personnel, low-income parents felt little control over their children's educational fate. When they went to school about problems, they were not confident that there would be acceptable resolutions, so they went to "let off steam" or "take care of business" when they "couldn't stand it anymore." I conclude that parents' generally passive reaction to disparities in educational conditions and outcomes was the result of experiencing inequalities and powerlessness in all aspects of their lives.

Low-income parents described almost complete isolation from their wealthier counterparts. They were uncertain about the location of high-income schools even though most had lived in the community all their lives. Nevertheless, they were convinced that the learning conditions were better in schools in affluent neighborhoods and believed that there was a stigma attached to having attended low-income schools. Although they worried that their offspring would suffer rejection in schools with heterogeneous social class enrollments, they idealistically preferred such schools. They did not, however, want their children to be a small minority in schools with predominantly affluent enrollments.

In recent interviews with high-income parents, preliminary analyses of my results reveal that such parents view their children (i.e., children of their social class) as substantially brighter and more competent than children of the poor. In fact, the "other" is a conglomerate of all the attributes that are distasteful and that they do not want to see in their own children, such as lack of motivation, low intelligence, and emotional disturbance. Since they describe their own children as superior, for these parents it logically followed that they should be educated in separate settings; that is, in good (predominantly high-income) schools or in advanced tracks in schools of mixed social class. They described advocacy for their own children as part of the "good-parent" role, and so they did not apologize for expecting—and pushing for—advantaged circumstances.

THE CONTEXT

Now that I have provided the rationale and the theoretical groundwork, it is time to turn to the context, details, and data of my study. The study was conducted in a midwestern city that will hereafter be called Hillsdale. Hillsdale has a population of about 60,000 people, of whom roughly 95% are of European-American heritage and 4.02% are African-American (United States Bureau of Census, 1992). The town has a distinct social class split, with low-income residents located on the west side and high-income residents on the east side.

Besides residential isolation of the social classes, there is a virtual lack of interaction between high- and low-income townspeople in all dimensions of their lives: They attend separate churches and social events and even shop at different stores. Since Hillsdale is dominated by a large state university (with 30,000 students), town–gown frictions also influence interactions. In Hillsdale there are large discrepancies in income levels and educational attainment among local residents. Social class distinctions are very salient.

In Hillsdale, elementary schools are located in neighborhoods and are predominantly social class homogeneous, serving either poor or affluent constituencies. The two junior high schools (which will be called North Junior

High and Loring Junior High) and two high schools (North High and South High) are on the north and south sides of the city, and therefore their attendance zones cut across the east–west, high-income–low-income residential patterns (see Figure 1.1). Unlike the elementary schools, the junior highs and the high schools have mixed social class enrollments.

THE DESIGN OF THE COMPREHENSIVE STUDY

Although this book is comprised primarily of analyses of interviews with high- and low-income teenagers, the adolescent study is grounded in a larger study, a comprehensive examination of social class relationships in the community, for which a multilayered research design was used. Since I periodically refer to the results of the broader study, a brief overview of the methods used should provide a helpful background.

Extensive School-Based Observations

During the past 12 years, while in the role of field experience supervisor, I have made a minimum of 4,000 hours of direct observations in local schools and have engaged in an equivalent number of conferences with teachers, student teachers, and administrators.

Familiarity with School and Community Customs

I gained information partly as a by-product of being a resident in Hillsdale and the parent of three children—eventually adolescents—who attended local schools. I garnered knowledge incidentally by going to school board meetings, school open houses, and parent–teacher conferences. Because of my interest in the relationship between social class and schooling, I constantly entered into conversations on these topics and made note of the casual remarks I overheard. Employment trends, arrests, birth notices, and obituaries published in the local newspaper were all of interest to me.

In addition, I conducted formal fact-finding missions into school policies and practices. Probes entailed examining school records and questioning school personnel to study zoning patterns; material and equipment distribution; faculty and staff hiring, placement, transfer, and dismissal; achievement test results; provision of subsidized lunches; school fee collection; pupil–teacher ratios; and special program (e.g., foreign language, remedial reading, summer school, Chapter I, special education) attendance. At various times, I asked school personnel to recollect the history and rationale behind local policies and practices and to discuss their personal opinions about them. One

FIGURE 1.1. Map of Hillsdale

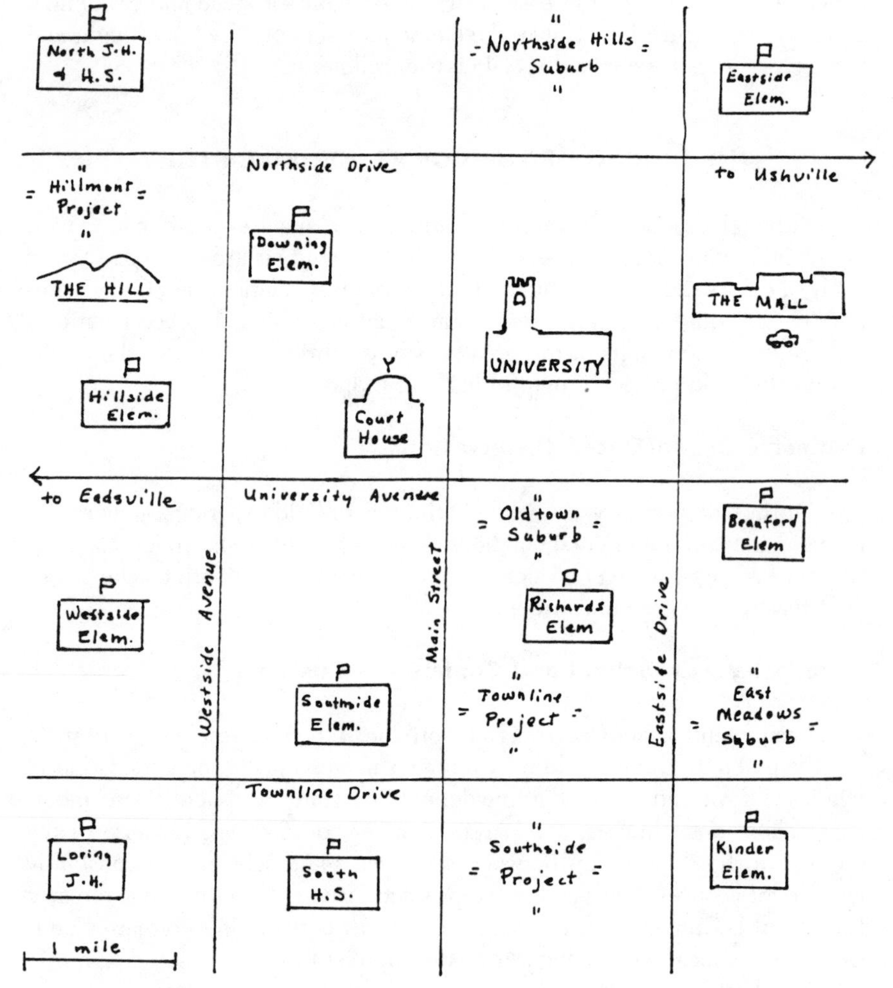

Project = where low-income participants live.
Suburb = where high-income participants live.

particularly revealing pursuit involved conversations with guidance counselors and principals responsible for tracking and special education referral in each of Hillsdale's schools. Another was studying the rationale behind the establishment of particular school boundaries. Such information resulted in my forming a very thorough mapping (and paper trail) of schools and community.

An Examination of Local Adults' Perceptions

Since perceptions, attitudes, opinions, and tastes of adolescents do not exist in a vacuum, another layer of investigation involved interviews with adults in the community. This part of the research project began with interviews of 35 low-income parents (E. A. Brantlinger, 1985a, 1985b, 1985c, 1986, 1987) and was subsequently extended to 20 high-income parents and 25 teachers and administrators in 1988–1992. Adult views were compared and contrasted with those of adolescents.

An Examination of Perceptions of Local Schools

Although I employed objective measures (e.g., the number of subsidized lunches, eligibility for Chapter I funds) to establish the social class nature of Hillsdale schools, the perceptions and attitudes of community members were also important. Hence I asked all participants in the adolescent, parent, and school personnel interviews about their familiarity with schools in the district, their judgment of the quality of these schools, their preferences for school attendance, and their estimate of the ratio of high- to low-income students in each school. That is, I asked them to categorize schools according to social class composition.

ADOLESCENT INTERVIEWS

The themes and information that emerged from the interviews with high- and low-income adolescents are the basis of most of the discussions in this book; therefore I will describe the nature of this part of the study in detail.

Participants

Low-income (l-i) adolescents (i.e., 13 to 18 years of age) were residents of three public housing projects (one older project is located on the north side of town in an area often referred to as "The Hill," and two newer ones are on the south side in the "Townline Drive" area) (see Figure 1.1). To be eligible for public housing, a local family of four must make less than $21,000 annually. The term *underclass* is used to describe a subset of those of lower socioeconomic status who come primarily from female-headed households, live in isolation from affluent families, and have few prospects for steady work (Kornblum, 1984; W. J. Wilson, 1987). This underclass contrasts with traditional working-class families who have tended to have secure jobs with modest incomes, stable family structures, and residential options. Although the term *underclass* sounds disparaging, it may aptly describe the conditions of most residents of public housing. An assumption underlying my selection of participants is that teenagers living in subsidized housing have been influenced by the conditions and stigma of poverty.

High-income (h-i) adolescents were also recruited from three neighborhoods, again one on the north side and two on the south side of town, so that approximately the same number of high- and low-income participants attended each of the four secondary schools in the school corporation. Based on a local realtors' guide, houses in these neighborhoods cost a minimum of $70,000 (and ranged from $70,000 to $275,000). The average house in Hillsdale sold for $60,000 in 1990. The dominance of the university in the city meant that a large portion of the parents of high-income adolescents had advanced degrees, thus coming from what Anyon (1980) has called an "affluent professional class." The sample included few "executive-elite" or "middle-class" individuals (white-collar workers with stable but relatively low salaries). Thus both high- and low-income adolescents were subsets of traditional social class groupings.

Identification Procedures. I attempted to avoid recruiting a skewed sample of adolescents, which often occurs when participants are found through clubs, agencies, or schools. The procedure used to identify participants might be called a "neighborhood census approach." Adolescents were located through (and interviewed in) their own neighborhoods. I felt that home-based interviews would be more productive in generating honest responses than school-based interviews based on the assumption that adolescents, particularly low-income adolescents, would feel more comfortable, and thus be more fluent and expansive, when interviewed on their own turf. The inescapable interaction between school personnel and researchers would inevitably link the two in adolescents' minds and likely inhibit truthful revelation of feelings. Moreover, school schedules would tend to impose time constraints, which would interfere with reflectivity.

Initial low-income participants were located by knocking on doors in subsidized housing. These adolescents were asked to name all other teenagers in the vicinity. Identified teenagers were contacted, interviewed, and in turn asked to provide names of other adolescent neighbors. In this way, all teenagers within a set geographical area were included. High-income participants were selected through the same residential census approach, although initial adolescents were individuals known to the researcher, and they were usually contacted by telephone.

The selection procedure resulted in a cross section of teenagers, including males and females, high and low achievers, blacks and whites, regular and special education students, and junior and senior high school students. By going through neighborhoods rather than schools, I included school dropouts and older (retained) adolescents who had not yet attended secondary schools. More than 75% of those identified were located and agreed to be interviewed. Of 49 low-income adolescents who were identified, 3 did not want to be interviewed and 6 were never at home (e.g., family moved, teen away for summer). Of the 41 high-income adolescents who were identified, 4 declined to participate and 3 were out of town for the summer.

Participant Characteristics. Forty low-income teenagers with a mean age of 15.3 and a mean grade-level completion of 9.1 were interviewed. Although it was assumed that students 13 or older would have attended secondary schools (i.e., seventh to twelfth grades), 2 low-income 14-year-olds had just completed sixth grade. Four informants had already quit school. There were 25 girls and 15 boys, 34 (85%) of whom were white and 6, black (15%). The 34 high-income teenagers had a mean age of 15.2 and a mean grade attainment of 9.8. The 19 girls and 15 boys included 1 Asian-American, 5 blacks (15%), and 28 white adolescents (85%). High- and low-income participants were about equally divided between the four secondary schools in the district.

Personal data collected from participants were consistent with those commonly used to determine socioeconomic status (Anyon, 1980; Havighurst, 1966). The educational attainment of the parents of high- and low-income adolescents varied dramatically. Because of the presence of the university, a large proportion of high-income parents had advanced degrees.

- Low-income mothers' education ranged from fourth grade to completion of a one-year postsecondary program. (mean = 9.7)
- Low-income fathers' educational attainment ranged from eighth grade to college graduation. (mean = 10.0)
- Six high-income mothers (18%) had doctorates, 10 (29%) had master's degrees, 13 (38%) had undergraduate degrees, and 5 (15%) had attended college without graduating. (mean = 4.8 years of college)
- Eighteen high-income fathers (53%) had doctorates, 5 (15%) had master's degrees, and 11 (32%) had undergraduate degrees. (mean = 6.7 years of college)

The occupations of respondents' parents corresponded to their educational attainment (see Table 1.1), with the exception of some high-income mothers whose occupational status was not commensurate with their academic credentials.

There were several differences in the family living arrangements of participants (see Table 1.2). A much higher percentage of low- than high-income adolescents were from single-parent homes. Furthermore, high-income adolescents whose parents were divorced had frequent contact with both parents, while many low-income adolescents had virtually no contact with the nonpresent parent.

In terms of residential and school-attendance stability, low-income adolescents generally had moved to different locations within the city or county (i.e., an average of 4.24 within-county moves in which a change of school was necessary). Nineteen high-income teenagers had not moved since they started school, eight had moved to different locations within the city, and seven had moved to the city from out of state (i.e., an average of 0.7 changes of residence and school). Low-income respondents mentioned numerous local

TABLE 1.1. Occupational Status of Participants' Parents

Low-Income	N	(%)	High-Income	N	(%)
Mothers					
Unemployed	17	(43)	Professional	17	(51)
Service	8	(20)	Business	7	(21)
Housewife	7	(18)	Housewife	5	(15)
Factory	4	(10)	Artist	2	(6)
Paraprofessional	3	(8)	Clerical	2	(6)
Vocational student	1	(3)	College student	1	(3)
Fathers					
Service	12	(30)	Professional	21	(62)
Factory	8	(20)	Business	12	(35)
Unknown	8	(20)	Artist	1	(3)
Unemployed	8	(20)			
Deceased	2	(5)			
Prison	2	(5)			

(Note: Due to rounding, percentage totals do not necessarily add to 100.)

TABLE 1.2. Family Living Arrangements of Participants

	Low-Income		High-Income	
	N	(%)	N	(%)
Parents married/living together	9*	(22)	24	(71)
Parents single/divorced	31	(78)	10	(29)
Frequent contact with other parent	2**	(6)	10**	(100)
Limited contact (once per year)	4**	(13)	-	
No contact with other parent	23**	(74)	-	
Unable to discern	2**	(6)	-	
Parent With Whom Participant Lives				
Mother	26**	(84)	7**	(70)
Grandmother	3**	(10)	-	
Father	2**	(6)	3**	(30)

*Includes stepparents when birth parent was not mentioned.
**Adolescents from single parent families only.
(Note: Due to rounding, percentage totals do not necessarily add to 100.)

extended-family members, whereas high-income respondents mainly referred to out-of-state relatives.

Selection of Questions

Reseachers have a tendency to ask questions that are mundanely common and require only mental association on the part of their subjects, thus trivializing human thinking. For example, the message that school influences social mobility is so predominant that it constitutes common sense. Based on the belief that individuals are able to use intellect critically to penetrate myths and make creative and insightful judgments about personal and social circumstances, I attempted to select and phrase questions so as not to trigger glib replies. In other words, in order to get reflective information, it was important to go beyond the level of questions likely to elicit automatic and routine responses.

I judged the interview methods developed by Glaser and Strauss (1965, 1967) to be a productive way to elicit accurate, unique, and deep information from adolescents. The questions were broadly phrased and open ended, requiring students to elaborate on their response. I considered it important to go beyond the initial responses by continually asking for clarification and explanation (e.g., "Why would somebody drop out of school?" "What reasons would you have for dropping out of school?" "Why have some of your classmates dropped out?" "How did you feel when they dropped out?"). Thus I added probes to get respondents to expand on ideas, conjecture about causation, and supply reasons for their replies. Additionally, instead of confining the interviews to conventional sets of questions, I asked adolescents to picture themselves in school, describe their images, evaluate their feelings in the scenes imagined, and discuss the reasons behind their actions.

Interview Procedures

On the grounds of potential to establish rapport with high- and low-income adolescents as well as general efficiency, three seniors in a teacher-preparation program were selected as research assistants. One was a returning student in her middle 40s and the other two were of typical undergraduate age but were from less affluent families than many of their cohorts. In return for three credits of education elective, the research assistants read and discussed selected articles and helped with the interviews. Their training involved a thorough introduction to the questions and probes, interview simulations with each other and the researcher, and pilot interviews with teenagers.

Interviews were conducted in the homes of respondents during the summer. Generally one of the research assistants went to the site with me and, after contacting willing participants, we split up to conduct the interviews separately. Potential participants were told that the researchers were future teachers (in the case of the research assistants) or a teacher educator (in my case) interested in what teenagers thought about school. If they agreed to be interviewed, they signed a consent form for audiotaping and for quoting them in publications. With the exception of a few with common names, respondents were assigned the pseudonyms that appear with direct quotations in this book.

Debriefing sessions were held immediately after the interviews, and notes were taken about the adolescents' response to the interview process as well as any observations that the interviewer felt pertinent to interpreting the response. I conducted approximately one-half (i.e., 22) of the interviews with low-income adolescents and one-third (i.e., 10) of those with high-income adolescents. The research assistants were not involved in transcribing the interviews or in analyzing the data, although they clarified meanings when necessary and verified the accuracy of transcripts.

Data Analysis

The interviews were audiotaped and transcribed. Whenever possible, quantitative results were derived from the data; that is, discrete categories were established and responses tallied. These figures are presented in tables or accompany the qualitative information, often in parentheses. Qualitative analyses involved perusing the narratives in search of recurrent themes or response patterns. Emergent themes in respondents' narratives were thematically coded and categorized and pertinent quotes—both representative and idiosyncratic—were identified. According to Erickson (1986), an inductive analysis of data from qualitative studies involves generating empirical asser- tions and searching for evidentiary warrant for those assertions by systemati- cally examining disconfirming as well as confirming data. So the next step was to interpret the results by looking for comparisons with the results of other studies and by hypothesizing about local meanings. Qualitative results are presented as summaries of responses and are illustrated by direct quotes rep- resenting majority, minority, and individual views.

In addition to focusing on what was directly said (face value, explicit meaning), my analyses involve examining messages embedded in the narra- tives in search of recurrent themes and meanings. I delve below the surface looking for subtle meanings and inferences. Thus I have scrutinized a num- ber of different aspects of responses, including emotionality, intensity, and tone (e.g., defensive, embarrassed, apologetic); use of significant terminology (e.g., "grits," "brains," "know-nothings," "piece of trash"); indications of iden- tification and affiliation (e.g., "They call us grits") as well as disidentification and disaffiliation (e.g., "The preppies, they . . ."); evidence of cognitive asso- ciations or underlying assumptions (e.g., viewing teachers as middle class, assuming connections between level of intelligence and social class); prob- able sources of response (e.g., dominant-culture messages, idiosyncratic views, perspectives associated with social class); response patterns (e.g., interactive effects of questions, generally flat or depressed responses); and reactions to the interview process (e.g., revealers/withholders, animated/passive).

PRESENTATION OF RESULTS

In organizing the report of results, I conform to very standard compo- nents of school, such as teachers, tracks, discipline, and parent participation. To set the stage for an understanding of students' social cognitions, Chap- ter 2 is an immersion into the social class dynamics of Hillsdale. It clarifies the forces of discrimination and segregation. Chapter 3 focuses on teenagers' informal clusterings—how adolescents from both social classes view themselves and each other—and their names for various groups. Chapter 4 covers adolescents' response to the formal organization of school, their views of the attributes of school personnel, and their reactions to the administrative arrangements designed to deal with pupil diversity. Chapter 5 examines adolescents' perceptions of themselves as students and their feelings about intelligence, particularly as it relates to schooling. Adolescents' views of trouble and its consequences are detailed in Chapter 6. Chapter 7 moves out of school to look at adolescents' relationships with family and friends. Teenagers' views of their own and other people's futures are dealt with in Chapter 8. Finally, Chapter 9 concludes the book by relating the most important findings to critical theory and by offering recommendations to educators.

CHAPTER 2

Poverty and Segregation

On a national level, an increasing segregation and isolation of social classes (i.e., bifurcation) has been documented, with poor and affluent people being less and less likely to have contact in community life (Levine & Havighurst, 1988; W. J. Wilson, 1987). Poverty is highly visible in large cities, but it is not confined to urban areas, as Schmuck and Schmuck (1990) conclude:

> The increasing poverty of small-town America not only influences the norms of life in small towns, it changes the character of students served by public schools. Most teachers and principals noted the rising population of emotionally and intellectually needy children served by today's school. (p. 17)

Social class interaction patterns in Hillsdale are similar to those described in the literature; that is, bifurcation is clearly in evidence. At the beginning of this chapter, I summarize my own observations of the influences of social class on social interaction patterns in Hillsdale. My views of schools and classrooms were formed during many years of supervising student teachers and practicum students. I also integrate the knowledge of the community that I gained as a long-term local resident. I provide a brief history of how school boundaries were established and describe the origin and extent of inequities among schools in various parts of town. I then move on to focus on adolescents' awareness of social class and their descriptions of their own social class affiliations. This includes their perceptions of the social class composition of various schools in Hillsdale and their judgments about the quality of these schools. Chapter 2 also includes adolescents' perceptions of wealth and poverty, their opinions about social mobility, and their preferences regarding the social class composition of schools they attend.

THE COMMUNITY

As in many other downtowns in the Midwest, tree-bordered streets are blocked in a square around a stately, domed, limestone courthouse. Dominated by the large state university, Hillsdale is a cultural and mercantile center; hence the Victorian buildings are not boarded up and decayed, as they are many other places, but are renovated and bursting with goods that appeal to college students and weekend visitors. Heading west from the town center, one arrives at the fringes of The Hill, where workers at the west-side factories and stone quarries live. Much of the nearby Hill with larger houses has been gentrified, but on a few streets farther west small cottages line the streets leading to the top of the hill, where Hillmont (government-subsidized housing) sprawls in its treeless, grassless surroundings. Because of industrial decline, many working-class homes are in disrepair and more projects have been added on the far west and south sides of town. The university takes over east of the square, with rows of dormitories, fraternities and sororities, and lecture halls. Then comes the mall, with expensive shops fringed by mammoth discount stores. Radiating from the university and the mall are the various suburbs, the vintage of which can be discerned by the comparative size of the trees and houses. In the newest suburbs, the trees are small but the houses are larger than in established neighborhoods.

Since elementary schools draw from their surrounding areas, they correspond to the social class nature of neighborhoods; thus four are primarily high-income (i.e., Beauford, Kinder, Richards, and Eastside), four are predominantly low-income (i.e., Hillview, Westside, Downing, and Southside), and the remaining four have either mixed or rural enrollments. Located on the north and south sides of town, the junior high schools (i.e., North Junior High and Loring Junior High) and the high schools (i.e., North High and South High) cut across the east–west residential patterns and have heterogeneous social class enrollments.

A survey of 94 adolescent and adult residents in the community revealed that high- and low-income people had very similar perceptions of the social class status of the various schools. There was a consensus that Downing, Hillview, Southside, and Westside were low-income schools and that Beauford, Eastside, Kinder, and Richards were high-income schools. Moreover, high-income schools were universally judged to be superior and low-income schools, "inferior," "second rate," or "bad." Jencks (1972) has observed that people define a good school not as one with superior facilities but as one with the "right" kind of students. Similarly, the quality of the local schools was seen to depend on their social class exclusiveness; but respondents also noted differences in the buildings, facilities, settings, locations, teachers, principals, curricula, and character—responses that revealed an awareness of the material and aesthetic differences in schools as well as the difference in clientele.

Local school segregation echoes neighborhood segregation; hence it might be argued that it is de facto segregation (i.e., unintentional segregation that results from circumstances). But there is also evidence of de jure (i.e., intentional or purposeful) segregation in school enrollments. Boundaries meander to conform to social class residential lines. Pockets of high-income students within low-income school areas are bused to high-income schools. School transfers are liberally granted to children of influential patrons. Thus school segregation by social class is not solely the outcome of recognizing neighborhood school concepts.

Administrators admit that boundaries were often intentionally drawn to create student bodies of homogeneous social class, but they claim that this is an artifact of attempts to meet the social class ratio criteria earlier required for obtaining Title I (i.e., Chapter I, Elementary and Secondary Education Act) funds. Initially, Title I provided funds to schools with concentrations of poor children; therefore it was financially advantageous to districts to preserve the social class exclusiveness of schools. Later, Chapter I policies changed to acknowledge the number of low-income children in the school system regardless of particular school ratios (Vaneck & Ames, 1980), but, supposedly, by this time the segregated zones were well established. An equally plausible explanation—guardedly admitted by a few administers—is that through the years influential parents were vociferously determined to have their children attend schools with predominantly affluent populations.

In the report of a local study (Hutson, 1978), a school board member was quoted as having said: "Only the educated vote in school board elections and the school board members know that. So the board plays to its supporters. The average board member's view is that the way to get along is to go along. . . . Decisions are often made to avoid no-win situations and maintain favorable public relations" (pp. 60, 62). Consistent with this position, a former superintendent wrote: "I believe that many parents in this community would be extremely unhappy if decisions made by the school board on school district boundaries required cross-busing as in the case of racial desegregation" (personal communication, September 28, 1984). To avoid contention and resentment, then, school administrators and board members have anticipated their powerful constituents' preferences and, at least at the elementary level, have zoned for social class homogeneity.

The charge of pressure by wealthy families is substantiated by a 1983 school closing. When board members suggested that children in the area be sent to Southside Elementary (low-income school), high-income parents demanded that there be a choice between Southside and Richards (high-income school). Although most lived closer to Southside and there was a safer walk to that school, most families chose for their children (i.e., 124 out of 130 children) to attend Richards. In spite of the intentions of the few parents who were committed to the idea of neighborhood schools regardless of their social class character, after a year only two of the six high-income children remained at Southside and at the end of 2 years none remained. Similarly, in 1984, when a high-income middle school was threatened with closure, a petition signed by 503 parents (virtually the entire school enrollment) was presented to the board requesting that their children not attend Downing (a low-income ele-

15/177

mentary school at the time of the study, but previously a middle school). Few of these parents had any acquaintance with children at Southside or Downing. It is likely that the general suspicion that Downing children were somehow different from their children influenced the active opposition to any mixing. Zoning to Downing or Southside would have resulted in schools of mixed social class with a majority of high-income patrons. It can only be conjectured whether these parents were insufficiently farsighted to envision integrated schools or if, in fact, they really wanted class-pure schools.

A 1983 decision to close four middle schools (i.e., made up of sixth, seventh, and eighth grades) and open two larger junior high schools (i.e., made up of seventh and eighth grades) resulted in secondary schools on the north and south sides of town with fairly balanced social class enrollments. Although social class desegregation was certainly not the specific intent of that decision, feelings connected with social class were likely to have precipitated it. As the district enrollment declined, the administration was compelled, for financial reasons, to close schools. Debates about which schools to close became very heated. High-income parents panicked at the threat of having their children zoned to low-income schools. A last-minute proposal made to the beleaguered administrators and trustees suggested that four middle schools be closed, zoning all seventh and eighth graders to Loring (a large new school located in a rural setting 4 miles southwest of the center of town) or to the underutilized new high school on the north side of town. One advantage of this proposal was that these schools were new enough and mixed enough in enrollment not to have the same stigma as that attached to other low-income schools, such as Downing. Another advantage was that by going to a junior high arrangement, sixth graders would fill the empty spaces in numerous elementary schools so that more of them could remain open. The proposal was one of many being considered, and at the time it seemed so preposterous that most people paid little attention to it. The vote was over before the protest could start. People grumbled, but the decision had been made. So, since 1984, students have attended large junior high schools and high schools with social class heterogeneous enrollments. In 1990, because of the increasing school-age population, the North Junior High student body was moved to the previous Downing building. There were few protests to this move, even though the building was located in the center of The Hill (i.e., low-income) area.

THE NATURE OF HIGH- AND LOW-INCOME SCHOOLS

Nationally, interdistrict disparities in funding are well documented. The tradition of using property taxes to finance schools has meant that high-income districts have considerably higher per-pupil expenditures. But social class inequities in resources exist among districts, among schools within districts, and among students within schools (Anyon, 1980; Goodlad & Oakes, 1988; Lightfoot, 1987). An abundance of information has been collected about disparities in school resources for children from different socioeconomic backgrounds (e.g., Bastian et al., 1986; Sexton, 1961). Jencks (1972) estimated that the per capita expenditure ratio for the most and least favored students was at least four-to-one. Moreover, recent reports indicate that school conditions have become increasingly disparate for members of different social classes: improving for high-income students and worsening for their low-income counterparts (Bastian et al., 1986; Newmann & Kelly, 1985).

Within-district expenditures are supposed to be the same; nevertheless, in Hillsdale, high-income schools are new, spacious, and well situated, whereas Westside, Southside, and Hillview are housed in old buildings to which new additions have periodically been haphazardly added. They are not aesthetically pleasing on the inside, outside, or in setting. Their playgrounds are small, often located close to parking lots, and are usually not well equipped. The classrooms are not carpeted or air-conditioned. Teachers' rooms are small and shabby; in fact, Hillview's teachers' room is adjacent to the boiler room in the basement of the school. Libraries have fewer books than those in high-income schools.

The resource disparities can be attributed to a number of factors. First, local schools collect fees from students for their books and supplies. In the past, individual schools were entitled to spend only what was collected from students. Low-income schools inevitably collected less money; therefore libraries and classrooms had fewer books and less equipment. Although in 1985 this material distribution policy was changed to a districtwide fee collection and fund distribution model, the smaller schools (i.e., the low-income schools) still received a smaller portion of the money available because the funding was done on a per capita basis. Even though this policy tends to be equitable in terms of the nonreusable supplies, durable materials remain unequal. For example, since libraries receive fewer books on an annual basis, their stocks become increasingly more disparate. Moreover, because of the history of unequal funding, in 1985 low-income schools started with proportionately fewer books, items of media equipment, and other supplies.

Second, school-based parent–teacher organizations (PTOS) are allowed to raise funds and give gifts to schools. As a result, high-income schools have such extras as stimulating playground equipment, prints and pictures in the halls, computers, auditorium features, art and music equipment, and media materials that come as gifts from their more affluent PTOS. Similarly, high-income schools have more parent volunteers for library or classroom aides. A pool of educated parents at high-income schools often come in to give special lectures or arrange field trips. There is no official foreign-language program prior to high school, but parents organize and sponsor classes for before- and after-school hours. Such programs have frequently been offered in high-income schools. A children's theater run by high-income parents is housed in a high-income school, thus very accessible to the local high-income clientele. A compelling argument for schools integrated by social class is the need to equitably distribute the enrichment available because of the expertise and affluence of more educated parents.

In addition to the allocation of material resources, there has been a history of inequitable human resource distribution. The central administration consistently assigned the most professional principals to high-income schools, while the unpopular ones with seniority end up at low-income schools. Staffing practices also push the most competent teachers to high-income schools. Both principals and teachers rank their choices (i.e., principals for teachers, teachers for schools), and the central administration matches them. Even if they do not prefer middle-class students, teachers sway toward the better facilities and more competent colleagues. Unequal staffing patterns are self-perpetuating: Schools that are initially of higher quality become the first choice of teachers in subsequent rounds of teacher distribution.

The teacher-transfer policy further adds to school disparities. If a teacher's performance is inadequate, principals have three choices: keep the teacher and try to remedy problems, dismiss the teacher, or give the teacher an involuntary transfer. Principals dislike the first two alternatives, so the third is frequently selected. Involuntary transfers go to schools with openings— hence less competent teachers often end up at low-income schools. Granted, excellent teachers often prefer low-income schools and intentionally select them; nevertheless, local staffing practices have tended to result in qualitative differences in school faculties.

Another inequality occurs as a result of the fact that three of the four low-income schools happen to be small. Larger schools have full-time music, art, and physical education teachers as well as librarians and nurses. Smaller schools have part-time ancillary staff who work on an itinerant basis, traveling from school to school. On paper, the student–teacher ratios seem equivalent, but a half-time librarian means that the library only stays open half of the day. Because of overcrowded conditions in the low-income schools, these teachers may conduct their classes in gyms, on stages, or in other teachers' classrooms. This limits the supplies used and the wall-display possibilities.

In some cases, principals of small schools are considered only half-time principals and may end up teaching or working in the library for the balance of the time. Yet the size of the school is not always an accurate gauge of principal workload. More special education classrooms have been located in low-income schools, and they entail extra effort in case conferencing, coordinating faculty, and often in student discipline or support. Furthermore, principals are responsible for collecting fees and taking the parents who do not pay the fees to court, as well as for collecting information to determine eligibility for subsidized lunch or breakfast. Such extra obligations are typical of principals' jobs in low-income schools. Additionally, for reasons stated earlier, principals must often work with problematic staff or figure out unsolvable space and scheduling problems. Subsequently, because of these conditions, principals often request high-income schools.

Over a number of years, schools with the largest numbers of low-income children usually had the highest student–teacher ratios in the system. The most plausible explanation for this discrepancy, again, was that central administrators catered to powerful patrons. High-income parents were likely to demand that a detrimental situation be altered, whereas they could get away with high enrollments at schools where parents tended not to expect ideal conditions or to confront school authorities.

The three public housing complexes where the low-income participants lived were in the catchment areas of Hillview or Southside. High-income respondents had attended Richards, Beauford, Kinder, and Eastside. Prior to the closing of four middle schools, students from Hillview had attended Downing, which at that time was a low-income middle school, and those from Southside went to Loring (a mixed outlying middle school) or Beauford, which was then a middle school with about 90% high-income enrollment. When Beauford and Downing became elementary schools, middle school students were redistricted to either Loring or North Junior High. Loring students eventually attend South High, and North Junior High students attend North High. Thus adolescents in this study had mainly attended social class homogeneous elementary schools and the older respondents had also attended the now-defunct social class homogeneous middle schools.

ATTITUDES TOWARD THE SOCIAL CLASS COMPOSITION OF SCHOOLS

Adolescents addressed a number of topics related to the nature of the student body and the quality of schools. They all showed considerable interest in the social class divisions in the schools and community; however, low-income respondents displayed stronger feelings and offered more detailed information about class differences—their responses were clearly embedded in a richer background of thought about social class. High-income respondents discussed social class issues in either an offhand manner, which conveyed that they felt they were not greatly influenced by the social class divisions in town, or a constricted manner, which communicated that they would rather not talk about them. Their responses reflected a politically correct etiquette of talking about social class; they deliberated in choosing the right words to say the right things. It is suspected that if they spoke with more candor, they would have revealed more disparaging attitudes toward their low-income counterparts.

Affluent adolescents claimed to have little contact with low-income schools or students. They could name some schools in poor neighborhoods but were unsure of precise locations and rarely knew students who had attended them. In contrast, all were able to name, locate, and reel off names of students who had attended other high-income elementary schools. Low-income respondents demonstrated the same social class isolation, being only vaguely familiar with high-income schools and students. There were gender differences in response: Some boys had become acquainted with boys of the opposite income level through Junior League baseball and, to a lesser extent, through Boys Club sports (basketball and soccer), although the Boys Club tended to form teams according to neighborhoods or schools and, hence, social class. Only a few of the girls had participated in such citywide programs.

High-income adolescents were somewhat evasive in even acknowledging that the schools in town did have an identifiable social class character (e.g., "I don't know—Kinder has the ordinary cross-section of kids as far as I know; it may be that Hillview has more disadvantaged kids, but I'm not sure; I'd say the schools are pretty much the same—but I'm not too sure"). They did, however, consistently judge high-income schools to be "good schools" and low-income schools to be of poor quality, citing both low academic standards and problems with discipline and drugs. Most focused on the nature of the student enrollment, not conditions at the schools or the quality of the professional staff. Although they did not always like the high-income schools—many had particularly disliked Beauford—they felt they were superior to other schools in Hillsdale and they were confident that others would judge their schools to be the best ones.

Low-income respondents indicated that elementary school attendance signified social class status (e.g., "That's where the hotshot kids go"; "It's mainly rich kids over there"; "The students are different at the different schools; some have rich kids; some have poor ones; Kinder and Beauford have rich kids"; "Most of the preppies at Loring went to Kinder before"). They appraised high-income schools as being of higher quality, some equating school quality with the social class affiliations of student clientele. Leejohn judged: "People I know from other schools know more than I do. This area is tacky. The schools are tacky. North Junior High has more high-class people." Louann, who had been to three low-income elementary schools and both Downing and Beauford for middle school, asserted: "People don't like Hillview or Downing. They're crazy if they like them. A bunch of low-class jerks go there." Most believed that high-income schools had more competent teachers, more varied and inter-esting programs, and nicer buildings (e.g., "Beauford is pretty fancy, pretty posh"; "I heard the teachers are nicer and more interesting at Kinder than at Southside—I'm not sure that's true, but that's what everybody says"). Tracy, who had gone to Downing (low-income middle school) for 1 year before going to North Junior High, contrasted: "North Junior High is better than Down-ing. The teachers are nicer. You do more things—more fun things."

Four low-income adolescents had attended high-income elementary schools for part of their school careers. Madalene confessed: "I would have liked to have stayed at Eastside. It seemed like teachers took more time to explain. They cared more that I caught on." Will recalled:

> At Eastside I had better friends. The people were nicer. I learned more there. Teachers were better. I was not happy about the move [i.e., to the Hillview area after his father deserted the family and his mother became eligible for subsidized housing]. Some schools seem better— they have a hell of a lot more money. Before I went to Hillview and Downing, people said there was gritty people there. I had second thoughts. Hillview was a bad school. Outsiders don't like it either. They think that Downing and Hillview are bad schools. They're prejudiced against Downing and students from Downing.

Thomas maintained: "Eastside is more open. You do more there. There are more different kinds of kids. Southside and Westside were more crowded." In contrast, four other low-income adolescents expressed nostalgic sentiments about their low-income neighborhood elementary schools. Stacy said: "I loved Hillview. There were too many preps at North Junior High." Tricia said: "I liked Hillview. The teachers understood. They know how you feel."

When asked about outsiders' evaluations of Hillview and Southside, 10 low-income teenagers refused to respond, stating either that they did not know students from other schools or that they did not know how others felt about their schools. Some of these noncommittal adolescents appeared to be genu-inely puzzled about how others felt. A tentative Max said: "People around The Hill like it. I don't know about other people. I suppose not." But most had a defensive tone to their replies. With a knowing smile, Teresa responded: "I couldn't tell you that."

Twenty-three low-income respondents (57.5%) stated that outsiders would consider their schools to be inferior, that there was a stigma attached to hav-ing attended low-income schools, and that there were status benefits from having gone to high-income schools. According to Tammy: "I heard that a lot of people talk about Hillview. They don't like it because of the people who went there." Wendy said: "Others look down on it because they know The Hill kids go there." Kit hypothesized: "A lot of people didn't like Hillview. Some teachers, the snobs, don't like it either. There is prejudice about where it's located." May simply said: "I don't think other kids think it's a good school." Stacy believed: "Grown-ups don't like it 'cause of where it's at." Beth felt: "Other students think their school is better." Rachel guessed: "They probably didn't think Southside was too good. They thought their school was better."

Two low-income respondents felt that the negative feelings against their schools were misguided. According to Dusty: "If they would have seen how it was they would have liked it. It's not what a lot of people think." Sonia concurred: "I believe Hillview was equal to other schools. Others kind of thought it was a low-class or middle-class school because they lived in a higher-class place. If they visited they could just explore and see our standards and how we were taught and everything." In contrast, Bret first said: "I don't know people from those [i.e., high-income] schools." Then he added: "I don't know, I expect they feel the same way I did. I hated Southside." He concluded: "I hope they don't go to Southside. I wouldn't have wanted them preps there."

The four low-income teenagers who had gone to high-income schools, as well as four others who had attended rural schools, had been directly exposed to outsiders' disparaging attitudes toward The Hill and schools on The Hill (i.e., Hillview and Downing). They also felt that rural schools were not held in high regard. According to Annie: "People look down on Eadsville [rural school 6 miles east of Hillsdale]. They call it a hick school." Will described a pecking order, maintaining that there was a bias against the Hill students but that students from rural schools "got the most flack."

Not only were students isolated in schools of homogeneous social class for their elementary years, but even at the secondary level, where a heterogeneous student body was physically present, few students described significant interaction with students who had attended an elementary school of the opposite income level. Participants said their friends were from their neighborhoods or their elementary schools; however, they did mix with others from elementary schools of similar income levels whom they had not known previously. Contact, then, was not limited to others from their neighborhood schools, but it was restricted to those of their same income level. High-income adolescents admitted to conscientiously avoiding sections of the schools or school grounds where the "grits hung out." Hence, social class isolation existed regardless of whether the students attended schools of homogeneous or heterogeneous social class makeup. Perhaps if they had attended integrated schools during their elementary years, there might have been more social interaction at the secondary level.

SCHOOL COMPOSITION PREFERENCES

Adolescents discussed their preferences for the social class composition of school enrollments. On an abstract level, the majority of low-income adolescents (32, 80%) were in favor of desegregated schools, giving idealistic reasons for their positions. Sonia said: "Kids should all be mixed. There is nothing different about them except for color and religion. Everyone is really the same." Nadia summarized: "Mix races, poor and rich. It doesn't matter." Tammy concluded: "Mixed schools are better for everybody all around."

The eight low-income teenagers who were opposed to either racial or social class desegregation (one was opposed to both) usually offered an incident or set of experiences that influenced their preference. Dean was in favor of social class segregation, noting: "Most blacks didn't give me problems. Whites did. If I had my way about that, different social classes would go to different schools." Tricia volunteered: "Kids with the same amount of money should go to school together. I'm not prejudiced, but then I wouldn't be teased as much." When asked why he liked "separate schools," a noncommittal Bret responded: "I don't know why. I just do."

Regarding racial desegregation, Sheila said: "I don't think there should be mixing of races. Mixing classes and religions is okay." Dusty stated: "Kids should go to school with the same race. I ain't prejudiced, but I don't like hanging around with black people and I don't like them around me. I do have some black friends but they ain't the type that acts bad like the others." Stacy, who had two racially mixed half-brothers, said: "I think they should mix races in school, but I'll never be like Mom and mix a family. But I love my brothers."

Some who advocated desegregation added conditions to qualify their position. Annie maintained: "Mixed schools are good if the students don't abuse it—like be prejudiced against others." Chrissy believed that: "Everybody should go to the same school, otherwise they won't learn to get along." But she added: "Preps that go to public schools and try to run the school should go to private schools like other preps do." Thomas vacillated: "I don't know about social class. To an extent it might be better to keep them separate. If you mix them, you have to make sure it's fair. It's probably best to mix them though."

The majority of low-income informants were definitively and emphatically for desegregated schools. Yet, throughout their interviews, these same adolescents said that their affluent schoolmates were snobbish and that the groups were isolated from each other or that there was unending friction between them. These contradictory responses revealed that idealistic views coexisted with more negative realism in adolescents' thoughts. They implied that "mixing" would spontaneously occur and that "being together" would automatically decrease prejudice. They waxed eloquent about integration in spite of this being counter to their experience. They were able to shift back and

forth between utopian ideals (in the abstract) and the reality of their circumstances fairly readily and, seemingly, fairly unconsciously. In other words, they
seemed oblivious to the contradictions in their responses.

Some low-income proponents of desegregation based their arguments on
criteria of equal opportunity or equal rights. Nick affirmed: "Schools should
have different kids together so that there will be more equal opportunity and
so that different people can meet and learn to be less prejudiced." Ruth
asserted: "Mixed. It's people's right. People should be able to go where they
want." Louann commented: "Blacks have the same rights. Social class mixing
doesn't bother me—preps and teachers might mind—but, we're not aliens."
Others took a social awareness stance (e.g., "People have a chance to meet
other people"; "So you can learn about other people—sometimes you just have
to learn to cope with other people if you can't get along with them"; "Being
with different people helps you learn to like everybody"; "It is good for all
groups to learn from others; it would be stupid to sit in class with the same
kind of people"; "Kids should all attend the same school because that's how
you get to know some interesting people"; "You need to know about others;
learn not to be prejudiced"; "You become sensitive to the problems of others"; "It's good to see others' points of view, how they live, what they're like").

High-income respondents were guarded in discussing social class, and
although most (32, 94%) supported integrated schools, it seemed this position was selected as being politically correct but not necessarily preferred.
They readily related details of what they felt to be improper and irritating
behaviors (e.g., fighting, chewing tobacco, smoking, driving outdated or
souped-up vehicles) or provocative appearances (e.g., "They wear those com-
bat boots and camouflage clothes"; "They dress like toughs"; "They look like
sluts") on the part of their less affluent counterparts. One of the two high-
income respondents opposed to schools of heterogeneous social class makeup
had an empathic perspective, saying: "It would be better if students were the
same, because then the poor would not be picked on as much." The other
asserted: "I'd prefer separate schools because I don't like being held back by
kids who don't want to learn." A third, who was generally in favor of mixed
schools, hedged: "We should be exposed to differences, but maybe not to
extremes."

Like their low-income counterparts, affluent students indicated that social
awareness should be among the goals of education, and they also implied that
social sensitivity would be the natural outcome of contact (e.g., "We need
exposure"; "Separate encourages prejudice"; "More opportunity educates you;
you get a better view of life"; "We should not be segregated; we should learn
to cope with different people"; "If we go to mixed schools, we won't have mis-
conceptions about others"; "We all need to get along despite our differences";
"If they're mixed, we grow up learning about other societies and people"; "We

should be together in school since we all live on one earth together"; "If you only go to school with the rich, you will not see the whole world"; "Mixed schools can offer more to everyone"). Unfortunately, their idealistic beliefs did not match the actuality of their actions or the reality of the situation.

PERCEPTIONS OF WEALTH AND POVERTY

Since poor people, by definition, have qualitatively different economic distributive experiences than do middle-class people (Enright, Enright, Manheim, & Harris, 1980), one might assume that they would have distinct views of the nature of social classes and the causes of economic disparity. Yet, twenty-three low-income adolescents (57.5%) indicated that poverty was due to negative attributes of individuals. Twelve (30%) attributed poverty to conditions beyond personal control, and five were uncertain. Twenty-four affluent respondents (70%) said poverty resulted from individual actions and ten (30%) blamed societal conditions. Since most adolescents named more than one cause of poverty, the total number of causal factors given are shown in Table 2.1.

The "personal" category included degrading or ambiguous descriptions of poor people. Typical of definitions offered by low-income adolescents were: "People who don't want to do things like succeed"; "They're the ones brought up on welfare, who will be on welfare when grown"; "People who don't want to do nothing"; "People that don't care." The "condition" category included responses that blamed factors beyond the individual's control (e.g., "No good jobs around here"; "They can get only low-paying jobs"; "Unemployment"). Low-income adolescents who blamed personal factors were usually explicitly derogatory about poor people, characterizing them as "lazy," "dependent on others," or as "just not trying."

Unlike the frank criticism of the characteristics of some poor people voiced by low-income respondents, high-income adolescents couched their answers in more objective-sounding terminology (e.g., "poor upbringing," "lack of initiative," "low motivation"). Six high-income adolescents stated that drinking, drug abuse, or gambling were causes of poverty; none of the low-income respondents mentioned these factors. Five of the seven high-income adolescents who listed "lack of school success" also mentioned "low intelligence." Again, none of the low-income respondents commented on intellectual factors, although one named "ignorance" as a cause of poverty. Responses categorized "education" revealed that for low-income adolescents "dropping out of school" was clearly associated with diminished life chances. High-income teenagers were more likely to allude to achievement criteria rather than persistence in school.

TABLE 2.1. Opinions About Causes of Poverty and Wealth

	Low-Income		High-Income	
	N	(%)*	N	(%)*
Causes <u>of</u> <u>poverty</u>				
Personal reasons	52	(75)	39	(78)
Motivation	16	(24)	14	(28)
Education	15	(22)	7	(14)
Family problems	13	(18)	11	(22)
Health	6	(8)	–	
Actions	2	(3)	7	(14)
Conditions beyond control	17	(25)	10	(20)
Work-related	14	(20)	9	(18)
Circumstances	3	(5)	1	(2)
Total causes of poverty	69		49	
Causes <u>of</u> <u>wealth</u>				
Personal reasons	49	(68)	46	(66)
Work/job-related	18	(25)	24	(36)
Education	16	(22)	7	(9)
Actions	6	(8)	2	(3)
Illegal/manipulation	5	(7)	2	(3)
Motivation	4	(6)	11	(15)
Conditions beyond control	22	(31)	25	(35)
Family	19	(27)	16	(22)
Chance	3	(4)	9	(13)
Total causes of wealth	71		61	

* Percentage of total number of causes given.
(Note: Due to rounding, percentage totals do not necessarily add to 100.)

Wealthy people were credited with being well educated, industrious, motivated, and wise in making financial decisions (see Table 2.1 for the total number of reasons given for wealth). Affluent people were described very favorably by 24 low-income respondents (60%) and 21 high-income adolescents (62%). Sixteen low-income adolescents (40%) pinpointed conditions beyond individual control, as did 13 high-income individuals (38%). Thus, like adults (Kluegel & Smith, 1986) and students elsewhere (Leahy, 1981, 1983), the majority of adolescents had individualistic explanations for achievement and status attainment.

Among the factors thought to precipitate wealth, "family connections" (e.g., "If the parents are rich then the kids will be rich"; "They inherit it") was a more prevalent response among low-income respondents than chance (e.g., "Win a lottery," "Being in the right place at the right time"). Only five low-income and two high-income respondents accused affluent people of illegal or manipulative means of becoming rich (e.g., "Pull strings," "Use influence," "Rob banks," "Get money off other people," "Cheat," "Some are selfish and take advantage of others"). With the exception of one black low-income and one white high-income adolescent who gave "racism" as a cause of poverty, responses were apolitical.

SOCIAL CLASS SELF-IDENTIFICATION

Given their negative perceptions of poor people and positive views of the rich, it is not surprising that regarding their own social class status only 11 low-income adolescents (27.5%) called themselves poor, whereas 29 (72.5%) claimed some version of "in-between." In addition to the 11 who identified themselves as poor, 7 more (i.e., a total of 45%) said that their parents called the family "poor." In my study of local low-income parents, all 35 referred to themselves as "poor." The discrepancy in self-disclosure rates for adolescents and adults may stem from adults' being desensitized to the social stigma of poverty because they are accustomed to identifying themselves as low-income in order to receive services. Adolescents had not had to characterize themselves as poor for official purposes. Adults might have realized that the researcher knew the housing projects where they lived were restricted to low-income people. Being less familiar with objective measures of poverty, teenagers may use criteria such as appearance or attitude in labeling themselves and others. The negative associations of poverty (e.g., "Grits dress scummy—they wear old, dirty clothes") are likely to have resulted in their avoiding the term *poor*. A couple of younger respondents declared that it was "not nice" to call someone poor (e.g., "I wouldn't call them poor since that would hurt their feelings, so I'd call them 'in-between'"). Another distinction made was between being "financially strapped" and "acting low-class" (e.g., "My family is poor in the amount of money we have but our way of living is not poor"). At any rate, at some time during the interviews, all low-income participants either referred to a lack of family funds or expressed annoyance at people who were biased against them (as poor people) or who called them "grits." Thus, indirectly, they all identified themselves as poor.

Twenty-two high-income respondents (65%) identified themselves as some form of "upper-middle class" (e.g., "We're not millionaires, but we're pretty well off"). Eleven (32%) called themselves "in-between," and one, who lived with his divorced graduate student mother, called himself "poor." Again, more (30, 88%) reported that their parents referred to the family as "high-income," "rich," or "upper-middle class." The adolescents who seemed the most affluent were often the ones who placed themselves in middle ground. Perhaps their families were oriented toward conspicuous consumption and then worried about finances, or perhaps they lived in the wealthiest suburbs and were thus aware of others who were wealthier than themselves. Since high- and low-income adolescents were substantially isolated from one another, in some respects the social referent of each group tended to be those of similar income levels; that is, they contrasted their own status to that of neighbors or friends (e.g., "Most of my friends have more money than my family—at least I'd guess they do; my mother doesn't work"). On the other hand, teenagers were also well aware of more general social class classifications, and they echoed them in their responses. As a low-income adolescent asserted: "What class you're in depends on who you're rated against. Around here—on The Hill—we're generally rated low class."

OPINIONS ABOUT SOCIAL MOBILITY

Adolescents challenged the concept of equal opportunity, with 33 high-income (97%) and 32 low-income youths (80%) expressing skepticism about all children having equal chances of getting ahead. The barriers to mobility most frequently mentioned by low-income respondents were family financial circumstances (e.g., "Preppies have more chances; they have rich parents to help them"; "Some kids don't have the advantages of others—like money!"; "Those with better lives and better education have more money; with more money they have even more chances in the future"; "Things are unfair—some people are poor"; "There's seldom any mobility; if you were born low class, you'll be low class"; "Some people are pulled, others have to climb"). Darcy observed: "They say you have the same chances, but you don't." Thomas was more hesitant:

> Things are close to fair. Some people get paid what they're worth, some are worth more than they're paid, and others are paid more than they're worth. It has to do with social class. To an extent you have equal chances, but in many ways you don't.

Besides family finances, low-income adolescents felt that family stability was an advantage and family problems, a hindrance (e.g., "People with close families that aren't in poverty have more chances"). Other reasons given were lack of personal effort (e.g., "Poor people and people who don't try don't have

very good chances"); disabilities (e.g., "Poor people, street people, and handicapped people have fewer chances"); and intelligence (e.g., "The smarts have
more chances than kids with low intelligence"). They also associated life
chances with school performance and educational attainment (e.g., "Poor
people with low educational levels have fewer chances"; "Some low-education people who don't try don't have chances"; "Some really poor people can't
afford to send their kids to school"). The quality (i.e., social class character)
of schools attended was felt to alter life chances, as Carol said: "All kids don't
really have the same chances, some quit school, some go to Kinder [high-
income school], and some go to schools like Southside."

A small number of high-income adolescents offered a similar range of
conditions likely to deter social mobility. Libby said: "Poor people can't get
ahead because they don't have the money to go to college." Marie hypothesized: "There just aren't that many good jobs." Some alluded to social class
reproduction, as Greg asserted: "Advantages are handed down through the
family." Angie maintained: "The poor are victims of their environment." Hilary
said: "Children's futures mainly depend on how they grew up—on how their
parents built for themselves." But the majority of high-income adolescents,
to some extent, blamed poor people for their lack of success. Lynette maintained: "The poor usually aren't motivated. If they are willing to work hard
enough, there are plenty of opportunities to get ahead." William said:

> I couldn't tell you why some kids don't get ahead, but I know there's a
> tendency to stay in the class they were born in except for those born
> with intelligence—they have more chances than the rest of the poor
> people. Some have a more ambitious attitude toward life, some are
> content with what they have.

Opinions about opportunity and personal life chances will be covered in more
depth and detail in Chapter 8.

CONCLUSION

Not only were respondents confined to class-exclusive family environments and neighborhoods, they were also relegated to separate school experiences. Adolescents were well aware of the class characteristics of the various
schools in the community. Their responses also revealed a mental association
that connected the class character of schools with their quality.

The stigma or prestige attached to having attended certain feeder schools
followed students into their junior high and high school experiences and
influenced interactions among students at the secondary level. The school of
attendance signaled social class distinctions—just as attending an Ivy League

college symbolizes intelligence and class, having gone to a high-income elementary school had status benefits at the high school level. To affluent adolescents, attendance at high-income schools credentialed certain fellow students as peers. Attendance at a low-income school was a stigma difficult to
overcome in subsequent interactions. Low-income respondents assumed that
schoolmates from high-income schools would look down on them—and they
did.

Respondents of both social classes were facile in vocalizing democratic,
egalitarian sentiments. When asked if they preferred segregated or desegregated settings, low-income adolescents inevitably expressed the belief that
putting people together would result in mutual understanding and even social
harmony. Yet they continuously complained about actual humiliating and
ostracizing relationships with schoolmates of higher income levels and about
second-class status in school. High-income adolescents furtively noted the
negative impact of having low-income schoolmates in the same school, but,
on an abstract level, when it came to choosing between segregated and desegregated schooling, their civic conscience bade them to speak unhesitantly for
desegregation. They glibly detailed the benefits of integration. Thus, with
multilayered and complex thought processes, adolescents' abstract musings
differed from their concrete observations or actions.

In discussing the potential outcomes of social class mixing, none mentioned enhanced achievement patterns for low-income youth, although
research indicates this to be the case (Coleman et al., 1966). There are a number of plausible reasons for better achievement by poor children in schools
of heterogeneous class makeup. Successful achievement patterns are observed
and imitated; that is, poor children learn middle-class styles, including the
linguistic and cognitive styles that are beneficial for getting ahead in school
and society. According to this theory, low-income students have access to the
cultural capital ordinarily available only to affluent students (Bourdieu, 1977).
Or prolonged, extensive contact with affluent schoolmates may give low-income
children more realistic perceptions of their own strengths than they had in
isolation; they see that the differences are not as great as they appeared from
a distance or as they had imagined them. In other words, myths of social class
uniqueness are dispelled. An equally credible hypothesis is that in middle-
class schools, low-income children are exposed to better physical conditions,
improved instructional materials, and more committed teachers; they are able
to take advantage of the better learning environments traditionally available
to middle-class children (Anyon, 1981; Lightfoot, 1983). But such advantages
are most likely to occur if students are significantly integrated from an early
age and receive similar and equitable treatment.

In the major study *Equality of Educational Opportunity*, Coleman and
colleagues (1966) found that the most significant variable in the achievement

of black students was attending schools with white students. Although these results focus on racial differences, research generally indicates that when social class variables are controlled, differences in achievement between races and ethnic groups almost disappear (Jeffrey, 1978; Levine, Kukuk, & Meyer, 1979). Thus the nature of the social class composition of schools influences achievement (Havighurst, 1966; Levine & Havighurst, 1977; A. B. Wilson, 1967), with low-income students more likely than middle-class students to be affected by peer-group effects (Beckerman & Good, 1981; Gronlund, 1979; Jencks, 1972; Ornstein, 1978). Yet in Coleman's (1976) opinion, social class desegregation is more troublesome to implement than racial desegregation.

In the context of race relationships, equal educational opportunity translated into desegregated schooling enforced through the Civil Rights Acts and Amendments. Many schools were racially segregated until forced by the courts and pressured by federal monies to desegregate. Public schools did not offer an education to children with severe handicaps until federal legislation (PL 94-142) withheld federal funds for noncompliance. There is little reason to expect schools to become more heterogeneous in social class makeup without similar external pressure. Yet in spite of the multitude of legislation and litigation relating to civil rights issues, none applies to discrimination according to income level. Although the indices for establishing social class status are clearer and can be more objectively defined than either racial or handicapped status, people of low socioeconomic levels are not given minority-group status by federal, state, or local governments. Unless the poor can be defined as a minority group, it is impossible, legally, to discriminate against them. Thus there is no legal handle to use against school systems guilty of social class segregation or discrimination. Nevertheless, a strong, principled administration and school board could influence school decisions concerning social class equity (Edmonds, 1982).

Related to adolescents' perceptions of social class, it was expected that poverty would be perceived differently by those most and least likely to feel its impact; however, the findings of this study replicate those of Kluegel and Smith (1986): Regardless of their social status, people have similar beliefs about the nature of social classes. It has been found that "underprivileged" people's views tend to reflect the general consensus about the status and image of groups (Moscovici & Paicheler, 1978; Tajfel, 1982). Consistent with this finding, in this study low-income adolescents gave more negative descriptions of low- than of high-income student groups. The views of subordinate adolescents reflected the perceptions of dominant students. Low-income adolescents adhered to standard views even though they were disparaging toward their own class. Damon (1975, 1980) also found that children focused on psychological or behavioral causes of poverty, with little political interpretation. They apparently accept institutionalized meanings and practices as personal perceptions of reality regardless of their status (Apple, 1982b; Gramsci, 1971; Rosenholtz & Simpson, 1984). Thus even victims blame victims.

Low-income adolescents' perceptions of social class, personal status, and social mobility revealed conflicts and dilemmas. Similar to Breakwell's (1978) finding, there was a disjunction between self-identification, perceived identification by others, and objective identification. By all objective standards they were poor; however, the majority did not identify themselves as such even though they admitted others would. Being overwhelmingly negative about the attributes of poor people, it is not surprising that they were reluctant to be affiliated with such a devalued group. Their negative feelings about their own class certainly obstructed class loyalty and precipitated a pecking order among low-income adolescents. At the same time, positive attitudes toward wealthy people provided the rationale for the uneven distribution of rewards in school and society.

Respondents humanized blame for poverty; that is, they attributed the source as poor people rather than societal circumstances (e.g., bad economic times) or biased institutional structures (i.e., that society is stratified). They did not depersonalize their observations to conclude that the present class structure meant that it was inevitable for some people to have comparatively less favorable situations. The frequent references by low-income adolescents to social class circumstances were generalized from individual (e.g., "Mom dropped out of school, so she can't find a good job") to collective levels (e.g., poor people are undereducated, thus unemployed). The narratives of all adolescents revealed a mind-set that linked poverty with lack of school success; both were the outcome of (negative) personal qualities. This tendency to personalize blame for situations resulted in both feelings of unworthiness and a basic tolerance for stratifying conditions.

In England, Willis (1977) found that working-class youths identified with their working-class fathers, proudly asserting their class affiliations and their counterschool, anti-middle-class sentiments. Adolescents in this study were mainly embarrassed and evasive about their origins. Clear-cut social class self-identifications are generally not evident in the United States (Simmons & Rosenberg, 1971). Apple (1982a) conjectured that one of the reasons that social class affiliations in this country are so complex is that individuals with unequal chances think of themselves as competing for elite positions. In other words, there is a faith in intergenerational mobility, thus a sense of fellow-feeling with elites among low-income people. This widespread belief in social mobility is considered instrumental in decreasing the intensity of class loyalty (Jackman & Jackman, 1983). Yet on one cognitive level, both low- and high-income adolescents in this study were pessimistic about social mobility, noting the advantages of present family status for future financial rewards.

CHAPTER 3

Social Sorting:
Student Identifications
and Affiliations in School

Isolation of adults of different social classes is fairly complete in the residential, religious, social, leisure, and political spheres of the lives of people in Hillsdale. Interaction through occupational roles tends to be defined by formal rules and boundaries that preclude much personal contact or empathetic interaction. Regardless of adult separateness, a traditional American belief holds that contact between members of different social classes should occur in comprehensive (i.e., socially inclusive) public schools during childhood and adolescence. Ideally, the common school is perceived as contributing to democratic processes by ensuring equal opportunity for purposes of social mobility and by enhancing understanding among diverse groups by bringing them together in a common setting. Yet, in spite of expressing lofty goals for student relations in school, the actual dynamics of student interactions may be nowhere near as positive as the ideal.

The literature describing segregation and differentiation of students from various social class backgrounds (e.g., Bourdieu & Passeron, 1977; Bowles & Gintis, 1976; Eder, 1981; Hallinan & Sorensen, 1985; Kohn & Schooler, 1983; Oakes, 1985; Rist, 1970; Scrupski, 1975) tends to focus on institutional practices such as tracking—that is, on the organizational aspects of school—but does not focus on the separation due to students' social perceptions and cognitions. Or studies of student relations restrict attention to such psychological factors as bias socialized in family or ethnic-group settings. The informal social context of school is portrayed as relatively unimportant in the development of interpersonal relationships and social perspectives. Causal implications or mitigating circumstances for patterns of behavior among members of different classes are ignored, as are unique perceptions of the social scene at school due to unique social class positions.

Some studies do provide insight into peer stratification processes. In an extensive examination (1961) and reexamination (1975) of high school life, Hollingshead found that students' groups were similar to their parents' cliques and that regardless of their ambitions, lower-class adolescents could not escape their status. In another midwestern study, Eder (1985) found that a stable hierarchy of cliques developed during the middle school years, so that by eighth grade seating patterns in the cafeteria isolating "grits" (i.e., low-income students) from "good kids" were firmly established. Eder hypothesized that students' stereotypes of one another and their fear of rejection prevented contact between the various groups.

Although their discussions were intertwined with allusions to social class, Hollingshead and Eder did not distinguish between the concept of clique (i.e., exclusive group of associates) and the concept of class (i.e., ranked or stratified divisions of people) in adolescent school society. A closer inspection of the results of both studies makes it clear that student group classifications referred to very global, multilayered clusters (i.e., layered according to prestige and status) of pupils closely resembling social classes in society. Students' classifications had little to do with personalized cliques. For example, Hollingshead observed that students made three levels of distinctions among each other, using the terms "elites," "good kids" (two-thirds of the school enrollment), and "grubbies," who were said to be "set off from the others by unfortunate family connections" and were considered "nobodies" in school social affairs. At the same time, he identified 259 cliques, which ranged in size from 2 to 12 individuals. Eder observed that students' classifications suggested a "two-layered social structure"; that is, the "good kids" and the "grits."

Schwartz (1987) reported "class-like" distinctions of adolescent groups, separating an "indistinguishable middle" (i.e., "straights") from the "greasers" (i.e., working- and lower-class youths). Regarding middle school informal groups, Castlebury and Arnold (1988) noted that certain classified students lacked sufficient cohesion to be considered "true groups" and suggested the labels implied social classes. Yet, in spite of observing that groups formed along social class (and racial) lines, Castlebury and Arnold claimed that members did not "make value judgments" of groups based on race or socioeconomic status.

Varenne (1983) stressed the importance of epistemology (i.e., participants' models of social reality) in his attempt to understand the structural and transformational interrelationships in processes of classification, segmentation, ranking, and segregation in high school. He started from the "cultural ground up," examining his informants' perceptions of their social world and the "quasi-mythical texts through which they communicated with each other about each other" (p. 9). He found that students differentiated themselves on criteria that were relevant to them and that their cohesive groups were "tangible organizational realities" reified by those who described them.

Varenne (1986) observed that the class system could be seen within the confines of schools and maintained that adolescents arranged themselves following their parents' social patterns in the community. His study, however, was conducted in a wealthy suburban school where social class variations among students were limited. In this school of homogeneous social class makeup, the hierarchical status of groups was not very evident and power struggles were fairly evenly matched. Varenne's "jocks" and "freaks" aligned themselves according to interests and tastes (i.e., not social class) and participated in school events having distinct, even complementary, roles. Varenne did identify a "small group of students whose parents were significantly lower-income" as the "most segregated" group in the school.

Focusing on 12 working-class youths in a comprehensive high school in England, Willis (1977) integrated theories of correspondence, relating the structures of school to the structures of society, as he explored the cultural and subjective levels of social relations. His "lads" were observed to have a "profound insight" into the conditions of social class under capitalism, being skeptical about their chances for upward mobility and rejecting the belief that effort in school would reap them personal rewards. Their relationships with school-conformists from their own social class (so-called 'earholes) and with students from higher-status backgrounds were conflict ridden. Because of substantial historical and social differences in British and American schools and society, parallels with the American situation, though suggested, may not be too clear.

Specifically illustrating the ritualistic and mythical nature of polarization and segregation in an urban high school, Shimahara (1983) maintained that segregation was stereotyped and symbolic. Similarly, Lesko (1988) identified main groups of students (i.e., "rich and populars," "mellows," "burnouts," "social outcasts") and discussed how they interacted through myths and rituals. She did not, however, discuss how such school behaviors related to the power structures in society.

GROUP CLASSIFICATIONS AND DIFFERENTIATION

When asked to talk about student groups in school, adolescents gave animated and lengthy responses. It was clear that this was a topic of great interest to them. Their names for groups, perceptions of interactions among different groups, and views of the reasons students belong to groups are all discussed in this chapter. But first, attention might be focused on the seven (i.e., nonlabelers) who did not name student groups.

Nonlabelers

Six low-income adolescents—that is, nonlabelers or alternative labelers—did not discuss student groups as their peers did. All six held positions that isolated them from the mainstream of social life and/or may have altered their perceptions of groups. Two 14-year-olds had not yet entered junior high school and so, to date, had attended only elementary schools of homogeneous social class makeup where social class sorting may have been less salient. These students seemed somewhat puzzled by questions about student groups and proceeded to name teacher-organized ability groups. Three respondents discussed their status as special education students and were preoccupied with peer rejection, which they felt was due to the stigma attached to their "handicap" label and special education placement. Diverted by special education, they apparently cared less about other types of barriers to peer interaction. The fifteen other students attending special education classes, however, named social class–related student groups in a manner similar to their nonclassified peers. The sixth alternative labeler was a 16-year-old black student who described race relations, which, apparently, were of greater concern to him. Again, the five other low-income black students provided the typical student group names. High-income respondents named peer groups, with the exception of Greg who was rather cautious and suspicious in responding. He insisted: "I don't really know names—I'm not big on stereotypes." (At other points in the interview, however, Greg used group names.)

Group Classifications

In response to being asked about the student groups in school, 34 (85%) of the 40 low-income adolescents named from 1 to 9 student groups, an average of 4.5 group classifications per low-income classifying participant (see Table 3.1). Some variation of "preppies" was named by all 34 low-income adolescents who named groups, and "grits" was named by 21 such respondents, with an additional 9 naming "headbangers" (i.e., recent classification of students generally associated with low-income status). A total of 46 distinct classifications were provided by low-income adolescents. Although many were subsets of more inclusive categories, the modifications appeared to be meaningful to the adolescents. True classification synonyms are in parentheses.

Thirty-three of the high-income adolescents (97%) named groups. High-income students named 35 distinct groups, with a mean of 3.8 per respondent (see Table 3.2). Twenty-four high-income adolescents named "preppies," and 22 named "grits," with 8 additional high-income adolescents listing other low-income categories (e.g., "stoners," "poorer students," "scum"), and 17 naming the "headbangers."

The low-income adolescents named 18 high-income groups, of which 7 were some form of "preppy," that is, "preppy" with a qualifying adjective (e.g., "big prep," "so-so prep"); 17 low-income groups, 6 middle groups, and 5 fringe

TABLE 3.1. Student Groups Named by Low-Income Adolescents

High-Income	Middle Groups	Low-Income	Fringe Groups*
Athletes	Middle kids	Grits	Weirdos
Jocks	Neutral people	Real grits	Acid rockers
Preppies	Nonpreps	Sort-of grits	Punk rockers
(Preps)	Inbetweens	Scummies	(Punkers)
Real preps	Everybody else	(Scums)	(Punks)
Big preps	Ordinary kids	Greasers	Nerds
So-so preps		Scuds	Loners
Almost preps		Hicks	
Would-be preps		Country kids	
Not-so preps		Headbangers	
Hotshot kids		(Bangers)	
Stuckup kids		Heavy metalists	
Snobs		Low-class kids	
Popular kids		Low-class jerks	
Mall rats		Rednecks	
Teachers' pets		Black kids	
High-class kids		Niggers	
Rich kids		Bullies	
Respectable kids		Poorer students	

*Nonmembers (categorized as individuals, not group members).

TABLE 3.2. Student Groups Named by High-Income Adolescents

High-Income	Middle Groups	Low-Income	Fringe Groups*
Preppies	Neutrals	Grits	Fags
Jocks	Average kids	Stoners	Punkers
Athletes	Normal kids	Poorer students	Geeks
Cheerleaders	Middle group	Rednecks	Prissies
Popular kids		Scums	Nerds
Rich jocks		Smokers	Loners
Bucks		Headbangers	Weirdos
The rich			Druggies
Trendies			Rebels
Brains			Hippies
Skaters ('boarders)			
College professors' kids			
Popular kids from the suburbs			
Good kids			

*Nonmembers (categorized as individuals, not group members).

groups. High-income participants named 14 high-income groups, 7 low-income groups, 4 middle groups, and 10 fringe groups.

Although there was considerable overlap in the categorization of school-mates by high- and low-income adolescents, the latter produced more than twice as many within-group names (i.e., classifications of low-income adolescents); that is, 17 low-income names compared to 7 low-income names produced by high-income respondents. Similarly, high-income teenagers observed and named more diversified special-interest groups among high-income class-mates. This is particularly true if the fringe groups are included in that count. Most of the fringe groups seemed to be categories of (alienated) high-income teenagers. In addition, adolescents gave more detailed descriptions of insiders; that is, they provided a greater variety of attributes for groups in their own social stratum.

A hierarchical status continuum of groups existed, which ranged from "big prep" to "neutral group" to "real grit" to "scummy." The adjectival modifications of the terms "grit" and "prep" implied that adolescents had a sense of a pure type; in fact, they frequently pointed out exemplars ("Muffy is a *real* prep"). The group classifications can be meaningfully divided into five general types:

1. High-status (dominant) groups associated with affluent families.
2. Middle-status groups, characterized by neutral and in-between positions or intentional nonaffiliation with either dominant or subordinate groups.
3. Low-status (subordinate) groups, linked with low-income families.
4. Fringe groups, which were outside the status hierarchy.
5. Nonmembers—that is, categorized individuals who were not members of groups.

Members of fringe groups tended to be high-income adolescents, but since they purposely dissociated themselves from high-status groups and did not compete for power positions in school, they were judged to be outside the mainstream of student groups, thus being categorized as fringe groups. Nonmembers (e.g., loners, weirdos) could come from either high- or low-income backgrounds.

Dominant and Subordinate Groups

Although adolescents used a variety of criteria to classify one another, there was considerable agreement both within and between groups about group names and their lifestyles, tastes (e.g., clothing, music), dialects, physical mannerisms, social interaction patterns, and relative social status. High-income adolescents described "preppies" as "smart," "rich," "outgoing," "good looking," "upper class," and "popular." Jessica, an eighth-grade self-proclaimed "preppy," elaborated: "All of my friends are preppies, like me. They're attractive and smart, but not really brains. We dress similar—nice clothes. We go to the mall, play tennis, and go to movies. Most of us are cheerleaders. My friends are all popular students." Andrew, a high-income senior who called himself a "college professor kid—not a prep," said: "Most preppies are popular kids from the suburbs. They never wear the same clothes twice. They've got everything going for them. They are really cliquish." Ian said: "Preppies are popular. They have the same clothes. They think the same and act the same. The real brains aren't preppies. They are sort of hippies or rebels."

Assumptions of social superiority by high-income youths were echoed in hegemonic ways by low-income adolescents, who assigned more positive traits to "preppies" (e.g., "dress nice," "dress better than the rest of the kids," "good in school," "smart," "rich," "good at sports," "good at everything," "popular," "have lots of friends"). The main flaw mentioned repeatedly by both high- and low-income youths was the preppies' social exclusiveness and snobbishness. Low-income adolescents also mainly attributed neutral or negative traits to "grits" (e.g., "chew Skol and smoke," "have holes in their pants," "look dirty," "love to fight," "like heavy metal music," "wear blue jeans," "wear sloppy clothes," "don't take baths," "vandalize," "don't care what they look like," "are scummy persons," "smell and dress gross," "don't do good in school," "be stupid," "are tacky"). Attributes of grits, for the most part, seemed intrinsic to conditions of poverty.

Social class–related criteria were evident in high-income respondents' views of grits. As Libby said:

> They don't have much money. They're all on welfare. I don't think they have cliques. They are lower class. I think that usually they're not real smart. I think most drop out of school. They wear ragged clothes—I guess because they have to. Most grits are from country areas. They chew tobacco and like cars. Some are rednecks. They don't get along socially.

Similarly, Marissa said: "Grits usually get bad grades. They have accents. They are not popular. They don't really fit in." Damon asserted: "Grits are country. They act weird. They're rejectees." Barbara clarified:

> Grits are usually hostile to people who aren't in their groups, they pick fights, smoke. They usually live on farms outside city limits. Punkers dress up in leather, spikes, chains. They have a live-and-let-live attitude; they are rebellious to authority. Preps are upwardly mobile. Most are

interested in having social groups that are tightly knit and hard to get into; they have a special dress code, language code, way of acting.

Both high- and low-income respondents volunteered very similar perceptions of the family financial status of groups. Twenty-three low-income teenagers directly stated that preppies were rich, and another nine alluded to expensive clothing or belongings. They also stated or implied that grits were poor. Only Adam (l-i) denied a significant correspondence between school groups and family money:

> Preps wear Polos, but they are not all rich. Most are snobby, some aren't. Grits smoke and do drugs. Sometimes you can tell them by the way they dress. They are into heavy metal and wear those shirts. Most are poor, but not all grits are poor. Some have money.

Less equivocally, and more typically, Leejohn (l-i) declared:

> Preps are rich people with gobs of money. They have fancy cars, rich houses, fancy clothes. Grits are poor people. They take what they can get: cheapest rent, cheapest car, cheapest clothes.

Twenty-one high-income respondents (62%) verbalized monetary connections when discussing groups, but they were also much more likely to focus on within-group wealth variations when discussing the financial status of peers (e.g., "rich jocks," "good kids"). Although "headbangers" were categorized as low-income by most high-income respondents, the social class connections of this group were less established than those of grits and their descriptions included fewer attributes directly related to poverty status. In fact, one high-income adolescent, Seth, a member of a heavy metal band, called himself a headbanger. The headbanger image was both more positive and more powerful than that of grits; they were said to: "be stoned," "tear up the school," "skip school," "be nice," "dress casual—no brand names," "dress tough like cycle groups," "smoke cigarettes and chew," "like heavy metal music," "wear concert T-shirts," and "wear earrings." Allusions were rarely made to their intelligence or hygiene.

To some extent, the gradation of groups within both dominant and subordinate classes echoed the multilayered class structure of the broader society (e.g., upper class, lower-middle class, working class, underclass). These layers could, however, be chunked into broader categories (e.g., subordinate, dominant, in-between). On the surface it seemed that there was a disparity in the number of main groups distinguished by respondents. Some maintained that a three-tiered system (i.e., high, medium, and low) existed (see Tables

3.1 and 3.2), whereas others identified only two (i.e., preps and grits). In the final analysis, for a number of reasons, major groups were judged to be dichotomous. First, even those adolescents who claimed an "in-between" status for themselves admitted that classmates would probably not identify them as neutral but rather as high- or low-income, respectively. "Middle" was used tentatively, even defensively, as if it were a status they would like to claim but realized it might not be credible to others. Additionally, when they spoke abstractly about peer relationships, they referred to two groups: preps and grits. "In-between" and "neutral" were added only when personal or close friends' affiliations were discussed and seemed to be a way to dissociate from undesirable group associations.

Adolescents used terms or phrases that implied bipolar relationships, such as "the haves and the have-nots," "rich and poor," or "high and low." The concept of a three-layered social class structure in society has been challenged (e.g., Dahrendorf, 1959). Semantically, the terms *neutral* and *middle* imply an ambiguous position in-between two real positions. Moreover, the visual image of group positions in relationship to one another is linear (and vertical), not triangular, with demarcations between groups including one or multiple cuts. Finally, a dichotomous image is more consistent with conflict theories of class relationships. Because of asymmetrical power relationships, the two groups are appropriately designated "dominant" and "subordinate."

Nonmember Students

Nonaffiliated students (e.g., "nerds," "loners," "weirdos," "isolates") were seen as being outside the social scene at school either because they were rejected or because they intentionally ignored their peers and did not conform to the social customs of other adolescents. For the most part, the term "nerd" was applied to high-income students who were believed to be intelligent ("they're brains") but who were also disparagingly called "grinds." Nerds were said to have "straight," unfashionable (adult-like) tastes and were unpopular. As Jeff (l-i) said: "Nerds are shy, sometimes really smart. They do weird things. I'm not saying that's bad, but nobody really likes them." It was believed that nerds chose to be bookish or scholarly; thus their lack of social behavior was somewhat excused on the basis of their having different, even enviable, agendas. But the term "nerd" was also used as a derogatory epithet for youths who were socially clumsy. Randy (l-i) bemoaned: "The girls call me a nerd. I don't get on much with girls my age; they call me 'nerd' or 'gross.' It gets me down sometimes."

In contrast to the asocial behavior of nerds, "weirdos," "isolates," and "loners" were more likely to be seen as antisocial. Some even appeared to be perceived as mentally ill ("really crazy," "God, he's really strange") and were felt to be dangerous and threatening. High-income adolescents were more likely than their low-income counterparts to call classmates "loners" or "weirdos," and they were more likely to pinpoint low-income students as exemplary cases.

Fringe Groups

"Punks," "weirdos," "fags," and "acid rock kids" were designated fringe groups because they did not neatly fit within the dominant or subordinate categories, although punks were generally described as high-income students. "Weirdo" fell into both nonmember and fringe group categories, depending on the context of usage (e.g., loner versus punk styles). Descriptions of fringe groups consisted almost exclusively of stylistic attributes (e.g., "The punkers have hair all over and play wild music and party a lot; they wear scarves on their heads"), not alliances and exclusions.

For the most part, respondents expressed amusement or indignation about punks, weirdos, and acid rock kids. Many claimed that punks had been common victims of violent, unprovoked attacks by "bullies" (usually low-income teenagers). In fact, two low-income youths bragged that they had "fought punks," and an additional two claimed that punks were threatening. Randy insisted: "They're tough. Don't mess with them or they will beat your brains out." Trent, who was about to start high school, admitted: "I heard that people there are just mean, like the punk rockers. They push you around. I'm kind of scared." The provocative appearance of fringe group members may have stimulated attack; however, a more viable explanation is that being unaffiliated with other high-income adolescents—even ostracized by them—punks were seen as powerless and defeatable high-income students. As such, they were acceptable outlets for the frustrations of angry low-income adolescents.

CLASSES, CLIQUES, AND SPECIAL-INTEREST GROUPS

Just as researchers have tended to lump together cliques, classes, special-interest groups (e.g., "band faggots," "jocks," "druggies"), and friendship clusters, adolescents vacillated between describing major groups (i.e., social classes) and naming subdivisions of groups of students who in some way "hung out" with each other. Nevertheless, it was clear that most group classifications referred to social classes, and that such classes were parallel to their parents' social strata; that is, they were roughly equivalent to the social classes in society. Furthermore, these school social classes did constitute the pools of students from which cliques, special-interest groups, or friendships could be drawn.

Adolescents claimed that it was virtually unheard of for cliques to cut across class lines, although special-interest groups (e.g., athletes, musicians) more frequently included students from both social classes. However, even if a low-income teenager was a star athlete, he was unlikely to be considered a "jock." The classification "jock" was reserved for high-income, popular athletes. Three low-income students (i.e., Will, Scott, Jeff, all black, fairly high-achieving athletes) had somewhat crossed social class boundaries, but they were only tangentially affiliated with high-income youths' cliques. All maintained that their real friends were peers from their neighborhoods. Friendship groups—that is, adolescents who claimed to like one another and spend time with one another (e.g., "We've been close friends for a long time"; "People call us Siamese twins because we're inseparable")—were also contained within social class boundaries but not always within cliques. (Chapter 7 will cover friendships in more detail.)

Each type of adolescent grouping had a unique function. Cliques had an identity-development function; that is, they served the purpose of establishing members' status. Clique membership signified the stamp of approval of certain adolescents; clique members were acceptable to others in the group. The status of the clique was tied to the reputation of clique leaders (e.g., "Doug's clique really think they are hotshots!"). Cliques were generally associated with special-interest groups, although special-interest groups contained several (levels of) cliques.

ORIGIN AND STABILITY OF GROUPS

According to low-income adolescents, major group distinctions were long-lasting, perhaps even permanent, with roots going back to elementary schools or neighborhoods. They described affiliation patterns as natural: they "just happened" (e.g., "Most kids hang around with their elementary school friends because they all live around each other and they went to the same school so they just stay friends"; "I always hang around with Hillview kids from the neighborhood; we know each other and we don't know anyone else"). Again, low-income adolescents alternated between offering a personalized, nonpolitical rationale for social class–exclusive patterns of group membership (e.g., "You more or less stick together with kids from your elementary school or neighborhood in high school because you don't know anyone else and you're kind of scared") and more political theories, which included explanations of social class elitism.

Similarly, high-income adolescents claimed that friends came from their "part of town"; thus it was implied that convenience was the reason for group exclusiveness. With further probing, however, they revealed that their cliques included high-income adolescents from all over town. In the end, both high- and low-income adolescents reported that their personal cliques were composed of students who had attended various elementary schools of the same social class composition as their own. Clique ties, then, were not so much characterized by early contacts as by social class exclusiveness.

Of the four types of adolescent groups, cliques were the most unstable. It was virtually impossible to change social class affiliations, and although connections to special-interest groups could be established or severed by starting or dropping an extracurricular activity, students indicated they usually stayed with the same activities over their secondary school years. Friendships were literally defined by long-term contact and loyalty. Respondents expressed concern about their status within cliques and talked about others being dropped from cliques. They could be affiliated with a clique and still be uneasy about the genuineness of friendships within that clique, still feeling vulnerable and lonely. To stay active in cliques, adolescents had to strive to maintain an image acceptable to others, especially clique leaders. Cliques could "drop" members or clique members could "rise" to better cliques and leave less popular peers behind.

An instance of the confounding of class and clique was the tendency for adolescents to believe that they had known others in their social circle since elementary school or that they had grown up in the same neighborhood. Many low-income adolescents initially stated that they met their friends "at Hillview" or "on The Hill," then proceeded to talk about friends who had attended other low-income feeder (to the secondary) schools or country schools. Apparently, they simply equated all low-income schools—they were merged in their minds as "our schools" and low-income neighborhoods as "our neighborhoods." Ultimately, "our" amounted to "our social class." People of their same social status, then, were perceived as "homefolks."

INTERGROUP PERCEPTIONS

Low-income respondents felt that they were stereotyped and ostracized on the grounds of being low-income or of having attended low-income elementary schools. As Will said:

> There were preps, punkers, hicks, grits, jocks, and nerds, with not much to do with each other. The preps are snobs; they have more money. I hang around mainly with kids from Hillview and Downing [low-income schools]. There is prejudice against kids from those schools. Other people say that gritty people come from Downing. The Ushville [rural elementary school located about 8 miles east of

Hillsdale] kids are most prejudiced against. The others stereotyped them as country hicks.

Although defensive in tone, a few low-income respondents claimed that *they* were the exclusive ones. As Chrissy said: "My friends come from Downing and Hillview. I avoid the preps—the rich people. I really avoid them." Then, more humbly, she added: "If someone talks to me I talk to them. They usually don't talk to me." It is likely that claims of avoidance stemmed from a motivation to save face when rejection was anticipated (Goffman, 1969).

High-income adolescents detailed the clique alignments and realignments of "popular" kids, but failed to mention association patterns among their low-income schoolmates. They seemed to perceive them as being rather socially anonymous. It is likely that they noticed only what interested them or was of personal concern. They clearly had little interest in low-income students. On the other hand, low-income respondents were quite likely to note the grouping arrangements of high-income adolescents. This may be partly due to the fact that high-income adolescents held most of the key school positions (i.e., "ran the school"), making their undertakings more visible. But it was also clear that low-income adolescents were in awe of the lives of their more affluent schoolmates. They were on the outside looking in at enviable lifestyles (of the rich and famous). Although the rudiments of cliques were apparent among low-income adolescents, their clique structure seemed looser and less intense. Apparently, the rewards of striving for status affiliations were too remote to bother with.

GROUP RELATIONS

As noted in Chapter 2, adolescents of the two social classes were significantly isolated from one another. A few politically conscious high-income adolescents blamed social class bias for group boundaries. According to Libby: "Preps are really snobbish; they don't even look at poor kids. If a lower-class kid sat next to them in the cafeteria, they would get up and move. They have a real thing about grits." Similarly, Carol (l-i) acknowledged: "Groups are already established by the time you get to high school. Different kids don't have much to do with each other. I try to watch my attitude toward people, try not to stereotype people; but a lot of people won't have anything to do with certain others." Adolescents described distinct school territories for groups (e.g., the "grit pit") and admitted to conscientiously avoiding others' areas. As Aaron (h-i) confided: "I once went out by the vocational door and got cussed out. I won't do that again."

Yet adolescents' unofficial clusterings coincided with—hence were reinforced by—segregating administrative arrangements such as academic track assignments or special education placement. As Carol (l-i) said: "Preps take like all those different kinds of math and different kinds of science—we just take general math and general science." Few low-income respondents were in advanced or college preparatory tracks, whereas all high-income respondents were. Adolescents were in the same classes as their neighbors, who had also been their classmates during the elementary school years. Thus there was an intersection of official and unofficial boundaries and barriers.

The consensus among low-income respondents (67.5%) was that high-income students formed cliques and rejected others. In fact, snobbishness and exclusiveness were usually the only negative attributes assigned to preppies (e.g., "There were mainly the preps and the grits; the preps split off and stayed in their own group; they were stuck-up and shunned others"; "Preps are not friendly; they think they're better than everybody"; "The preps are too snobby—stuck-up—too much; they think they are in their own little world"). As Kit, who transferred from North to South her sophomore year because of "fights, discipline problems," said: "At high school there were more cliques. I thought: 'What you turning your nose up for?' The popular kids hang by themselves. They don't associate with others."

Some high-income adolescents claimed that they avoided low-income teenagers because of their undesirable personal characteristics (e.g., "smoking," "being druggies," "looking gross," "the way they act," "being foulmouthed"). Thus class exclusiveness was blamed on out-group inadequacies. Other high-income respondents admitted that pressures from like-group adolescents prevented cross-class affiliations. As Lynette said: "If I hung out with them, some of my friends would not like it." Thus out-group contact was con-sidered contaminating by high-income adolescents. Most denied any personal feelings of elitism, but they did acknowledge giving in to social pressure.

Low-income teenagers objected to being invisible to preppies; nonrecognition was painful and humiliating, but they also maintained that they had been the victims of verbal and physical abuse from their high-status schoolmates (e.g., "The preps smart off, call us grits"; "They're always bumping into us—on purpose"). Even those who did not identify themselves as grits claimed to have been prey to preppy scorn. For example, Louann elaborated:

> I hated South [high school]. I hated Beauford [predominantly high-income elementary school]. The kids were snobbish and stuck-up. The teachers were definitely stuck-up. South is the same as Beauford: snobby kids and snobby teachers. There are different groups: snobs and preppies. There were ones that weren't preppies—that's definitely where I fit in: not so preppy. There were grits—lower-class jerks—and

punks and weirdos. I got along terrible. I was always arguing and fighting. At South there weren't too many nonpreps there. That's why I didn't like it. The first time I heard the word "grit" was at Beauford. A grit is someone who doesn't have fancy clothes and a fancy car. I always thought of what I'd say if someone called me grit: "If you don't like the way I dress, then you go buy me fancy clothes." At Beauford I couldn't avoid the preps; they were in most of my classes. They got mad because I ignored them, and they left me alone. At Downing [low-income elementary school] there were greasers. They wanted me and a friend to join up. But there were too many vandalizers in that group; tearing up lockers and beating up kids.

At another point in the interview, when asked why she quit school, Louann replied: "I couldn't handle the snobby kids."

One prominent form of interclass conflict described by many adolescents is what Thorne (1986) referred to as "borderwork." Borderwork consists of one group venturing into another's territory with taunting or another form of friction-arousing behavior. As Trent (l-i) recalled: "Sometimes walking in the hall the preps would bump into me and laugh—just to be mean, to start trouble." Leejohn (l-i) related: "There's a lot of fighting between the groups. The preps will push someone else into you or just bump into you and a fight will start." In gender relations, contact with a devalued group is seen as resulting in contamination; for example, boys are said to get "cooties" from girls. These same motives seemed to be behind this pattern of interaction among adolescents of different social classes.

High-income adolescents confirmed low-income teenagers' views that it was generally their peers who initiated negative interaction, but they also claimed that low-income adolescents reciprocated (i.e., overreacted) with explosive verbal and/or physical attacks. Some criticized their peers, either as a group or as individuals, for being cruel to low-income ("rejected") students. Others asserted that low-income students acted in ways that provoked them, and thus were to blame for the friction. Inevitably, however, each high-income adolescent denied any personal wrongdoing, although they were fluent in describing peers' actions regarding out-group adolescents.

Low-income adolescents might be expected to fight as a reaction to rejection or because of frustration about their inferior status. As Wexler (1988) conjectured, subordinates' social action might be perceived as resistance against the preexisting social order. But such a theory does not account for aggressive actions by dominant-group members. Perhaps high-income adolescents were asserting their authority and establishing their power—even marking their territory. Or they might have been physically distinguishing themselves from low-income schoolmates in the process of establishing their own (more prestigious) status. Displacement theory might also explain their behaviors: Low-income students were acceptable outlets for frustration and anger. There is said to be a brutalizing trend among both males and females during adolescence, with an increasing acceptance of being physically hurtful to others (Cairns & Cairns, 1986). Supposedly, an increase in abrupt and explosive acts is the case for middle-class, nonaggressive, nonincarcerated youth as well as those with a longer history of aggressiveness (Perrin, 1981).

Adolescents showed a fascination with friction among schoolmates. Some respondents described feuding among the classes as a permanent state of affairs. The oppositional nature of dominant and subordinate groups, apparently, resulted in a very dynamic social situation. Twenty-three low-income respondents claimed to have fought preps in school. As Les said:

> Some kids were friendly. Some were pains. There are preps and headbangers at Loring. A prep dresses up, is rich. Headbangers wear sloppy clothes and earrings. I was in with the headbangers. Now and then I would help them fight when they needed it. I don't really consider myself in a group. The others realized that I wasn't really in a group. I do consider myself to be more of a headbanger than a prep. I got along with the headbangers, and I didn't really get along with the preps. The headbangers fought with them. I had a couple of friends who were in the headbangers permanently. I used to help them fight.

Similarly, Chrissy said: "I only know kids from The Hill. The preps aren't friendly. They think they are better than poor people. I get into fights with kids who make me mad; the snobs and preps call me names and I go at them."

Low-income adolescents considered their retaliation to be a defensive reaction to derision or aggression, yet many were embarrassed that the necessity for fighting had arisen. They expressed considerable guilt and worry about friction between social classes and clearly felt themselves to be on the losing end in the interaction. Most complained that preppies escaped detection and/or punishment, whereas they received severe disciplinary consequences for fighting. A few detailed their fights with high-status students with a certain amount of pride, conveying that their status as fighters incurred respect from peers. They had been brave enough to stand up to the abuse from more powerful youth. As Bret related:

> The higher-class kids hang together and the lower-class kids do too. The preps think they're upper class, rich people. They laugh at people with less money. A headbanger is someone who goes by the rules. He don't like people who think they're better than other people. They are

a fighting group—against preps, mostly. Preps start by calling other
people names.

Fights, then, were seen as legitimate reactions to infractions of a moral code
(e.g., "go by the rules"). Satisfaction resulted from having "taken care of business" or having "taken a stand." Some such fighters were annoyed that others
misconstrued their actions and accused them of being bullies.

Although their anger was real, it is suspected that the extent of fighting
was exaggerated. For one thing, in describing friction, adolescents often
recalled fights that had occurred several years earlier. Furthermore, they
categorized threatening postures and facial expressions as "fights," even if contact had not occurred. It seems that fighting was something many low-income
adolescents frequently felt like doing, especially in response to certain situations, but may not actually have done.

SOCIAL CLASS SELF-IDENTIFICATION

When asked whether they considered themselves to be rich or poor, only
about one-fourth of the low-income adolescents said they were poor, whereas
almost three-quarters claimed to be "in-between." Similarly, they avoided ver-
balizing the humiliating term "grit," with its negative associations with poverty. Randy emotionally recalled:

Most of my friends are from Southside [low-income elementary school].
I haven't really gotten to know the others. If you wanted to hang
around with certain kids, you couldn't. There was name calling and
fights. There were the preps, headbangers, and the grits. I guess I was
a headbanger because I don't like no preps and I hate it when people
call you a grit, because I'm not a grit. Grits don't take baths and stuff
like that. Preps are snobs. There were a lot of people I didn't like at
that school. So, I had a lot of fights.

Since being either a grit or a prep was unacceptable, many low-income
respondents said they belonged to "middle" or "neutral" conglomerations or
claimed no affiliation. Jeff asserted:

Headbangers like heavy metal music and wear concert T-shirts and
earrings. Preps are assholes. Grits smell and dress gross. Rednecks are
the same as grits. Punks have weird hair. I get along with all except the
preps, but I don't see myself as belonging to any of these groups.

Thomas maintained:

> Preppies and mall rats feel that they are better than everyone else. The
> bullies were brought up to be unfriendly. The grits are too busy
> showing their muscles and four-wheel drives. I'm not in any group. I
> just hang around with my friends.

Yet respondents did admit that classification had two dimensions: labeling oneself and being labeled by others. May's response demonstrates this
dual perspective:

> Preps have nice clothes and they talk and act different. They don't like
> to get their hands dirty. They talk about things that aren't important.
> They brag about themselves. Grits are scummy persons. I'm neutral. I
> think others think that I should be a prep because I dress nice, but the
> preps don't think I'm a prep!

Given the negative image, it is not surprising that adolescents objected
to being identified as low-income or classified as grits. Most denied the fit of
the term, but Dean dryly said:

> The preps smart off, call us grits and stuff like that. It didn't bother me.
> I just fought them. The preps ran the school. I didn't have much of a
> part in school. I had some friends. We stuck together. There was
> punks. They were smart alecks. We avoided them. They started
> trouble—never got along with us. Rich kids thought they was better
> than everybody. I guess I am a grit. Others would call me a grit.

Reluctantly, Max said:

> They are more or less scared of me because I come from The Hill.
> They don't mess with me—won't fight me. I don't fight unless they say
> "nigger" to me. Some of the rednecks aren't friendly. I just don't
> associate with them. One-half of the kids are high over there [at North
> High School] and some teachers too. I don't like the prejudice against
> blacks and poor people. That place over there thinks they're so high-
> class. They would probably call me a grit because I'm from The Hill.
> (*Note:* Max was not African-American, but most of his friends were.)

Although they did not identify themselves as grits, neither did low-
income respondents classify themselves as preps. For example, Tracy said:
"The heavy metallers and acid rock kids like the same music. Then there are
the country hicks. I'm in-between the country hicks and heavy metallers. I

wouldn't want to be a prep and think I'm better than everybody else." Three low-income respondents admitted that they aspired to be preps. Madalene said: "If I succeed in what I want to do in life, I will become a prep, but not a snob!" A more ambivalent Carol confessed:

> I don't call myself a part of any group. K-Mart has the same clothes as the mall, only the mall is more expensive. I do want to be in a prep group but then I don't, because they're snobs. I'm not lonely, but I'd like to be more popular.

Striving for "the good life" was confounded by a worry that such aspirations might be interpreted as wanting to be a prep. Low-income adolescents were adamant about wanting more material goods and better neighborhoods but were less ready to confess that they wanted to change their group affiliation. There was a certain amount of loyalty to peers of the same social class. For example, May claimed:

> A grit doesn't do good in school, is a sloppy dresser, and doesn't care what they do or act like. A prep has a lot more money, dresses good, is good in school, and has a lot of friends. My group is not grits, not preps. I try to get along with everybody—be neutral. I would like to be part of the prep group and be high class, but I want my friends to be there too.

Although annoyed and defensive about low-status identification and clearly envious of more affluent adolescents, low-income respondents were undecided about ideal group membership. Such ambivalence undoubtedly interfered with social class cohesion among low-income youths.

On the other hand, high-income adolescents were fairly glib in stating their group affiliations, although many gave interest-group rather than status-group names. Two called themselves "skaters" (i.e., skateboarders) and one, a "headbanger." Seven called themselves "preps"; six, "prep/jocks"; two, "jocks"; one, a "conservative kid"; one, a "brain"; one, a "college professor's kid"; and, in a somewhat nervous but good-natured manner, Mario referred to himself as a "nerd." Four claimed to be "neutral"; three, "average"; and two, "normal." One of those who called himself "normal," added: "Or maybe punk." Three high-income students said that they did not belong to any group.

High-income adolescents seemed relatively unconcerned about how others would classify them; they were, apparently, confident that others would not speak disparagingly of them or that applicable labels were not offensive. There was a fairly high correspondence between how high-income adolescents classified themselves and how they felt others labeled them. A few,

however, did not want to be categorized as preppies. Two of these were consciously counterculture, saying they deliberately avoided anything preppy (e.g.,
brand-name clothes, hanging around in the mall), and both wore ill-fitting,
ragged clothes. Andrew was delighted that he had been dubbed "odiferous
Andy." Involved in music and academic organizations, he scorned the activities of popular peers and bragged that he had never attended a sporting or
social event at school. The other, Vanessa, intensely disliked school and
shunned the whole school social scene. She claimed a very high rate of
absenteeism. At the time of the interviews, although only 15, she dated a
college student. Both Andrew and Vanessa considered themselves to be
politically left.

INTRAGROUP DIVISIONS

Vertical distinctions (i.e., a hierarchical ranking of subgroups) existed for
both dominant and subordinate groups, with some discrepancies among
respondents about the nature of the hierarchy. During an interview that took
place on the front stairs of her house, Leejohn (l-i) greeted a passerby in a
perfunctory manner and whispered to the interviewer that he was a "grit,"
"tacky," and "typical of kids who live on The Hill," which was why she wanted
to "get off The Hill." During her interview, in turn, a neighbor of Leejohn's,
Madalene, talked about Leejohn: "I don't want to sound mean, but she is not
a nice person. I don't know, she is kind of a sleazebag, I mean, you see the
way she dresses and the way she acts. She doesn't care about school—she'll
quit. There are a lot of kids like that around here." Thus insiders were aware
of a hierarchical ranking (i.e., a pecking order) that might not be evident to
outsiders.

There appeared to be more horizontal divisions among high-income
youths; that is, they described groups with distinct images and lifestyles that
were fairly equivalent in status. Such interest-group divisions were stylistic in
that they evolved around hobbies and tastes. Although not exactly synony-
mous with cliques, interest groups tended to be composed of students with
roughly the same social class status. The two who referred to themselves as
"skaters" wore unique (to skateboarding) styles of clothing and earrings, and
sported unusual hairdos. Although they assured the interviewers that others
would not think of them as preppies, they still considered themselves to be
popular and high-status. Their cliques centered around skating accomplishments, and they referred to peers who imitated their appearance but did not
skate well as "pseudos" or "'posters" (i.e., imposters). There was no female
equivalent to 'boarders, but they tended to hang around with preppy girls or,
put more accurately, such girls were said to hang around them.

Others (Eder, 1985; Eder & Stanford, 1986) have provided evidence that students (i.e., junior high school girls) make a distinction between high status and popularity. Similarly, in this study, popularity and high status were somewhat distinct. Although the majority of respondents judged that preps had the most friends (i.e., a sign of power), a few claimed that an in-between group was the most popular. Barbara (h-i) contended: "The most popular group is the middle class. They dress nice and act better than preps—they are not so stuck-up. They are friends with everybody and don't care about their image. I think I'm in this group." May (l-i) tentatively said: "There is a middle group. We can go back and forth between both grits and preppies. We are the most popular of all because we know the most people."

INTERGROUP MOBILITY

A few younger low-income respondents believed that social mobility between groups was possible. As Jeff volunteered: "You get to be popular by hanging out with popular kids." But most low-income adolescents judged the high-status levels of the group system to be closed to them (e.g., "The groups are closed; you can't get in because they are from different class groups"). Pressure from peers was rarely mentioned by low-income respondents as inhibiting mobility; they were more likely to say that elitism and gatekeeping on the part of high-income students kept them in their place.

Even low-income respondents who the interviewers thought might pass as affluent on the basis of appearance, manners, speech, and school achievement, still felt like outsiders. Madalene said:

> Most preps are snobs and care only about those that wear brand names. I try to fit with the styles, but we're not in a condition where we can have brand-name clothes. If people think that you're really, really poor, then most of the time they try to avoid you or look down on you. You're put into a category of people like you.

Similarly, Les (l-i) hypothesized:

> There is an undecided group, a middle group—they're younger and haven't decided which group to join or can't decide. You can change groups by hanging around with other groups. It is harder to become a prep than a 'banger. Kids form groups to act big and impress other people, and then they stay in that group because they make friends there. I belong to the headbanger group. I could change if I wanted. To change I would hang around the preps, change my attitude—become

snobby, and change my dress style. If they found out you were poor
they would throw you out unless you were real friends with the preps.

On an abstract level low-income adolescents believed in social mobility
for all children, but on a personal level they were likely to see barriers. At
first Randy said: "I know a couple of people in every group that I don't get
along with, but I've got friends from all kinds of groups. I just basically talked
to everybody. I don't feel left out." But later he confessed:

I got in trouble for fighting and being late to classes. I could have rode
the bus, but there were stuck-up people on the bus that I didn't get
along with, so I rode my bike through snow and rain. I couldn't stand
that group of people: stuck-up preps! I couldn't get along with them.

When asked about the local deterrents to social mobility, the majority of
high-income adolescents blamed some inadequacy on the part of their low-
income schoolmates (e.g., "They don't take school seriously so how can they
get ahead? They just don't care"; "Most aren't smart enough to get into advanced classes, so we don't see them"; "They like to stick with their own kind").
Bourdieu's (1984) "taste of necessity" theory illuminates how poor people are
seen as having a "natural taste" for the disadvantageous conditions to which
they are condemned. For example, because they were mainly not in high-
track sections, low-income adolescents were seen as "not caring about school"
or "sticking with their own kind." Only a few high-income adolescents mentioned that biased practices might act as barriers to social mobility for low-
income students.

GROUP POWER

According to low-income respondents, high-income students wielded
power in a variety of ways (e.g., "running the school," "taking over," "being
on all the teams," "being teachers' pets," "getting to play all the time," "only
ones teachers call on," "having the right answers," "getting good grades," "never
getting punished," "getting away with everything," "the ones to get picked,"
"winning all the elections," "getting awards," "keeping in their own little world,"
"doing good in school," "having lots of friends," "snubbing everybody," "not
caring what anybody else thinks"). Similarly, numerous phenomena signified
their own lack of power (e.g., "punished unfairly," "flunking in school," "disliked by teachers," "being unpopular," "having no friends," "never getting
picked").

High-status positions were said to be monopolized by high-income adolescents, and thus were inaccessible to others. Jocks were described as an elite preppy subgroup, and, as Max observed: "There's no need to try out; even if you make the team they won't play you." Carol noted: "Grits can be athletes if they're *real* husky." Randy asserted: "The preps thought it was their school." And Chrissy bitterly complained: "They thought they were better than us. They thought they could take over the school and everything. They thought they ran the school." Later she suggested: "Preps who go to public schools and try to run them should go to private schools like some other preps!"

Low-income adolescents detailed incidents of social class discrimination and indicated that there was collusion between school personnel and high-status students. They even classified teachers as preps. They were angry about the reality of discrimination they observed, as it clashed with their idealistic views of school as neutral territory. Carol complained:

> Mrs. D. put the preps on one side of the room and the grits on the other. I stood up to her and said, "It's not fair to put preps on one side and grits on the other." I mean we're all the same except for clothes and color (I mean race) and attitude. Other students agreed. I told Mrs. D. that she had a big attitude problem.

When asked what side of the room she had been put on, Carol's disgruntled reply was: "With the grits!"

High-income adolescents saw privileging phenomena as the natural outcome of their superior qualities, not deference to their status. They attributed the differential participation rates in activities to an uneven distribution of skills and talents in students. They took it for granted that they, as well as other members of their social class, were generally more capable than low-income students. Unfortunately, many low-income respondents held the same beliefs. Many were resigned to inferior status, but they were still depressed about group memberships and relationships at school. Darcy sadly responded: "I don't belong to none of them. I just stay by myself. The kids are not real friendly." When asked how she would like to change her life, she said: "I'd like to be smarter, have better clothes, know more people, and have more friends." Rejection and discrimination were frequently cited as the rationale for quitting school (e.g., "I might quit because I thought I didn't belong"; "I quit because of the snobby kids, snobby teachers"). Stacy, a dropout, said: "I liked Hillview because no one looked down on me." Annie analyzed:

> Money makes you have power. If you don't have money, you can't conform. If you can't conform in high school, they don't like you.

School has introduced me to people I don't like. I'm alone most of the time. I've been depressed. I need to make more friends.

Many low-income adolescents offered strategies to cope with discrimination and rejection. Sheila's approach was: "When they call me names like 'stupid' or 'grit,' I solve it by calling them something. You don't tell on them or you'll be called a narc—that way you'll get a bunch of people mad at you." Adam's strategy was planned ignoring:

The preps are rich and dressed better than the rest of the kids. The grits don't care about what they look like. I stayed in the middle. I didn't get involved with either group. I don't believe in classifying people. I found friendly people and if others weren't friendly, I didn't notice.

Yet the emotions apparent in their voices undermined the credibility of their detachment.

The stronger and healthier teenagers were indignant about inequities and injustices. They were the fighters who blamed the system and retaliated physically, verbally, or through manipulation. Thomas volunteered: "That stuff doesn't cut it with me—it's like medieval social classes!" Carol self-righteously voiced:

In school there are the preppy kind that think they're too good for us. Grits are poor kids. I think that kids are the same. God made us equal. They don't have the right to call us grits!

CONCLUSION

Adolescents constitute a small society, a subculture with their own jargon and special symbols and values (Varenne, 1983). They enter school with notions about the relative status of groups (Katz, 1983), and their group memberships and peer relationships subsequently act as socializing agents (Bourdieu, 1984; Eder, 1985; Festinger, 1954; Maccoby, 1986). Adolescents' cognitive mapping of social relationships was integrally related to their social status (Bourdieu, 1984; Willis, 1977). Although respondents mentioned cliques, cliques were described, not named. Their group classifications, with the exception of some that pertained to special-interest groups, referred to stratified layers of students roughly equivalent to social classes in adult society.

The universal disposition to classify is biased toward confirming rather than rejecting hypotheses about the social world (Forgas, 1981; Katz, 1983), with social image being largely based on social class (Schwartz, 1987). Adolescents' narratives were fraught with myths about the "other"—myths likely to influence current and future discourse. Negative images were associated with low-status groups and positive images, with high status groups.

On the other hand, group classifications were not static. It was clear that the naming of groups was a dynamic, ongoing process; that group classifications were in a constant state of flux. Fluctuations reflected social class struggle; that is, anger about oppression and subordinate status resulted in resistance (Giroux, 1983, 1986). Reclassification and, to some extent, regrouping evolved as a result of the ongoing discourse among adolescents of different classes. For example, although the origin of the word "grit" was disputed (e.g., "no idea"; "form of hominy," signifying Appalachian or southern heritage; "something to do with gravel" and the local stonecutting industry), the label signified negative images of mythical proportions. Clearly, "grit" was a very effective dominant-group put down of low-income adolescents. Yet, in turn, low-income respondents denied the term's applicability to themselves by claiming to be "in-between," or they escaped it by changing their image and reclassifying themselves as headbangers.

Of recent emergence, the headbanger group had somewhat less definitive social class associations than the grit group. Headbangers had a flashy, aggressive, and powerful image (e.g., earrings, 'cycle outfits, heavy metal music, jeans and jean jackets, headbands, concert T-shirts), perhaps even that of a warrior class. Adolescents' denial of grit affiliation and the development of new, more acceptable allegiances were certainly acts of resistance to the pejorative classifications imposed on them by dominant students. Social class conflict played itself out not only in actual intergroup interactions, but also in intergroup classifications and reclassifications.

Resistance was not limited to classification denial and self-reclassification by subordinate groups. It was also used offensively. Although primarily positive in connotation, the term "preppy" also conveyed materialism, superficiality, and elitism. It was used with envy, but also scorn. The simple act of applying ambiguous labels to elite classmates was a means of undermining their status, and thus a weapon in social class conflict. Social class conflict and solidarity were apparent in the adolescents' processes of naming and renaming themselves and others. Adolescents had a highly differentiated lexicon for talking about groups in school—it was clear that language played a constitutive role in their perceptions (Bakhtin, 1981).

Theories of reproduction are very relevant to this analysis; however, rather than being perceived as transmitted solely by institutionalized policies and practices, the class structure is additionally reinforced through the self-determined groupings of adolescents from different social class backgrounds and the classifications for groups. The mythical aura surrounding group alignments in school and the very nature of the language pertaining to groups separated students and conditioned them for inequitable adult roles. But, simultaneously, low-income students learned to evaluate, struggle, and resist while involved in the dynamic social scene of school. Reluctance to identify with low-status groups obstructed social class solidarity, but low-income adolescents were united in antiprep sentiment, were defensive about their own groups, and were active in developing positive new self-classifications and in their collective use of ambiguous and negative labels for high-income schoolmates.

CHAPTER 4

School, Tracking, and Teachers

As with any social institution, schools have an official purpose and formal system that convey what is supposed to occur, and, generally, these can be articulated by their constituencies. But there is also an informal system—a hidden curriculum—that is not always fully apparent to those within the system (Calhoun & Ianni, 1979). Whitty (1985), in fact, distinguished three curricular levels: overt (publicly stated, ideal), in use (real), and covert (hidden). Smith (1984) maintained that students and teachers follow scripts (expected sequences of behaviors) without thinking much about what is happening. Existing forms of school are seen as permanent, natural, and commonsensical (J. B. Thompson, 1987), just as a sense of the appropriateness of certain student behaviors—and the inappropriateness of others—governs social order within schools (Keddie, 1971).

In spite of the numerous observations of daily life in schools by ethnographers, students' voices tend to be inaudible; that is, little is known about their impressions of school phenomena (Nicholls, Patashnick, & Nolen, 1985; Nicholls & Thorkildsen, 1989; Perlmutter, 1986; Prawat, Lanier, Byers, & Anderson, 1983). Some information about the perceptions of unsuccessful students has come from studies of dropouts (e.g., Alpert & Dunham, 1986; Ekstrom, Goerts, Pollack, & Rock, 1986). Many such researchers maintain that dropouts are students with multiple problems such as failing grades, grade-level retentions, and disciplinary problems. Fine (1986, 1991) and colleagues (Fine & Rosenberg, 1983; Fine & Zane, 1989), however, argue that dropouts are often astutely aware of the lack of job market benefits of obtaining a diploma, whereas those who stay in school may be depressed, conforming, and reluctant to take initiatives in their own behalf. They further contend that defining dropouts as losers undermines the legitimacy of their criticism and rejection of schools. Concurring with this view, E. E. Cashmore (1984) found that high school graduates who had unsuccessful school careers retrospectively categorized their school experience as worthless. These studies shed light on the views of unsuccessful students, but less is known about the perceptions of more successful teenagers. Metz (1978) did report that high-track students have a variety of opinions about how schools should be run and feel that school is there to serve their needs, whereas lower-track students take school the way they find it—they endure it—and do not believe that they can affect the school's operation in a way that would meet their own needs.

The literature also has not addressed students' views of the administrative arrangements (e.g., tracking, ability grouping, special education) developed with the purported intent of meeting individual needs and/or dealing effectively with pupil diversity. Although they accommodate different achievement levels and behavior patterns, these arrangements also segregate, isolate, and stigmatize students. Furthermore, they divide students not only by supposed ability or achievement but also by race, ethnic background, and social class (e.g., Amato, 1980; Brady, Manni, & Winikur, 1983; Hallinan & Sorensen, 1985; Oakes, 1985; Rist, 1970; Rist & Harrell, 1982; Sleeter, 1987).

There is some empirical evidence about students' perceptions of teachers, their relationships with teachers, and the influences of social class on interactions. In England, Willis's (1977) working-class students felt that teachers had treated them "roughly" and those in Furnham and Gunter's (1989) study wanted teachers to make school more interesting and goal oriented. Jenkins (1983) claimed his Irish lads rejected school and teachers. In the United States, MacLeod's (1987) black adolescents were optimistic about the benefits of schooling and strove to please teachers, while the white youths were negative about school practices and school personnel. Metz (1978) found that low-track students felt that teachers were tolerable if they were "fair" and "nice."

Students have been found to be aware of inequitable treatment of themselves and others by teachers (Balch & Kelly, 1974; Fine, 1986; Fine & Rosenberg, 1983; Marshall & Weinstein, 1986; Rosenholtz & Simpson, 1984). Although definitions of ideal teacher characteristics are readily available in the literature, they have traditionally not come from those who interact most closely with teachers and those who are most affected by teachers; that is, students. Of the research on students' subjectivities (e.g., their values, attitudes, opinions), few relate directly to their evaluations of school or teachers. This chapter attempts to fill these gaps.

SCHOOL

Affect Toward School

Adolescents' attitudes toward school were explored by asking them to describe not only their feelings about school but also the attitudes of their friends and parents. It was assumed that adolescents would gravitate toward those who performed similarly in school and shared views of schooling

(Festinger, 1954)—asking about friends' attitudes was a way to test that hypothesis. It was also anticipated that respondents would project their feelings onto these significant others and would perhaps be more honest in discussing friends' feelings than in revealing their own. Thus the indirect approach was a way to delve further into adolescents' thoughts. Furthermore, asking about significant others was a way to examine the roles and influences of parents and peers; for example, participants' perceptions of their parents' feelings about school could provide insight into intergenerational influences.

There was a full gamut of attitudes toward school, with quantitative analysis showing a roughly parallel spread in high- and low-income adolescents' affect (see Table 4.1); however, with few exceptions, low-income respondents counted in each category were substantially more negative than high-income youth. For example, both of the following responses were counted as ambivalent. Nicole (h-i) responded: "I enjoy the learning. School is someplace to go. It's a lot of hard work but I like it. The curriculum could be better but since I'm learning things, it's fine." In contrast, Will (l-i) said: "Mostly I like it—well, sometimes I do, but I'm getting tired of it. It doesn't seem to be going anywhere."

As in MacLeod's (1987) study, the African-American low-income students were fairly positive about school regardless of their school careers. Besides Will, the five others were judged to be positive. Scott, a college-bound athlete, expressed an unconditional "I like it a lot." Nadia, who struggled in school and was placed full-time in a classroom for students classified as learning-disabled, similarly rejoined: "I really like it. You learn about stuff." Jeff, Kit, and Madalene all "liked school." The nine white low-income teenagers classified as positive were less enthusiastic (e.g., "school's okay").

TABLE 4.1. Attitudes Toward School

| | Low-Income | | | | | High-Income | | | | | |
| | Self | | Friends | | Parents | | Self | | Friends | | Parents | |
	N	(%)	N	(%)	N	(%)	N	(%)	N	(%)	N	(%)
Positive	15	(38)	11	(28)	14	(35)	10	(30)	10	(30)	31	(91)
Mixed	15	(38)	12	(30)	13	(33)	18	(54)	16	(48)	2	(6)
Negative	10	(25)	17	(43)	13	(33)	6	(18)	8	(24)	1	(3)
Total	40		40		40		34		34		34	

(Note: Due to rounding, percentage totals do not necessarily add to 100.)

Many adolescents seemed unable to disentangle personal feelings from
their overriding persuasion that school was necessary and important. Angie
(h-i) replied: "It's not very exciting, but I understand the importance of
going." Seth (h-i), classified as learning-disabled, said: "It's not fun, but I guess
there is some use to it. I forget everything once I get home. That's a pain."
Honor student Mario (h-i) said: "I don't have feelings about it. I think of it as
a necessary evil." Sheila (l-i) said:

> Well, last year was my freshman year and I didn't like school. I thought
> it was boring. I didn't understand what they taught me. I flunked a
> couple of classes. Then I started thinking about the future and decided
> to get my rear in gear—next year, when I go back, I'll do better.

Carol (l-i) volunteered: "Well, I like it. It's important to get an education and
finish school. You won't get anywhere if you don't." Carol's recollection of a
conversation with a friend also demonstrated her attitude: "April don't like
school, she quit the day she turned 16. She was in eighth grade. I told her
'April, you'll never get a job.' I said: 'These days people want a diploma with
your application.'"

A saving virtue of school was its social nature. According to Leejohn
(l-i): "It's not my favorite thing, but I have a lot of friends there." Similarly,
Sonia (l-i) said: "I like it. You get to meet friends." Teresa (l-i), a junior in a
program for mildly mentally handicapped students, replied: "It's okay. Teachers
get on your case, but I like the kids." Hilary (h-i) admitted: "We see school as
a place to be with friends; we don't think much about the scholastic side."
Libby (h-i), a straight-A student, remarked: "I like school—being with other
people—but I don't like the homework. It's all too much alike." But the social side of school was not always positive. Tyler (h-i) believed: "You meet
people, but they're both cruel and nice."

Ambivalent attitudes toward school (e.g., "It's fun; at times it's boring";
"It's okay; sometimes a drag"; "All right; sometimes it's a pain") were prevalent. Note the negative qualifier inevitably followed an original positive evaluation. Tyler (h-i) confessed: "I like to learn things, but it gets to be a real drag
after 9 months." Chrissy (l-i) wavered: "I don't really like it because of the
teachers. I guess I liked some subjects."

Ambivalence about school often revolved around feelings of competency.
Stacy (l-i), who had quit school, recalled:

> When I went to junior high school it seemed like you didn't get enough
> help or attention. I'm good in school if I really try. But it seemed like in
> junior high school they could never put anything into words that I
> could really understand. I needed help and I really didn't get it. I loved

school in elementary. I got good grades—above average. In junior high
I didn't do enough to pass.

High-income adolescents' feelings were also linked to performance. As Marissa
said: "I like it. It's very important. All my friends like school a lot—they are
all smart." Jeremy, a skateboarder, said: "I feel good when the work is done
or when I do well on a test. My friends don't try. They hate it."

High-income adolescents, even those with mediocre grades, took pride
in attacking the rigor of school. A recent high school graduate, Andrew, said:
"High school was a joke. It was easy. Most things weren't taught well. It was
boring. Oh, some of it was relevant. Sometimes what you learned opened your
mind. Most didn't." Honor-student Barbara hedged: "It's okay. Nothing's
especially good, nothing's really bad. My friends think it's a joke. Some take
it seriously."

A few adolescents who were lukewarm about school still believed that
school was better than certain alternatives. Trent (l-i) was upset that his grandmother "had to work so hard in a factory" while he was "just in school." Sonia
(l-i) conjectured: "This is the easiest time I'll ever have—I'll have to get a job
when I'm out of school. I wouldn't mind staying in school till I graduate."
Tammy (l-i), who had attended classes for mildly mentally handicapped students since elementary school, confessed: "It's hard to say how I feel about
school. I wish I hadn't quit. I'd like to go back now. The only thing I do is
babysit. I'm bored. I'd like a better job. People's tried to get me to go to Wee
Willie's Restaurant, but I get nervous. I think I couldn't do that work."

Conducting the interviews in the summer is likely to have tilted affect
toward school in a positive direction, because a number of respondents, particularly the low-income ones, said that they were bored and lonely and there
was "nothing to do." Beth (l-i) stated: "I like school. It's not boring. I'd rather
be in school right now." Max (l-i) admitted: "It's better than sitting at home."
Similarly, Darcy (l-i) said: "I'd rather go to school than sit around here and
be bored all the time." Celestine (l-i), who was spending much of her time
babysitting, said: "I can't wait until school starts again." Lynette (h-i) said:
"School's all right; it's better than staying at home." Similarly, Joe (h-i) said:
"It's okay—something for us to do."

Responses categorized as negative were global rejections of all aspects
of schooling (e.g., "hate it," "don't like anything about it"). According to Bret
(l-i): "I wish all of them would burn! I just don't like it. I never have since
first grade. School's just a waste of time." Seventeen-year-old Dean (l-i), who
quit on his sixteenth birthday, said: "I hated it. Teachers hassled me." Louann
(l-i), another dropout, simply said: "The only grade I liked was kindergarten."
Vanessa (h-i) bitterly remarked: "It's something I *have* to do, not something I
have to enjoy. I think of it as something I have to get through."

Perceptions of Friends' and Parents' Attitudes

There was considerable correspondence between personal feelings and perceptions of friends' feelings, as Chrissy (l-i) elaborated:

> There is one friend who is in most of my classes. She does about as well as I do. She likes school. At first she really didn't like it. She moved in from G. County [rural school] and our school was more advanced. She had trouble with the work at first and she didn't like school. She improved. Now she makes pretty good grades and she likes school.

Chrissy's response demonstrated the validity of a number of hypotheses: She and her friend were in the same classes, received comparable grades, had similar feelings about school; and their attitudes were related to their performance.

Even though most respondents described friends' feelings as similar, as predicted, respondents—particularly low-income respondents—were more negative in the "indirect response" (i.e., describing friends' reactions; see Table 4.1). Audrey (h-i) confided: "He has a little different attitude than me. He dreads it more. I don't care. I don't like getting up or doing the work, but I like being with my friends." Sarah (h-i), who "sort of liked school," analyzed: "My friend feels it's just routine, but she's expected to do well by her parents and so she has to work hard. It's tough on her. She works hard even when she hates a class."

Projection was very evident. Randy (l-i) initially talked about his "friend," then simply resorted to saying "I." In response to queries about his own feelings, Randy blandly said he "liked school," but regarding "his friend" he replied: "I'm not sure. He kind of likes it but then he doesn't. Like me. I don't like to do all that crap. I like it that I'm with friends but I don't like the work I have to do. School was getting me down." At first, 14-year-old Randy seemed nervous and anxious to please the interviewer, but within a short time he became a revealer rather than a withholder of information. Unfortunately, what he revealed were insecure and troubled feelings about life at home and at school.

J. Cashmore and Goodnow (1985) claimed that the best predictor of adolescents' position regarding school is their perception of their parents' position. Almost all high-income adolescents believed that their parents had liked school as children (see Table 4.1). Those who were negative themselves still believed their parents had been happy in school. A case-by-case examination revealed little correspondence between low-income adolescents' personal feelings and their judgments of their parents' feelings. Fewer than half (i.e., 47.5%)

described their parents' attitudes as being the same as their own; 10 felt their parents were more positive and 11, more negative. Many low-income parents had dropped out of school, and this was interpreted as a sure sign of "not liking" school by adolescents.

Regarding support for the schooling of respondents, parents perceived as negative were criticized as "not caring," "just lazy," or "peculiar." It was clear that low-income adolescents believed that the "correct" position of parents should be one of encouragement and positive attitudes. In fact, their views of parents' roles were identical to those Lareau (1987) attributed to middle-class teachers. They had an ideal, but in some cases their parents' behaviors did not match that ideal.

School Images

When directly asked how they felt about school, many adolescents' responses appeared to be normalized perspectives or echoes of dominant views. To encourage reflection on their own circumstances and a more genuine revelation of feelings, respondents were asked to picture themselves in school and describe how they would be feeling in the scene imagined. The task of creating a school image still stimulated ritualistic details, but affective response seemed somewhat more heartfelt.

Teenagers who described academic contexts were more positive when they pictured active rather than passive pursuits. Barbara (h-i) was "taking a test. I'm not having any trouble on it. I'm doing good work. I feel pretty good." Scott (l-i) was "in Spanish learning vocabulary. The teacher is in front of the class lecturing. I just came from lunch and I'm happy." Madalene (l-i) was "in class answering a question—giving my opinion. I feel okay." Aaron (h-i) was "sitting at a desk writing. I'm busy, happy." Les (l-i) was simply "working, happy." Many claimed to feel "tired," but May (l-i) was the only one to use it in a positive context: "I'm studying, busy, feeling tired and happy." Four low-income teenagers, who typically were disgruntled about school, expressed positive feelings about nonacademic situations. Dusty was "working in art. I feel pretty good because I like art." Darcy was "sitting at a table doing ceramics. Feeling okay." Sonia was "in band playing the clarinet—feeling pretty good." Kit was "running track, feeling happy."

Nine active images were neutral or combined negative and positive affect. Dean (l-i) qualified: "I'm going to class—working. I feel okay if no one is messing with me." Celestine (l-i) was "writing at my desk. The teacher is at her desk trying to explain the work. I don't feel happy or sad, just in-between." Karen (l-i) was "studying alone—concentrating—devoting myself to getting work done so I can have the evening free. I'm not really feeling any way. I'm just thinking about the work." Damon (h-i) said: "I'd probably be studying a little bit—maybe talking to Saul. I'd probably feel pretty good, but in school you feel up and down. If you get a bad grade you feel bad." Chrissy (l-i) said: "It's the first day of school and I'm listening to the teacher lecture. I'm trying to soak it up—figure out in my mind what she's talking about. I feel sort of interested. Not too bad. Probably wishing it was still summer vacation."

Active teenagers with negative affect included Andrew (h-i), who said: "I'm trying to get my homework ready at the last minute. I'm feeling frantic—a little scared. I'm on the brink of being bawled out by the teacher. Typical scene!" Thomas (l-i), who claimed to like school, said: "I'm working fast on last night's homework, listening to the teacher rattle on, thinking 'Why am I here, I know this stuff,'" Randy (l-i) was "in writing skills class trying to think of something to write. I'm struggling, frustrated, unhappy."

"Bored," "blah," "feeling nothing" were echoed repeatedly by those who imagined passive roles. High-achieving John (h-i) said: "I have a pencil in my hand. I'm at my desk writing. I'm bored, uninterested, tired." Jeff (l-i) was "listening at the end of the school day. I'm just feeling ready to get out." Teresa (l-i) was "in English—sleeping. 1 don't feel anything." Will (l-i) was "sitting in class looking at the board, not doing anything. I'm feeling hungry, bored." Nicole (h-i) was "sitting in a boring lecture feeling bored." Bret (l-i) was "just sitting there, doing nothing, feeling bored." Mario (h-i) was "in class, aware of the teacher, feeling bored, just bored." Annie (l-i) was "paying slight attention, feeling blah!" Dropout Louann (l-i) was "probably sleeping, bored, wishing I was home watching 'Days Of My Life.'" Another dropout, Stacy (l-i), was "sitting behind a desk feeling awful. I wouldn't like being there."

The "bored and tired" motif permeated teenagers' discussions of school images: Fifteen high-income respondents used the word "bored," an additional eight gave some version of "tired," and three shrugged "nothing," for a total of 76% of the high-income teenagers. Eight low-income respondents used the term "bored," five said "tired," three said "nothing," three gave some version of "wishing I was somewhere else," and one said "blah" for a total of 50% of the low-income respondents. The relatively fewer bored reactions from low-income adolescents was undoubtedly due to the higher frequency of social or nonacademic images among them. When scanning the entire interview transcript for all respondents, it was found that every participant claimed that school was boring at least once and three students (two l-i; one h-i) used the term "bored" more than ten times.

Adolescents (three h-i, twelve l-i) who pictured themselves in social situations were mainly positive. Jeremy (h-i) was "goofing off with my friends, happy." Sheila (l-i) detailed: "I'm greeting friends in the hall by my locker on the first day of school. Feeling great. Glad to see everybody. But it's about time for the bell to ring for the first class. Yuk!" Tammy (l-i), who had quit school but mostly regretted it, said: "I'm going to my locker to get paper and a pencil. I'm happy to see everybody." Among the ambiguous social situations, Max (l-i) speculated; "I'm in the lunchroom eating lunch. I've got decent clothes on. How I feel depends on how the day's gone." Tricia (l-i) detailed: "I'm in the office straightening out classes at the beginning of school. I'm trying to keep out of fights with kids. I have on jeans and a shirt—I don't want to look like no prep. I hardly have any dresses. I'm feeling good about still being in school."

Four low-income teenagers imagined problematic social scenes. Trent was "getting yelled at. It feels terrible." Jim was "getting kicked out—I feel awful." Wendy was "trying to figure out a grade; trying to straighten it out with the teacher—I'm worried. I'm just trying to get along." Nadia's image was complex:

> I'm working. Sitting at my desk. The teacher is giving an assignment. Some kids are bugging me. I tell the teacher. I don't really try to get them in trouble. I just want to do my work. Someone tries to copy my work. I yell at them. The teacher sends us to the principal. He talks to us. He tries to figure out who's lying, who's telling the truth. He yells at us, then he sends us back to the classroom. I'm mad. I get blamed but it's not my fault. I'm real mad.

Contrary to the assertion that certain students "enjoy" disrupting others or intentionally instigate social friction, these teenagers were decidedly unhappy about social conflict.

Adolescents who mentioned appearance stressed the importance of "looking good." Hilary (h-i) elaborated: "It's the first day of school. I've got on new clothes. I'm spasmatic with friends. We're happy to see each other again. I'm real happy." Sherry (l-i) had "on jeans, a T-shirt, and hightops. I'm talking to friends. I feel good." Ruth (l-i) was "jerking around in the hall having fun. I have on jeans and a T-shirt and my hair is nice." Leejohn (l-i) claimed: "My hair and clothes are better than usual. I'm having fun." High-income respondents rarely mentioned their appearance; perhaps it was not an issue because they had the wherewithal to "look good" on a daily basis.

Evaluations of School

Adolescents were vague and relatively inarticulate when discussing the purpose of school. Sheila (l-i) felt that "a good education is learning things you don't know." Sonia (l-i) introduced the element of choice: "Teaching you things you don't know and would like to know." Carol (l-i), again, stressed the importance of school and warned: "To learn. To get an education. There's no fooling around. It's business."

Thirty-six adolescents (49%) indicated that school's mission was teaching (some form of) basic skills (see Table 4.2). High-income teenagers usually referred to skills in the context of preparing for college, while low-income students alluded to becoming literate. Barbara (h-i) said: "To educate us in the basics and older, more specific, fields. Get us ready for college." May (l-i) maintained: "The purpose of school is to teach you to read and do math and things so that you can get along all right in the world." Like high-income students, low-income adolescents implied that what they were presently learning was not inherently useful but was important as a prerequisite. As Nick (l-i) put it: "Children need to learn things to base further learning on." An underlying assumption was that at some point school learning would begin to be relevant and useful.

Although they did not diverge far from a basic academics theme, 29 felt the purpose of education was vocational preparation. Ruth (l-i) responded: "To learn what you want to do when you get out of high school." Les (l-i) said: "Learn things to help on the job." Beth (l-i) recommended: "Learn to

TABLE 4.2. Opinions About the Purposes of School

	Low-Income		High-Income	
	N	(%)	N	(%)
Purpose of School				
Basic skills	21	(53)	15	(44)
Vocational preparation	15	(38)	14	(41)
Other	4	(10)	4	(12)
Undecided	–		1	(3)
Importance of the Curriculum				
Important	16	(40)	16	(48)
Somewhat important	15	(38)	13	(39)
Unimportant	6	(15)	2	(6)
Undecided	3	(8)	3	(9)
Future Directedness of the Curriculum				
Future oriented	22	(55)	18	(54)
Somewhat future oriented	5	(13)	7	(21)
Not future oriented	8	(20)	7	(21)
Undecided	5	(13)	2	(6)

(Note: Due to rounding, percentage totals do not necessarily add to 100.)

try to become something—make something of yourself, accomplish things." Bret (l-i) felt that school should "make it easier to get a job." Karen (l-i) said: "School gives you the chance to get ready for a good job." Libby (h-i) replied: "School teaches discipline—self-discipline. You need it for growth and for a successful career." Damon (h-i) stated: "To be better prepared for the job market."

Four "prepare for the future" ("other") responses were not specifically vocational. Adam (l-i) said: "Teach you stuff to get you ready for your life." And Annie (l-i) replied: "Educate you for the world." Hilary (h-i) felt that school's purpose was to: "Help you get through society easier." John (h-i) said: "Helps us learn to succeed."

Categorized "other," Andrew (h-i) responded, "Keep kids occupied—out of trouble" and Marissa (h-i) said, "To make sure ignorant people aren't running around the streets." Then she added: "When they're in school children have less free time to get in trouble." Two "other" responses by low-income adolescents referred to moral development. After confessing she had recently been to court on a shoplifting charge and had previously gotten into trouble in school for cheating and theft, Celestine (l-i) said school was "to teach you right from wrong." Michael (l-i) believed "school is to help you learn to be a good person in the world and make something of yourself." Thus they granted school moral authority over their lives.

In judging the importance of school, 32 teenagers (43%) glibly indicated that it was "taken for granted" that what they learned in school was important, yet there was considerable dissent (see Table 4.2). There was also some ambivalence about whether school was future-oriented. Particularly low-income adolescents were not convinced that the time and effort put into school would "pay off" on the short or long run.

In spite of their lack of satisfaction with the present curriculum, 16 low-income adolescents (40%) could not think of anything that they would like to be learning in school that presently was not covered. As Randy said: "Not really. There are some things I could do without. I'd like to be an electronics technician for the government. I can't do creative writing or art, and I don't think they'll help me in the future. I don't like those subjects." Sonia replied: "Probably nothing. I think I'm learning more than I need to know right now." Four sarcastically indicated that they were doing too much already, and another's "everything" conveyed that she was presently not learning much. Half of the low-income teenagers wanted more and/or better vocational training. Seven others wanted more of a certain kind of academic work to overcome deficits or meet certain needs.

High-income adolescents furnished a multitude of suggestions for improving school—often wanting to eliminate things that were difficult for them. Polly complained:

Science is never interesting. I can't see the point in it. Math is a big
chore. I know I need to know this stuff to make decisions for college,
but a lot of it is boring and I really wonder if I need to know it. Languages are important. I'd like more languages, and I'd like to start
them earlier. I don't like the way most of the classes are set up. I like
to read and I like learning, but I don't like being tested. I forget most of
what I learn as soon as I get home.

In contrast, Simon said: "Some things are important, like science; it's usually
interesting. I feel like English is more of the same—I don't see myself being
able to use my ability to pick out nouns and verbs in the future. Languages
are a pain. I hate the memorizing." Probably because they were in college
preparatory classes, high-income adolescents were less critical of the types of
courses they were taking than the way they were taught.

The suggestions of both high- and low-income adolescents conformed to
present school practices; they wanted more of the same, less of the same, or
the same in a more stimulating format. Conforming to outsiders' (e.g., teachers, general public) perceptions of their capabilities, low-income adolescents
claimed to want very basic and practical curricula. They conveyed that they
needed to "get by" but not achieve or compete.

STRATIFIED CLASSROOM ARRANGEMENTS

Tracking

The local school corporation uses ability groups, tracks, and special education, supposedly to accommodate the diverse achievement levels and behavior patterns of students. Chapter I reading and math tutorial programs
exist in the low-income elementary schools for primary-age students. There
are special education classes for "learning-disabled" (three to five classes per
secondary school), "mildly mentally retarded" (one to four classes per school),
and "emotionally handicapped" (one to three classes per school). All four secondary schools also have classrooms for students with moderate and severe
disabilities.

Because there are no central administration policies about tracking, I
contacted building administrators to find out about tracking and ability-group
practices. Interviews with them revealed widely divergent tracking patterns
with distinct rationales, techniques, terminology, and criteria for pupil assignment. One principal cited inclusionist principles ("I think it's best to keep
students together") for avoiding tracking; another cited administrative ease

("I've found tracking to be a headache—more trouble than its worth"); and another maintained that random grouping avoided "concentrating all the trouble-makers in a few classrooms."

The method used to determine tracks at Beauford Middle School was first to divide students into three categories (based on their fifth-grade achievement test scores, grades, and teacher recommendations), then split the middle group "randomly" between the high and low sections. The rationale offered was to avoid "putting too many low-achieving disciplinary problems together"; hence the better-behaved middle-status students could buffer the behaviors of their lower-functioning classmates. It was volunteered that family name, address, feeder school, and parental preference also entered the decision-making process. Parental requests were "almost always respected unless the student is miserably low." The administrator went on to complain that many parents were "pushy" in demanding high placements for their children. According to student and teacher rumor, the children from low-income feeder schools and the black children were inevitably assigned to low sections. The administrator admitted that low tracks included mainly low-income children but maintained that this was due to the nature of the children and/or the quality of their elementary schools. She also argued that the children were divided according to those who typically attend college and those who do not— a division she said would occur in high school anyway. Tracks were openly referred to with the semantically loaded "high" and "low." The administrator asserted that there were "no problems" with this system and stated: "I believe that we are accomplishing as much with homogeneous grouping as could be accomplished in heterogeneous classes." Even high-income people in the community complained that Beauford was elitist and catered to the most affluent children.

The high schools had four track levels, referred to as honors, advanced, general, and basic (remedial). Gifted-and-talented sections and advanced-placement (in which college credit is given) arrangements were created on an ad hoc basis by certain teachers for certain courses. Middle school counselors and elementary school faculty worked collaboratively to determine track placements, referring to students' grades, scores on standardized achievement tests, and teacher recommendations, supposedly in that order. But counselors and principals readily admitted that parental requests were respected "if there was room in the section," "unless the student was real, real low." (The direction of request was apparent from that statement.) According to school personnel, high-income parents routinely made such requests.

With the exception of social studies, all high school academic courses were tracked; however, even in social studies, certain courses were traditionally taken by college-bound students and others by general-track students.

Moreover, once students were tracked for some courses, scheduling convenience usually meant that enrollments in untracked classes were congruent with those of tracked classes.

Adolescents discussed the nature of grouping in the schools they attended, their typical group assignment, and their opinions about grouping practices (see Table 4.3). Twenty-nine low-income adolescents discussed homogeneous grouping, while 11 claimed not to understand the question or were evasive or noncommittal in responding. It was obvious from the courses and teachers they talked about that most low-income respondents were in general or basic tracks; still, 18 could not "remember" or did "not know" their track placement.

A number of explanations for this amnesia about grouping are plausible. Students might not have been cognizant of grouping, they might have genuinely forgotten about earlier grouped situations, or they might have failed to connect questions about grouping with what had occurred in their schools. Teachers and counselors attempt to handle ability grouping discreetly. Research, however, indicates that students are fully aware of grouping arrangements and that they make a lasting impression on them (Eder, 1981; Jones, Erickson, & Crowell, 1972; Mehan, 1979; Page, 1991). Hence it is more likely that participants were reluctant to talk about the topic because of distressful memories or that they deliberately concealed this embarrassing part of their school careers. They found it easier to say "I don't know" or "I don't remember" than to reveal their humiliating group status.

Many seemed oblivious to the fact that high school tracking was a deliberate grouping practice. The tracks may have seemed so permanent and intrinsic to the schools that they were not perceived as resulting from human decision making. In contrast to the impervious high school tracks, the reshuf-

TABLE 4.3. Attitudes Toward Tracking

Attitude	Low-Income		High-Income	
	N	(%)	N	(%)
Liked tracking	11	(28)	17	(50)
Disliked tracking	9	(23)	5	(15)
Neutral about tracking	2	(5)	12	(35)
No awareness of tracking	11	(28)	0	
No opinion about tracking	7	(18)	0	
Total	40		34	

(Note: Due to rounding, percentage totals do not necessarily add to 100.)

fling of students for ability groups at the elementary level were more salient, so many of them focused on elementary school practices. Nevertheless, in spite of some confusion about the general nature of grouping, low-income adolescents did know that preppies were not in their classes (e.g., "Preps take different kinds of science and different kinds of math; we just take regular science and math"; "The high-class kids take all those hard classes") and, at one point or another in the interviews, most complained about the second-class feel of their programs or courses. The few who were in college preparatory classes proudly announced this; it was clear they were well aware of the status differentials of various tracks.

High-income adolescents quickly understood questions about ability grouping and, with the exception of four, claimed that they had been in high (e.g., "honors," "advanced," "gifted-and-talented," "top," "advanced-placement," "upper-level," "fast") or above-average tracks. The majority (i.e., 26) were in favor of homogeneous grouping, evaluating it as something that could not be done without. Those opposed to tracking usually admitted that through the years they had worried about staying in advanced groups or said that their average-group assignments made them feel "mediocre" and "inadequate." Some recalled that the high-income schools "did not have low tracks," but it was obvious to them that "middle" tracks had been established for the less competent. Two disdained the peer competitiveness that tracking encouraged and expressed empathy for students in low tracks.

Attitudes about tracking reflected adolescents' track status. The seven low-income adolescents who said they had been in average or advanced levels generally judged ability grouping practices to be fair. Scott said: "Yes, it's fair. You can work at your own pace." Will said: "I don't mind them. You learn more in the high groups." Madalene elaborated: "It's done according to your ability—if kids do good then they can move up. If the low readers are with the others, they'll get discouraged and give up." Others who claimed advanced-group status were not as ready to endorse the system. Louann ventured: "I was in the top group. I always liked to read. But I always felt sorry for the ones in the lower groups. They felt sorry for themselves. I tried to help them, like in the lunchroom or at recess." Trent said: "They're okay. I was in about the highest [in special education]. I would feel bad if I was in the lowest."

The seven adolescents who admitted to being in low groups were inevitably ambivalent or negative. Stacy divulged: "I usually got put in the dumb groups. It was awful. I hated it. It did not seem like we were really that bad." Kit admitted: "The highest group felt proud, we—the lowest—stupid." Adam complained: "The teacher made a big deal out of making up silly names for groups. If you were in the low group everybody would tease you with that name. The names for the slow groups were the worst." Sheila asserted: "I really don't like that. They put you on different levels and then the teachers say: 'Well, this level is not as smart as this level.' I wasn't always in the lowest groups, but others would still say they were smarter than you." Celestine flatly stated: "I preferred no groups."

Some noted the connection between track level and social status. Darcy (l-i) thought: "The low group felt bad. The high groups felt snobby—better than everybody else." Carol (l-i), who had been "embarrassed and ashamed" in low groups, conjectured: "I guess they want the other ones to learn—for the good to get better." Randy (l-i) said: "Usually I was in the medium, where I was supposed to be." He did not directly state that he had also been in lower groups but noted: "People in lower groups feel bad. Other people look down on you."

In talking about the long-term stability of group membership, Thomas (l-i) noted: "They expected you to stay in the same group. There was no opportunity to improve—no chance for change." Karen (l-i) recalled: "Sometimes teachers didn't give you a chance to move to a higher group. I don't know why." In contrast, Chrissy (l-i) explained: "Once I was in a higher group, and it felt weird to be separated from my friends. I got confused, so they put me back down in the low group."

In spite of resenting tracking, low-income respondents were rarely critical of judgments made by school staff, begrudgingly indicating that tracking decisions were "accurate" or "fair." Max felt the practice prevented some students from "flunking." Some stated that tracking was necessary, stressing the criterion of convenience (i.e., tracks made it "easier for the teacher" or "easier for the students"). Tracy optimistically projected: "If all groups are treated the same, all the groups will get better."

More high- than low-income respondents favored tracking, but more also argued that they had been incorrectly placed, that others were placed in higher tracks than they deserved, or that the placements of students often reflected bias on the part of school personnel. As usual, they challenged authority, especially school personnel's judgments about themselves. Those in advanced tracks claimed that with increased effort or parental request they could move to honors sections, asserting that there was not much difference between those levels. High-income adolescents were skeptical of an intelligence and track correlation for the higher tracks, but they were vehement that students in advanced tracks were academically and intellectually superior to those in low tracks (e.g., at the high school level they referred to general or vocational tracks). Only a few acknowledged social class–stratifying or discriminatory aspects of tracking. Andrew said: "It's pretty predictable who's going to be in which group. They might as well just ask what your parents do and make the placements." Sarah said: "All the poorer kids are in the low classes. I wonder who decides where different kids should be."

Special Education

Like tracking, special education for students classified as mildly handi-capped evolved as a result of pupil heterogeneity and is, in essence, a highly formalized track system. Federal law (PL 94-142) and various state statutes mandate set procedures (i.e., due process) for referral, pupil evaluation, and decision making about services provided. Children from low-income families are especially likely to be educated in special education classrooms (Carrier, 1986; Gerber, 1984; Kugelmass, 1987; Ysseldyke, Algozzine, & Richey, 1982).

In spite of the fact that special education numbers have increased steadily over the past two decades (Carter & Sugai, 1989), Greer (1989) and Thiessen (1987) have noted the lack of research focus on students' attitudes toward special education. It is known that students placed in special education are confused about their labels (Sachs, Iliff, & Donnelly, 1987) and that they experience considerable stress about placement decisions (Dupont, 1989; Esquivel & Yoshida, 1985). Moreover, research reveals that up to 50% of students receiving such services drop out of school prior to graduation (deBettencourt, Zigmond, & Thornton, 1989; Wolman, Bruininks, & Thurlow, 1989; Wyche, 1989).

Consumer participation in special education placement decisions is man-dated; nevertheless, students and their families may not have sufficient infor-mation about school options or their own rights to make sound decisions. Although they may not prefer special education settings and handicap classi-fications for their offspring, parents may consent because they are frustrated by the negative circumstances (e.g., low grades, disciplinary measures, teacher complaints) their children encounter in regular classrooms or they may not know that they have the right to disagree with professional wisdom (E. A. Brantlinger, 1985c, 1987). Moran (1984) stated her belief that low-income parents perceive the professional judgment of school personnel as legitimate authority and feel relatively powerless during interaction, even when their opinions are supposed to be solicited.

In this study, adolescents' definitions of special education and percep-tions of students classified as handicapped varied according to social class. In describing special education students and services in their schools, most high-income respondents alluded to students with severe handicaps (e.g., "The ones in wheelchairs and stuff are in a class by the home ec. room"), whereas low-income respondents referred exclusively to students with mild disabilities (e.g., "Sometimes people are put there because their grades are low; it's not that they're dumb, but they need extra help"). Many high-income adolescents were unaware of the presence of programs for students classified as mildly handi-capped or they had little information about them (e.g., "I don't know about special education; I haven't really thought about it; I usually don't converse with them because of different schedules").

The distinct perceptions according to social class were likely to be the result of the different rates of classification and placement among high- and low-income adolescents (see Table 4.4). In addition to the eighteen low-income students who were receiving special education services at the time of the interviews, four had previously been placed and four had been referred but not placed. In contrast, only two high-income students had been classified as learning-disabled (LD), and both went to resource rooms one period a day for support for their college preparatory courses.

Because of the social class distinctions in rates of classification and placement, there were also distinctions in exposure to classified peers. Low-income respondents had siblings and "lots of" friends in special education, while few high-income adolescents could name any. Low-income adolescents used personal referents in discussing special education students (e.g., "My sister is in an LD class"), while upper-income adolescents used the impersonal "them" (e.g., "Some people are slow learners; special education helps *them*"; "I guess it's a good thing for kids that can't do all right otherwise—so *they* don't have to go without an education; it helps *them* lead a normal life"). One high-

TABLE 4.4. School Careers of Adolescents

	Low-Income		High-Income	
	N	(%)	N	(%)
Above grade level	0		6	(18)
On grade level	11	(28)	28	(82)
Retained 1 year	9	(23)	0	
Retained 2 years	6	(15)	0	
In mildly mentally handicapped class	3	(8)	0	
In emotionally handicapped class	1	(3)	0	
In learning disabilities class	10	(25)	0	
In LD resource	4*	(10)	2*	(6)
Previously in special education	4*	(10)	0	
Classified but not placed	1*	(3)	0	
Referred but not placed	3*	(8)	0	
Total classified handicapped	23	(57)	2	(6)
Total	40		34	

* Also included in first four rows.
(Note: Due to rounding, percentage totals do not necessarily add to 100.)

income student claimed contact through being a "peer tutor in a moderate classroom."

Attitudes toward special education varied according to both income level and special education status. Twenty-seven high-income respondents were positive about special education. With little firsthand information, high-income adolescents spoke abstractly and seemed to be quoting parents, teachers, or the media rather than forming their own opinions (e.g., "I think it's good because some can't get into the mainstream of school and this gives them the special attention they need"; "To my knowledge it's going well; it may have funding problems"). The rationale for special education provided by high-income adolescents was that schools should accommodate differences in learners (e.g., "Special education gives them a chance to do better at their level"; "I think we really need to educate people according to their ability"). They saw special education as a benevolent and helpful service for others.

Of the 22 low-income adolescents who had received special education services, only 2 were entirely positive about it. Les (classified as emotionally handicapped) was particularly fond of his teacher: "I like special education. They treat you better. I think it's a good thing. Mr. W. has turned me around. He's helped me. Special education gives you more chances." Les's father had previously been imprisoned for abusing him. Thomas (LD), who had gone to resource rooms while in elementary school, said: "I was in special education and it helped me. I was glad because I was not doing well by myself. It's helpful. They shouldn't put people down for being in special ed." He then added: "I'm glad they decided I don't need it anymore."

Five respondents, including three of the four served in resource rooms, were ambivalent. Two thought special education was necessary for them because, as Tracy put it: "I don't like special ed., but I don't think that I could do the work in regular high school. It would be hard for me, and I wouldn't pass. I would never graduate." Trent said: "I guess the smaller classes help me. I'd rather avoid it. I used to hate it. Now I just don't think about it, but I don't like it when people call me stupid." Kit and Darcy were negative about the placement but positive toward teachers (e.g., "I felt bad when I heard I was going to be in special education; I'm sort of used to it now; it's embarrassing to be in special ed., but the teachers are better—they're not as mean"; "I feel good about some of it; some of it I don't; the teachers are nice"). The two high-income (LD) students were neutral (i.e., "I guess it's okay"; "It doesn't bother me").

Fourteen classified low-income students (67% of those in special education) were negative about special education—most unremittingly so. Tammy said: "I hated it. That's why I quit school. I couldn't take another year there." Dusty complained: "It's awful. When you first go they say it will only be for awhile, but you never get out once you're there." A few started out neutral

(e.g., "It's okay") but became progressively more animated, intense, and critical as they talked. Nadia first said: "It don't hurt me none. People are different—they're born that way. That's just the way it is." Later, she confessed:
"To me, you see, being in special education makes a difference. To me, intelligence makes a difference. I try to be smart. I study hard. I try to prove myself
to the teacher. I would really like to be smart. Maybe other kids don't care.
Being in special education tells other people that you're dumb."

The most intensely negative sentiments were expressed by adolescents
who had been in special education placements the longest. Many of the 14
presently in self-contained classrooms had spent most of their school careers
in such placements. Dusty (LD) related: "I started in special when I was in
fifth grade—12 years old! I've been in it ever since. I don't like it. I'm supposed to be getting out. It's nice to have because it helps some kids, but
everybody makes fun of you. I can't take that. I would learn more in regular."
At another point in the interview, in response to being asked about his life
goals, Dusty replied: "To get *out* of special education!" Tammy, classified as
mildly mentally handicapped, had quit school on her sixteenth birthday.

Tammy: I went to special ed. when I was at Hillview. I could tell the differ-
     ence. I felt like I learned more in regular. I was upset at first. Mom and
     Dad didn't want me to be there. I wished I could have been in regular. I
     could have succeeded without special ed. Special ed. was not really
     that good.
Interviewer: What about your classmates. Did they need to be in special
     ed.?
Tammy: More of my classmates could have done regular education. The
     whole idea of special ed. is not good. I was embarrassed being in
     special. I pretended I wasn't. I told people I wasn't in special ed.

The feelings expressed by the adolescents who no longer received services were similar to those presently in special classes. Adam (LD) asserted;
"I hated it. I don't know, maybe it helped me. I'm glad I'm out." Kit (LD)
said: "It was too easy. It didn't really help me. You're labeled there. Other
people think it means that you are stupid. I can't help it if I'm kind of slow.
It does hurt my feelings." Nick (LD), whose mother had refused to grant
permission for him to continue in special education, speculated: "It might be
okay if it was handled right. It was not handled right for me. It did not help."

The responses of low-income adolescents depended somewhat on their
classification/placement status, but even those who had never been in special
classes were more negative about it than their high-income schoolmates (e.g.,
"I don't know; I guess it's good for people who need extra time, but a lot of
kids in it don't like it"; "If I needed it, I wouldn't mind—it's helpful for kids

who need it; but my friends there don't like it; they don't think it does much good"; "It's a good thing to try to help them, but when they graduate they will not know the same things that others know"; "I've never been in it; I don't think they should have it; my friends are only doing first- or second-grade work; I have heard you don't learn much"; "I don't know exactly what happens in it, but they're way behind").

Those who were not doing well in regular education were particularly wary of special education (e.g., "It's probably good for people that don't understand, but I don't think I'll need any classes in it"; "It's a slow class for people who don't quite do the work, but it's not for everybody who has problems in school; you have to have, well, real bad problems with learning, you know, special problems"; "That's when they put people who can't do that good together; most have problems; everybody in those classes has the same intelligence"). When asked if special education might alleviate their problems, they emphatically denied the possibility. Chrissy said: "It's good for people who need it, but people who don't need it shouldn't have it. Because of my grades they were going to put me in special education. The school informed my Mom. They gave me a chance to repeat a year instead." Undoubtedly these adolescents were similar to classified peers; nevertheless, they alluded to mysterious differences between themselves and those labeled. They also accepted the standard school definitions of their classified peers.

A unique perspective was given by Leejohn: "I did too good on the tests to get into special. I went to summer school. Special ed. could help me, I think. Special ed. does help the type who need it." In contrast, school dropout Stacy recalled:

> No, I was never in nothing like that. I knew a lot of people who was. I had to go to pre-first. Then I flunked again. I flunked again in eighth— that's when I quit school. I didn't feel that the school's helping them was fair. They wanted to put me in special education, but my mom didn't like it. She wouldn't let me be in them classes.

When asked if special education might have helped her, Stacy replied: "No. I wouldn't want to be in with them. All they done was act like little kids. They did stupid stuff."

Special education was perceived as stigmatizing, and peer rejection and lack of popularity were attributed to special education status. Adam admitted: "I felt bad when I heard I was going to be in special ed. Everybody in school laughs at you." The few who said special education status did not influence relationships with nonclassified peers mostly claimed other special education students as friends or complained they had no friends. Darcy (LD) divulged that she and her classmates "felt embarrassed" about being in special classes, so they discreetly slipped in and out of the special education class-room and asked the teacher to keep the door closed and the door window covered so they would not be seen. Others told how they avoided certain peers from their special education classrooms who "looked retarded" or "acted dumb."

Nine of the fourteen in self-contained classrooms felt that they were not learning as much in special education as they would in regular classes (e.g., "It keeps repeating itself"; "I learned the stuff way back at elementary school"; "They treat us like babies in special ed!"). Although none of the respondents felt that they were learning more, five stated that they were "doing better," that is, they received better grades in special education (e.g., "I'm not failing now"). Three of the four in resource rooms thought the support they received was somewhat helpful; the other said: "I don't think it does much good; I'm still failing."

The three classified as mildly mentally handicapped were evasive about their exact label, using only the generic term "special education." (Their clas-sifications were traced through the names of their teachers.) They referred to themselves as "slow" and "backward." It is unclear if they were really con-fused or if they simply disliked and avoided the term "mentally retarded"; however, the latter is suspected. The terms "mental" and "retard" are among the most commonly used derogatory epithets among local teenagers. Simi-larly, Les, classified as emotionally handicapped, never used that term, but talked about special education in a fairly neutral manner. In contrast, those classified as learning-disabled seemed content with that label but avoided using "special education," which they appeared to associate with emotional distur-bance ("acting crazy," "being weird") or "mental retardation" (e.g., "I'm not exactly in special education, it's something a little different—a little better"; "I used to be in special ed., but now I'm in LD resource").

Mainstreaming

Perhaps because of the close comingling among low-income students who were in special and regular classes, low-income students had little to say about mainstreaming. The term usually had to be defined, but even then they seemed unsure of the rationale for and significance of the idea. When asked more generally about the integration of diverse students, however, 32 (80%) whole-heartedly endorsed the idea of pupil heterogeneity, stating the belief that different kinds of children should attend integrated school settings (see Chap-ter 2).

High-income respondents, more distant from special class students, had more definitive—even if abstract—reactions to mainstreaming. Twenty-four were positive (e.g., "They need special attention because of their handicaps, but I don't feel they should be secluded all the time"; "They should take normal classes—the ones they can handle—with normal kids"; "I don't get to see them; I think it may be bad for them"; "I'm not sure what goes on in those classes because the teachers and the students in it are separated from the rest of the school; I think they probably should mix more"; "I suppose mainstreaming would get them with other kids; it doesn't bother me; I see them as regular people"; "It's a good idea to mix them in with society since they live here").

Ten high-income adolescents were hesitant about endorsing mainstreaming, with seven focusing on the treatment of special education students (e.g., "Special education itself is good, but they are tormented so much at school"; "They shouldn't have to go to the public school and be subjected to the kind of treatment they get here"; "It makes me mad when people make fun of them"; "I don't think it's fair for them to go to a school like Loring Junior High; they get harassed—made fun of; I understand that they want them to be with normal kids, but it is just not fair to them"). The remaining three admitted that they were opposed to mainstreaming because they disliked personal exposure to people with disabilities (e.g., "They should be in this school, I guess, but the way they act bugs me"; "Personally, I'd rather not have them here"; "They're embarrassing; I guess it's good for them to be with us though").

TEACHERS

Perceptions of Teachers

Just as a quantitative analysis of "feelings about school" made the attitudes of both groups seem fairly similar, a fine-tuned perusal of narratives about teachers revealed low-income adolescents to be considerably less positive (see Table 4.5). Among the "mixed" replies, high-income adolescents liked "all but one or two," whereas low-income teenagers provided lower ratios (e.g., "about one in four of them," "last year maybe two out of seven"). Fairly global in his dismissal of teachers, Dean (l-i) confided: "I never did like school or teachers. Me and teachers didn't get along. Some was all right. Most was snobby." Similarly, Sheila (l-i) summarized: "Teachers were too defensive—worried about discipline. I'd say 'no' to liking teachers." Trent said: "No. Not really. Teachers give me a hard time."

Although on one level special education was resented, in the context of "liking teachers," the large percentage of special education students among low-income respondents clearly inflated the positive "attitude toward teach-

TABLE 4.5. Attitudes Toward Teachers

	Low-Income		High-Income	
	N	(%)	N	(%)
Affect Toward Teachers				
Likes teachers	17	(43)	18	(52)
Ambivalent toward teachers	16	(40)	15	(45)
Dislikes teachers	7	(18)	1	(3)
Teacher Affect Toward Student				
Affect positive	16	(40)	24	(72)
Affect mixed	16	(40)	8	(24)
Affect negative	8	(20)	2	(6)
Teachers' Caring Personally About Student				
Caring	11	(28)	15	(44)
Somewhat caring	15	(38)	15	(44)
Uncaring	14	(35)	4	(12)
Relationships with Teachers				
Positive relations	23	(58)	22	(64)
Mixed relations	9	(23)	10	(30)
Negative relations	8	(20)	2	(6)
Total	40		34	

(Note: Due to rounding, percentage totals do not necessarily add to 100.)

ers" response (i.e., 13 of the 17 with positive affect were students in special education). Teresa, classified as mildly mentally handicapped, recalled and hypothesized: "Teachers were nice to me and I was nice to them. If you are nice to them, they're nice to you." The most negative affect was expressed by 15 low-income teenagers (37.5%) in regular classes who had repeated one or two grade levels and were currently not doing well in school.

The importance of teachers' attitudes toward them in the formation of student affect was very evident, as Stacy (l-i) recollected:

I didn't like one teacher. Everything she said was so fast. You couldn't understand her. And she was real snotty. If you couldn't do it, she'd say you were stupid. I liked Mrs. H. She liked me and she explained things well.

Similarly, Louann (l-i) remembered: "Mrs. K. at Hillview treated us like her kids. I loved that woman. I never got into any trouble with her." Nadia (l-i) recalled: "I had one who was really nice. She was a beautiful teacher. She taught me a lot. You could talk to her like a big sister. She was nice to me. Once she took me and another girl to dinner. I still see her sometimes."

Unfortunately, only 40% of the low-income adolescents felt that teachers liked them, and only 20% felt teachers cared about them personally (see Table 4.5).

Wendy: Teachers don't like me. They don't care about what happens to me.
Interviewer: Can you think of any who do care?
Wendy: No!

When asked if teachers had liked her, Louann, a dropout, initially said: "No, not really." Then she remembered: "Oh, maybe Mr. M. at South. He'd talk to me. He'd say, 'If you don't come to school, you'll get in a lot of trouble.' He tried. It didn't do any good." Categorized "affect mixed" and "somewhat caring" (see Table 4.5), Thomas quietly observed: "Some of them might care about me personally—one or two. Most don't. Most ignore me." Chrissy summed up: "Generally teachers did not like me." Trent said: "No—well, my art teacher last year liked me. She praised me. She thought I was a good artist." Les said: "No, not many. I had to work hard at getting along."

Unlike their low-income schoolmates, high-income adolescents conveyed a confidence that teachers would naturally like them and, perhaps more importantly, that they were worthy of being liked. Only two accused teachers of negative affect. Seth, classified as learning-disabled, complained: "Most don't like me. Not every teacher likes every kid. I really don't get along with many teachers. They are stubborn and want me to do things only in their way." Vanessa, a 15-year-old senior who "hated school," asserted: "Teachers stereotype and overgeneralize about certain types of people. I think most think I'm weird and obnoxious."

Among the various symbols of teacher affect were grades. As Trent (l-i) remarked: "The art teacher liked me. She gave me good grades." High-income adolescents' discussions centered around rounding a grade up or down. Hilary said: "Like I have a friend in one class who is really the teacher's pet. We get the same grades on tests, but she always gets better semester grades. It really makes me mad." Low-income adolescents talked about large discrepancies in grading. Wendy, who had been retained twice, bitterly confided:

"No, I doubt that teachers like me. They just care that you get your homework in on time. They don't care what grade you make as long as they get paid. It don't matter to them if you pass or fail." Sheila said: "I don't like teachers' attitudes. They don't care. I've had teachers say: 'I don't care what you do; it's your grade.' One way I get good grades is if I like the teacher. Teachers make a difference."

The frequency, type, and severity of punishment received by students were also interpreted as signs of teacher affect. Low-income respondents felt they had received more than their share of punishment, while many high-income teenagers bragged that they "got away with" various misbehaviors. Furthermore, in describing ways that they had been punished, high-income teenagers said teachers "talked to" them, whereas low-income adolescents had been "yelled at," "put in the hall," "sent to the office," "whacked," and "suspended"—types of punishment that embarrassed and angered recipients. Several years after the event, Nadia remained bitter about a fifth-grade teacher who had accused her of stealing: "She wasn't being fair on me that one. She could be nice, but evil too." Annie was bothered by a teacher who "was very unfair and always talked down to me." Max complained: "I do one little thing wrong, and they throw the book at me." Ruth summarized flatly: "Discipline depends on how much the teachers like the student."

In describing their interactions with teachers, the majority of immediate responses referred to positive relationships (see Table 4.5), but, among low-income adolescents, negative details surfaced as they talked. The strain between public sentiments and private feelings was evident—honest reactions followed socially acceptable ones (i.e., that relationships should be positive).

Problematic relationships with teachers reported by high-income adolescents typically included only one or two teachers and involved such events as a dispute over a grade or a philosophical or stylistic difference that was discussed relatively calmly. Jeremy (h-i) was mildly perturbed that a teacher had "cut his grade" for his reaction to being pestered by a peer during an exam. Whereas Jeremy shrugged his shoulders and smiled as he talked, an intense Nick (l-i) angrily blurted out: "I got along with a few teachers, but most teachers are not fair. They do not like me." Negative situations with school personnel described by low-income teenagers were more generalized, intense, long-lasting, and personal. Dean (l-i) poignantly related:

> Some was helpful. If you didn't understand, they didn't treat you like you was a piece of trash. Mr. E. was a real cool teacher. He helped you out if you had a problem. Miss B., she don't like me. The only thing she cared about was being on time. We argued a lot. I wouldn't understand. She'd get mad and say, "I showed you how to do it." She'd make you feel dumb. She said: "You'll flunk if you don't do your

work." She was hard on me. Most teachers were hard on me. Mr. E. cared about me. Most didn't.

High-income adolescents not only claimed to have congenial relationships but often admitted that teachers were partial to them. As Nathan said: "They might be a little biased toward me. I guess I'm a teachers' pet. I can usually bend the rules—especially with some teachers." Tyler confessed: "I have a good relationship with teachers. Even when they get mad at something, they don't take action." High-income participants took smooth relationships for granted, indicating that it was the natural outcome of their superior status. It was apparent that they felt entitled to the respect and humane treatment they received from school personnel.

When asked whether they could improve relationships, low-income adolescents were doubtful. Stacy said: "Maybe, if you could sit down and talk to them. But they don't have no time. They talk at you. They don't listen to you. I tried to talk to a counselor once about things. She wouldn't talk no more. She never called me back." Will explained: "I tough it out. I try to straighten up. Last year I tried to improve my relationship with Mr. B.—but it didn't do nothing." Tammy (l-i) timidly conjectured: "Teachers don't really want to change." Low-income adolescents were frustrated about their perceived powerlessness in controlling the nature of relationships.

High-income adolescents, on the other hand, felt that their personal actions influenced their relationships with teachers. Vanessa complained that teachers were "uptight and conservative," but admitted that the negative interactions resulted from her own decision not to conform or be humble. Describing peers who manipulated teachers, Andrew said: "Some of my friends butter-up to teachers. It irritates me that they're just doing it for grades. I guess I could force myself to do that too. That's not really my style though." Similarly, Marissa said: "I know some kids who always have their nose in the teachers' grade book. They pressure teachers. They let them know they're keeping track." Although these behaviors were described with disdain, Marissa and Andrew conveyed that they could also successfully use such tactics.

Low-income adolescents discussed problematic relationships with teachers with strong emotions; the few who claimed not to care had a defensive tone. As Ruth put forth:

No, I don't have good relationships with teachers. They don't try to make school good for you. They just care about getting paid. Sometimes I stand out as a troublemaker, all right, but other times I try not to talk so much or stand out or make smart remarks. It doesn't make any difference. I can't change things. They don't respect me. I don't care what they do.

Sheila expounded:

> Most don't like me. I had one teacher that really didn't like me. I don't
> know why. Every time I'd ask to do something that she let the others
> do, she'd say "No, get back in your seat." We disliked each other a lot.
> They had it in for me. I couldn't have changed them. I wouldn't want to
> change. I didn't want to talk to them. There are teachers that spread
> rumors—they talked to each other about you. One lady was nosy. One
> teacher got the idea that we were talking about her because we didn't
> like her. She'd say "one more smirk; one more noise." In general, I
> don't communicate with some people. I don't really care what they
> think.

The agitation as Ruth and Sheila talked belied their indifference; their manner revealed truer emotions than their rhetoric.

Teacher Attributes

Although high- and low-income adolescents shared many views of teachers, there were class-related distinctions. High-income teenagers were pro-
lific in talking about generic teacher characteristics (e.g., presentation styles,
behavior-management skills), producing about twice as many traits as their
low-income schoolmates. Low-income respondents gave more detailed and
animated accounts of particular teachers.

Seventy-two percent of the low-income teenagers' responses, in contrast
to 39% of those of high-income adolescents, concerned teachers' attitudes.
Moreover, their focus was on teachers' attitudes toward students rather than
toward subject matter or teaching—both of greater concern to affluent youths.
Celestine (l-i) stated:

> I like teachers who are fair about everything. Who show they care. Who
> put up with kids who are a pain in the butt. They expect you to get
> your work done. They push you. They like to hear new ideas from
> people. They like to make school the best way they can so that people
> won't quit. Some teachers make everybody think that they are intelli-
> gent. They think well of anyone who will put forth an effort.

Similarly, Randy (l-i) liked:

> Somebody willing to listen, to understand. Sometimes when they tell
> me to go up and read something in class I can't do it. My voice starts
> cracking, I start sweating, I pass out. In creative writing, I wouldn't read

in front of the class. I'd take the bad grade instead. It's insecurity—
stage fright! I need a teacher who understands.

Darcy (l-i) appreciated: "Teachers who listen to you, have patience, and
understand." Beth (l-i) liked: "The ones who don't give up on you." Will (l-i)
felt: "Good teachers can communicate with you. They understand kids. They
talk with you—laugh at your jokes."

For low-income youth, the most disliked teachers were the ones who
humiliated students. Thomas said: "When you ask for help, some respond
'Weren't you listening?' They accuse you of doing something wrong. Most are
not very helpful." Chrissy liked: "Ones that make you feel like they want to
help; that take time to teach and don't make you feel dumb." Tricia concluded:
"Bad teachers don't make you comfortable in their classes." Providing a positive example, Madalene said: "Like my math teacher. She has a sense of
humor, which most don't have. If you have a question, she doesn't look down
on you like you're dumb. She has you work at the board, and you're not
embarrassed in her room." Virtually no high-income adolescents accused teachers of humiliating them or of looking down on them.

Adolescents made numerous suggestions for improving teaching competencies. Since "boring" was constantly on their tongues, it is not surprising
that responses focused on what teachers do to relieve the boredom of school.
Scott (l-i) said: "Some teachers care to talk—to make it interesting. Some just
say 'Do the assignment.'" Polly (h-i) felt: "Good teachers can talk—embellish
on the material. They lead interesting class discussions." Humor was also
important. Barbara (h-i) judged: "Good teachers are funny and make classwork
interesting, not boring. But they're serious about school." Will (l-i) volunteered:
"Good teachers let you have fun in class. They crack jokes and tell funny stories. Everything is not so serious all the time." Hilary's (h-i) least favorite
teacher was "not creative. Bored us to death—droned on. Learned everything
he knew from books."

Some students enjoyed hearing teachers' personal anecdotes, whereas
others did not. Karen (l-i) said: "I had one man and one woman teacher who
really made things interesting. Sometimes they broke off from a subject and
told personal experiences. They liked to discuss politics, and we'd have a good
class discussion." On the other hand, John (h-i) complained: "Some teachers
bore us with their personal experiences. Who cares!" And Marissa (h-i) said:
"Teachers talk about the past all the time. I don't know why they think I should
be interested in something they did in 1942."

Conveying subject-area information effectively was a common concern,
with high-income responses centered on knowledgeable lecturers and creative
assignments. Libby responded: "Good teachers continue to learn about what
they are teaching. They lecture in an organized manner so you can take good

notes." Ian said: "I don't like teachers who just write your assignment on the board and expect you to do it in the same old way. Or if they want you to do it just their way. Good teachers are good explainers. They actually teach so that you don't have to read all you learn." Andrew clarified: "I like teachers who know what they are doing, who know the subject well, and know how to teach it."

Low-income adolescents usually discussed teachers' making subject matter comprehensible. Regarding assignment clarity, Will complained: "Bad teachers don't explain the work. When you had a question, they said: 'Look it up in the book!' Lots of time I did that and I still did not understand." Randy felt: "A good teacher is somebody who can explain stuff. Sometimes I can't understand directions no matter how many times I read them." Ruth was bothered because: "One teacher said everything too fast. I couldn't understand her. She used big words and thought we should know them." Sheila believed: "Good teachers are willing to help you when you need the help. They want your opinion and listen to what you say. They teach at your level instead of teaching only to the higher levels." Chrissy elaborated:

> There was some teachers, when you don't know how to do something, they'd just force you to do it. The math teacher helped me. She had me come after class for extra help. She was a good teacher. Good teachers help people after class. They don't just say "Do so and so" or "Read this and that" or "Do the worksheet." Some don't even go over it. They just say "You should know how to do it." Mrs. L., she helps you after she explains. She calls certain people up for help. She's very helpful.

Responses indicated that high-income adolescents perceived themselves as capable of understanding; hence they focused on teachers' roles in relaying information appropriately. In contrast, low-income respondents conveyed a mind-set that they were not always capable of understanding—that not understanding was their own fault. Therefore they focused on the importance of teachers "helping" them comprehend. Whether these divergent stands were the result of dominant myths or the result of an accumulation of school experiences is not known; however, it is clear that most low-income adolescents worried about their ability to understand what was taught.

All respondents appreciated teachers who had clear and reasonable expectations. Barbara (h-i) liked: "Teachers who get things done but don't overload work." Damon (h-i) complained: "Some teachers don't know how to teach a subject, but they still expect a lot from us." May (l-i) asserted: "I get tired of some teachers. On some days you just sit around, then, all of a sudden they pile on the work. You never know what they're going to do. My grades suffer when teachers are like that."

There was a consensus that good teachers were organized and consistent. Jamie (h-i) complained: "Some are disorganized and let problems go by in class." Darcy (l-i) fretted: "Mrs. B. sometimes just throws papers on her desk, and sometimes she loses papers and stuff. I did my 20-page paper on drugs. My mom took me to the library. I worked very hard. She gave me a D. It did not seem fair." Celestine (l-i) was bothered that: "Last year I had a teacher that was a pain in the butt. I got my work in and he lost it. He didn't give me credit. He failed me. He was not fair. He's careless. He done it to lots of kids last year."

Fairly equivalent numbers of both groups appreciated teachers who were effective in classroom management. Sonia (l-i) said: "Good teachers joke around, but they discipline you when you need it. They get the point across." But more low-income adolescents mention the impact of poor discipline on their own school experience. As Carol (l-i) expounded:

> When they teach us and kids act up—if the kids keep it up—I expect them to do something about it. We're trying to learn and they're disturbing us. I expect the teacher to tell them to be quiet or spit out gum. If there's a fight, the teacher shouldn't sit and watch. Good teachers know how to do things like handle kids—discipline kids.

Similarly, Thomas (l-i) clarified: "Some people hate school. They make it worse for everyone by getting in trouble. Some teachers don't know what to do about them. They have to stop teaching for them. You don't get through as much as you need to."

Adolescents distinguished between strictness and meanness. According to Andrew (h-i): "Good teachers are friendly—but they don't have to be your best friend. They're strict because they want you to learn, but they're not mean." Tracy (l-i) liked "teachers who were real nice" and disliked "teachers who were real mean." Leejohn (l-i) said: "I loved my English teacher. She was strict, but I really enjoyed her class. Some teachers don't teach, they just yell!" Like Leejohn, more low-income adolescents described teacher behaviors that could be called unprofessional. They complained about teachers yelling or otherwise overreacting. Low-income youth were also more likely to mention fairness.

References to teachers' personal and personality attributes, such as appearance, mannerisms, and speech patterns, were much more prevalent in the narratives of high-income adolescents. Angie disliked a teacher who "thought she was perfect, took things too seriously." Sarah said a teacher "was a fake on top of being mean." Hilary complained that a teacher "talked weird. It bugged me." Ian said: "Mr. C. speaks in a monotone. It puts me to sleep." Polly volunteered: "About half of the teachers down there talk with a southern twang. They sound real ignorant. It seems like being able to speak English right should be one requirement for teaching, but I guess not!" Jessica complained: "I don't like this one teacher who always dresses like she's going to a cocktail party. She wears more makeup in one day than I wear in a year. She really gets on my nerves." Marissa remarked: "There's this one teacher who dresses like a dork. He could get a prize for worst dresser."

Nine high-income adolescents remarked on teachers' intelligence or literacy in their discussions. Tony said: "Some teachers are pretty dumb. I really think the students know as much as they do. But if you correct them, they get pretty nasty. They resent it." Andrew said: "I had a science teacher who seemed intimidated by students. I think he thought we were smarter than he was—he was probably right!" Polly responded: "I get annoyed at ignorant teachers. I really do. I've even had some teachers grade me down because they can't understand what I'm talking about."

Expansive in delineating generic teacher qualities, most high-income teenagers were somewhat indifferent when asked to discuss particular favorite and least favorite teachers. Libby said: "I don't really have a favorite. They are all pretty much the same. There's nobody I particularly dislike either." Ian volunteered: "They're all pretty mediocre. Nobody stands out as being especially good or especially bad. I guess I like a couple of my math and science teachers better than the others." Sarah remembered being afraid of a third-grade teacher because "the lady threw temper tantrums. She even threw things around the room. But in some ways she was a good teacher. We did interesting things in her class." High-income adolescents' descriptions of specific teachers were typically brief and vague.

Low-income teenagers had no trouble singling out preferred and least preferred teachers, and they gave vivid accounts of individuals. Carol expounded: "I like Mr. G. He's nice. He's real funny. He jokes around with you a lot. He lets you write on the board, take notes to the office—everything. I go up and touch his head—he has a brush cut. He says: 'Don't mess with that, it might not stand back up!'" Usually negative about school, Sheila remembered:

> I had a favorite teacher. He explained if you didn't understand. He really tried to make you understand. He was happy when you got good grades. There would be fun times—someone would say something funny and everyone would laugh and he wouldn't be mad. He'd give you a chance to talk things out, but he wasn't nosy. If you saw him on

the street after school he'd say "Hi, how ya doin'?" He was real friendly, real nice. I really liked him.

Sheila also described a disliked teacher:

I had one teacher that really didn't like me. I don't know why. Everytime I'd ask to do something that she let the others do, she'd say "No, get back in your seat." We disliked each other a lot. She was nosy. She spread rumors about me. She got the idea that we were talking about her because we didn't like her. She'd say "One more smirk! One more noise!" I really hated her. I used to skip her class. I just couldn't stand to see her.

CONCLUSION

There was a consensus among adolescents that the outcome of school attendance should be a broad constellation of skills and knowledge that were essential prerequisites to subsequent enterprises (e.g., college, work, citizenship). They conveyed that they were gradually working through a morass of mainly uninteresting, presently irrelevant but potentially important, subject matter. Regardless of their negative accounts of daily activities, adolescents still assumed that what they were learning would at some time become relevant to their lives. As in Everhart's (1983) findings, adolescents perceived school knowledge as linear, relatively unproblematic, and given; thus they placed themselves in the role of passive recipients. Analyses of adolescents' narratives also give credence to LeCompte's (1978) conclusion that school settings stress authority, time, work, achievement, and order. Everhart's (1983) claim that the content of classroom instruction constitutes reified knowledge (i.e., the subject matter and typical methods of instruction are transformed from ordinary to essential) is replicated by the results of this study. Respondents repeatedly verbalized dominant beliefs about the importance of school.

Accruing school credentials enabled high-income adolescents' college plans; whereas endurance in school was a way to avoid being labeled ignorant or illiterate for low-income youths—graduation would provide them with a stamp of respectability that might allow them to obtain jobs and have a modicum of pride. Even those whose school careers lacked luster optimistically held to such beliefs. If the curriculum was unintelligible or remote, low-income respondents attributed this to their own faulty comprehension, while high-income teenagers attributed it to the instructional inadequacies of teachers. Similar to Ogbu's (1981) findings, the favorable perceptions of the linkages between school and work opportunities seemed to lead to favorable perceptions of school. In spite of the fact that there are continually fewer career possibilities for people not going to college (Howe, 1988), to some extent adolescents, just as in Kickbusch and Everhart's (1985) study, believed in the power of school and had a commitment to technical knowledge.

MacLeod (1987) described inverted values among low-income youth, where the ideology of individual achievement (i.e., if you work hard, you will get ahead) was spurned and a prison record was regarded as prestigious. There was little evidence of this among my respondents, except on a rhetorical (defensive) level. In this study some respondents claimed "not to care" about their performance or that they "couldn't wait to leave school," but at various other points in their interviews, there were signs that school was important to them. Willis's (1977) youth equated manual labor with masculinity and mental labor with social inferiority and femininity. Again, there were no signs of such cognitive associations among participants in this study. Low-income adolescents conveyed that it was prestigious to be "smart" or high-achieving. They were frustrated and embarrassed about not doing well in school.

Teenagers had complex feelings about school. They claimed to be happy when they had positive social relationships and successful academic careers— they disliked social friction and failure. Most unhappy were adolescents who felt lonely or rejected, or who were in trouble in school. In analyzing their responses, it became apparent that threads of dominant messages about the purpose of school and the importance of literacy were interwoven with more personalized negative reactions to school circumstances. In other words, it was difficult to disentangle sincere reactions to school from well-ingrained messages (i.e., common knowledge) about school. However, regardless of the topic, there was a persistent tendency for low-income adolescents to start out with glib, standard replies and advance to negative, emotional discourses. At some level of their thinking, there were cracks in the dominant ideology. There was considerable evidence of critical thinking about school circumstances. Such thinking, however, remained largely fragmented, intermittent, and even incoherent. Since dominant ideologies worked for high-income adolescents, they prevailed from the beginning to the end of their discussions.

There is a tendency to depoliticize school curriculum; as Apple (1987) and Giroux (1992) contend, people think of education as a technological task, asking "how-to" rather than "why" questions. Aronowitz (1980) challenges the perception of scientific (and school) neutrality by arguing that science is con-figured in social relationships and therefore is a form of social knowledge, and thus ideological. The practiced and mundane in the organization of everyday life in school become ideological in that they are sanctified; thus school rituals, with distilled meanings embodied in their rhythms and gestures, are part of a historical–cultural existence, which is inherently political (McLaren, 1987). Even though schools' stated goals are couched in the context of individuals' need for technical training and job credentials, Shor and Freire (1987) accuse dominant classes of setting up a delivery system to market official ideas that correspond to capitalist ideology; "the dominant ideology living within us" (p. 113) is made complete and definitive by schools. Likewise, Berman (1984) maintains that school is the most visible arena in which capitalist hegemony is disseminated to a captured clientele.

It became clear in my study that the significance of school was reified to the point that adolescents accepted its unflattering definitions of themselves (e.g., as low-track, as retarded, as disturbed, as unintelligent) and allowed it to encroach upon their lives with boring, repetitive, and humiliating routines, which were unlikely even to facilitate their personal goals for the future. School as a definer of right and good was illustrated by low-income adolescents assigning it a correctional role (e.g., schools were to help students become honest or better behaved) and granting it moral authority over their lives.

Imagery pertaining to school revealed standard props (e.g., desks, lockers, offices), traditional postures (e.g., raised hands, sitting at school desks), and mundane tasks (e.g., spelling, writing, math problems). Regarding schoolwork, getting it done or "over with" was emphasized. Although vociferous about dissatisfactions with school (e.g., "Listening to the teacher drone on"; "Sick of filling in worksheets"), neither high- nor low-income adolescents were radicals in terms of school restructuring—many could not even be considered reformists. There were no references to modern labs, cooperative groups, or computers. Suggestions for changing schools showed little imagination; apparently respondents could not fantasize beyond their present circumstances. Clearly the structure of school was thoroughly familiar to them—the rituals so automatic that they were unable to envision their developing lives in other activities or other settings.

Peer influence is a consistent correlate of educational outcomes, but the academic advantage for low-income students of being in comprehensive schools depends on being in close proximity to high-income schoolmates (Ide, Parkerson, Haertel, & Walberg, 1981). In spite of the fact that the advantages of integrated schooling for low-income students are well known to school personnel, locally, at the secondary level, tracks split the social classes just as had their own informal social clusterings. Studies have documented that school personnel have negative attitudes toward and less positive interactions with children classified as mildly handicapped who have been mainstreamed (Fox, 1989; Garvar-Pinhas & Schmelkin, 1989; Parker, Gottlieb, Gottlieb, Davis, & Kunzweiller, 1989; Sabornie, Marshall, & Ellis, 1990). Although the flawed nature of regular education settings for students classified as handicapped has been brought to light (Bender, 1988), there is also a scarcity of reliable information about the value of special education for children who tend to be placed there (Carlberg & Kavale, 1980; Edgar, 1988). The message of bifurcation of students into tracks or special education surely widened the schism between the social classes and reinforced their respective self-images.

School's sorting of students is integrally political. In spite of claims that school offers equal opportunity, Ogbu (1986) argues that school socialization is geared toward the development of instrumental competencies required for adult economic and politically structured inequalities. School and workplace for low-income people correspond in that both are bureaucratic, impersonal, hierarchical, routinized, and motivate performance with external rewards (i.e., grades and wages) rather than depending on the value of the enterprise (Carnoy & Levin, 1985). The everyday structuring in schools is similar to requirements in workplaces, with schools or classes for elite groups requiring more creativity and personal control and those for children of subordinate classes dwelling on routine tasks and conformity (Anyon, 1980). Knowledge and skills leading to social power are made available to advantaged social groups but withheld from the working classes, who get a more practical curriculum. Such curricular distinctions legitimate and perpetuate a given social order by making social hierarchies appear to be based on merits or attributes (Bourdieu & Passeron, 1977).

Adolescents described tracks as being correlated with social class, but they still, somewhat hesitantly, maintained that track placements were fair and that tracking was probably necessary. Insight into the class-biased nature of the system was likely to have been clouded by the behind-the-scenes approach to the staging of tracks (i.e., track placement was determined covertly without their input and without their access to either the criteria used to track or information about how such criteria are applied) and by the commonplace nature of social class separation. Tracking was consistent with well-established views that students from different classes were very different from one another. Thus adolescents did not really expect to be together; in fact, they would have been surprised to find themselves on common ground or equal footing. Similar to Jenkins's (1983) finding about youths in Belfast, adolescents in this study took the legitimacy of their class position in school and society for granted. Although Jenkins's lads showed resistance to school routines, they rarely challenged basic disparities among people. In this study, social class reproduction was evident, and stratification was thoroughly described by respondents. But such inequities in power were inevitably translated into themes of individual differences. Students questioned certain aspects of the learning environment, but this did not lead to their questioning of stratifying practices at large. Kickbusch and Everhart (1985) also found that student epistemologies included a conformist belief that explained school sorting phenomena and discouraged a search for more fundamental explanations.

In an attempt to explain why students were so uncritical of the basic structures of school in spite of being critical of daily existences in school, J. B. Thompson's (1987) four-factor model of successful domination might be applied to this analysis.

1. *Legitimation*: School as a system of domination is sustained by being represented as eminently just and worthy of respect (e.g., school was touted as essential to social mobility—as the way out of poverty).
2. *Dissimulation*: The relations of dominance are concealed and obscured (e.g., adolescents were made to feel that if they were worthy they would have chances to succeed).
3. *Fragmentation*: Groups that might have common perceptions are placed in opposition (e.g., low-income adolescents were divided into various tracks and special education placements, which created a pecking order among them).
4. *Reification*: A transitory historical state of affairs is presented as permanent, natural, and commonsensical (e.g., adolescents viewed the curriculum and curricular tracks as predetermined, set, universal, and unchangeable).

Differential treatment of students at various track levels has been well documented (e.g., Bullough, 1987; Eder, 1981; Evertson, 1982; Hallinan & Sorensen, 1985; Page, 1991; Pink, 1982; Rowan & Miracle, 1983; Vanfossen, Jones, & Spade, 1987; Veldman & Sanford, 1984). Bayer (1981) found that the organizational strategy of stratified grouping influences informal social interaction patterns—as early as the first grade a social hierarchy corresponding to reading accomplishments develops. With less successful school careers, low-income respondents in this study had been continually subjected to subordinate levels of stratifying grouping arrangements. Whereas researchers (e.g., Eder, 1981; Oakes, 1985) have found that students are acutely aware of the status of their groups, many of the low-income respondents in this study appeared to have concealed or repressed any memory of grouping. In some cases, the trauma of special education classification and placement apparently overshadowed and obscured that of tracking. Even those in average or advanced tracks nervously conveyed that they felt like imposters or worried that they might end up in low groups at another point in their school careers. They also felt like outsiders, like they were not an integral part of the higher groups.

High-income respondents had little personal exposure to students in special classes and saw them as being very different from themselves. They spoke calmly and positively about special education, describing it as a beneficial service, but one they were unlikely to need. In contrast, special education was an immediate reality for more than half of the low-income respondents. Although they voiced appreciation for caring teachers and passing grades, with few exceptions, low-income adolescents resented their labels and placements. Special education signified failure to them, as had other inadequacy-confirming experiences (e.g., low grades, grade-level retentions, low-track placement, teacher hostility). The closer and longer the contact with special education, the more negative the response of adolescents.

Another important finding was the large percentage (i.e., 55%) of low-income adolescents who had been classified as mildly handicapped at some point in their school careers. At the time of the interviews, 18 (45%) were receiving services, 14 of whom were in self-contained (full-day) classes. Even this lowest figure is twice the national average for the combined categories of handicap.

Schools have been accused of finding it easier to label and segregate children whose families wield little power than to consider the context of school as an influential variable in children's school careers (E. A. Brantlinger & Guskin, 1985, 1987; Gartner & Lipsky, 1987; Mehan, Hertweck, & Meihls, 1986; Poplin, 1988; Pugach & Sapon-Shevin, 1987; Sleeter, 1986; Stainback & Stainback, 1984; Tomlinson, 1982; Wang, Reynolds, & Walberg, 1986). Although special education may generally be perceived as designed to meet the needs of classified children, Reynolds (1988) maintains that such children are placed in special education not because of evidence that it will enhance their lives but because it is difficult to tolerate them in regular classrooms.

Far removed from difficult school careers, most high-income adolescents viewed low tracks and special education as charitable arrangements for the less capable. They believed in the common school—in social mixing, at least on a theoretical level—but given their attitudes toward low-income youth, it is likely that their approval of heterogeneous social class arrangements (e.g., detracking, mainstreaming) would exist only as long as such practices did not touch them personally.

Although there was considerable within- and between-class variation in adolescents' descriptions of teachers and their relationships with teachers, the basic teacher role took on conventional forms in the narratives. Teachers were to present academic subject matter in an interesting, easy-to-understand format and were to be consistent and fair in responding to students. The greatest class distinction was that low-income adolescents were attuned to teachers' attitudes toward students and high-income respondents made critical judgments and disparaging remarks about teachers' personalities and pedagogical characteristics. Since high-income teenagers were generally successful in school, they took positive relationships with school personnel for granted—their strivings for competence and belonging had been met. Emotionally secure, they were relatively indifferent to teacher attitudes and were not particularly concerned about their relationships with specific teachers.

Adolescents saw teachers as members of a social class that, for low-income adolescents, was different from their own. Their narratives included details of how members of the other class felt about members of their class—themselves included. A variety of teacher behaviors were interpreted as being snobbish and rejecting. Thus adolescents' interpretations of events and views of people were filtered through subjectivities influenced by social class.

Adolescents had a tendency to humanize experiences; that is, they had personalized interpretations of what happened in school. Low-income adolescents internalized blame, apologizing for their own inability to meet dominant standards, or they embellished on teachers' acts as transgressors. Only rarely did they attribute their status to institutional structure. They construed what happened in school as resulting from personal inadequacies or projected institutional bias onto teachers.

A parallel set of beliefs predominated among high achievers. They held themselves personally responsible for—and thus entitled to—advantages and high status. On an abstract level, high-income participants talked about equity and fairness and criticized teachers who favored others or discriminated against certain groups. At the same time, they were annoyed at teachers who did not give them the preferential treatment they expected. As Mickelson (1990) found, much of the idealism expressed by adolescents appeared to have little impact on concrete relationships. Olson (1983) and Sieber (1982) also document that in spite of idealism about democratic principles, high-income school patrons expect preferential treatment in school and act in ways to secure such treatment.

Thus adolescents responded to teachers not only as members of a social class but also as personifications of the institution of school—which, for low-income adolescents, was an institution that did not work well for them. This meant that teachers took on multifaceted and complex persona, bearing the burden of a collective history of class relationships. The literature on teacher expectancy has recommended that teachers acknowledge themselves as members of a social class, race, or gender whose perceptions of groups are influenced by myths and preconceptions. Not only should teachers be aware of their own feelings toward members of different social groups; they must also be sensitive to the ways that social class affiliations and the unique experiences of members of different classes influence students' subjectivities.

It is important to delve below the surface of students' immediate behaviors and rhetoric in order to understand them. It is often assumed that low-income students do not care about school or teachers, but in this study low-income teenagers spoke in animated ways about teachers—both those they liked and those they disliked. The pretense of not caring by some appeared to be a defensive reaction to anticipated rejection—the emotional manner in which they asserted their indifference belied such claims. Low-income adolescents were less confident in school and felt more vulnerable with teachers. On the outside looking in as school facilitated the agendas of high-income students, low-income teenagers were grateful to teachers who were kind and upset at teachers who humiliated them or appeared uncaring. Teachers were important to them, and they showed definite preferences for particular teachers.

CHAPTER 5

Self as Student

The literature on students' school experiences and school outcomes has demonstrated that regardless of factors measured or criteria used to evaluate, low-income students have less positive school careers than affluent ones. They receive more frequent and more severe discipline for infractions (Balch & Kelly, 1974; Marotto, 1986), and they are likely to be shunned by schoolmates (Eder, 1985; Schwartz, 1987) and rejected or ignored by teachers (Good et al., 1987; Goodlad, 1983; Weinstein, 1983). Their intelligence and achievement test scores, grade-point averages, class rank, and educational attainment are lower (Apple, 1982a; Ogbu, 1986), and they are likely to be in the lowest ability groups and tracks (Anyon, 1981; Eder, 1981; Granovetter, 1986; McNeil, 1987; Mitman & Lash, 1988; Oakes, 1985; Rist, 1970; Winn & Wilson, 1983) or in special education (Brady et al., 1983; Gartner & Lipsky, 1987; Gerber, 1984). Over the past two decades, the rate of children being classified as emotionally disturbed and learning-disabled has increased dramatically (Gerber & Levine-Donnerstein, 1989; Zill & Schoenborn, 1990). At the same time, the school dropout rate went from 22.8% in 1972 to 29.1% in 1984 (Rumberger, 1987), and it has been projected that this rate of growth will continue (McDill, Natriello, & Pallas, 1986).

There is considerable information about the relationships between self-concept and school experiences and outcomes (Birksted, 1976; Brookover, Thomas, & Patterson, 1964; Faunce, 1984; Wang, 1987), yet little is known about how students from different income levels feel about performance distinctions or, more generally, how they see themselves as students. Supposedly people have implicit theories of intelligence (i.e., commonsense notions) that they use to evaluate their own intelligence and that of others (Sternberg, 1984; Sternberg, Conway, Ketron, & Bernstein, 1981), but there is limited information about nonpsychologists' views of intelligence (Yussen & Kane, 1983). Elementary school children use school-related cues, such as grades, work habits, speed, and specific task performance to assess ability (Blumenfeld, Pintrich, & Hamilton, 1986), but little is known about adolescents' beliefs about qualitative associations with intelligence, the impact of nature versus nurture, and the constancy or malleability of intelligence (Wagner & Sternberg, 1984).

In order to gauge the impact of school on students, it is important to explore their perceptions of themselves in student roles. This chapter, then, will address adolescents' feelings about their strengths and weaknesses as students. The way they view connections between their performance in school and their personal intellectual characteristics was of particular interest. In interviewing adolescents, I attempted to discern whether their definitions of intelligence included school-related criteria; that is, whether they defined themselves the way school would probably define them. It also seemed important to try to understand the nature of their appraisals of their own and others' intelligence, particularly if their perceptions had social class overtones.

STRENGTHS AND WEAKNESSES AS STUDENTS

In describing their attributes as students, work habits were the most frequently mentioned by low-income adolescents, with 14 (35%) mentioning them as strengths and another 14 (35%) as weaknesses. Adam's strengths resembled a rule list posted on the wall: "I'm quiet. I pay attention. I don't fight. I do my work." Celestine said: "I don't tarry. I like to get my work done right away." Max divulged: "I work hard if I like a subject." He then added: "If I don't like it, I don't work." In terms of strengths, May boasted: "I'm a good listener. I pay attention. I keep out of trouble." About weaknesses, May replied: "I don't think I have any—I'm strong in almost all subjects." Michael admitted to being a procrastinator.

Work-habit strengths (10, 30%) were second to subject strengths (17, 51%) for high-income youth, and also second as weaknesses (i.e., 12, 36% and 15, 45%, respectively). Perhaps already gearing up for specializing in college, many high-income adolescents believed they had special talents in certain subject areas. Andrew claimed: "Math comes easily for me." Polly said: "I've always been a good writer—I've won some prizes, but I am lousy in math and science, and I don't like them either." Rather than discussing subject-area knowledge, most low-income adolescents focused on skills. Thomas and Carol claimed to be "good readers," whereas Darcy, Les, and Nick felt they were "not good readers." This social class distinction might have been the result of differences in the groups' curricula—lower tracks and special education classes are typically more oriented toward skill than knowledge acquisition.

Attitudinal attributes listed as strengths by five low-income respondents included "open to learning," "caring," and "concerned about school." Annie, whose responses typically diverged from her peers, said: "I think for myself, I concentrate well, and I have fun." Michael claimed: "I'm a good thinker. I have good ideas. I don't get in trouble a lot." On the problematic side, Randy felt that his "insecurity about reciting" was an emotional block that gave him difficulty in school. Karen, too, said: "I'm afraid to speak up in class." Three high-income adolescents talked about being motivated (e.g., "caring about school") or, for two with less than top grades, unmotivated. Some low-income respondents focused on their ability to understand. As Tammy said: "I catch on to things pretty easy." But Stacy complained: "I just didn't understand much." Responses of adolescents who used school criteria to evaluate themselves revealed that they had bought into the routines and mores of school.

Only two low-income and three high-income adolescents alluded to social skills as positive characteristics. Generally altruistic, Carol (l-i) was unique in evaluating herself as a "good friend." She added: "I'm a good listener if someone has a problem." Rachel (l-i) spoke of attempts to avoid trouble by "getting along with everyone and not getting into fights." On the other hand, problematic social behaviors were listed by twelve low-income teenagers (30%). Somewhat playful, Jeff "goofed off" and Will "fooled around." Nadia confessed: "I talked to classmates when I should have been listening." Trent had been scolded for "talking out of turn." Tammy had "sassed back; misbehaved." Sheila admitted: "I talked back. Didn't listen." Annie said: "I talk out too much. Don't listen enough. Tend to lose my temper." Similarly, Sherry revealed: "I get angry fast. I have a hot temper." Adam said: "I was moody, tired." Wendy said: "I get into fights. I fall asleep." Tricia said: "I get mad at preps and fight them over name calling. I should have just ignored them." Louann succinctly summarized: "I was terrible."

THE IMPACT OF SCHOOL

Low-income adolescents were much more likely to describe problematic school careers, and, although it was apparent that school greatly influenced their self-definitions and self-esteem, they rarely noted any negative impact of school. They blamed themselves—not school circumstances—for their problems. School was important in socializing a sense of inadequacy as well as deficiency relative to others. In contrast, high-income adolescents appreciated school as an arena in which they could establish personal efficacy. Sarah said: "I did well on my SATs. I think school prepared me for them." Similarly, Mario said: "I have been in advanced science courses since my freshman year, so I have the background I need for college." Barbara felt that "school has given me a background that I can expand on in college."

As indications of school's positive impact, low-income adolescents concentrated on literacy and basic academic skills (e.g., "learned to read and write," "free education," "taught me a lot of stuff," "taught me to do stuff like divide, read, pronounce words better," "nothing, except an education"). They conveyed that reading, writing, and mathematical accomplishments were essential not only for survival but also to establish their "respectability," perhaps even their humanity. Teenagers did not want to be embarrassed by a lack of literacy skills or by being thought of as ignorant, uneducated, or stupid.

Some low-income adolescents focused on broader issues than academic effects, but most still confined their responses to school criteria (e.g., "I learned to learn and to study more"; "I learned how to think"). Madalene explained: "This year has taught me how to study. I was in advanced math, and I had to work hard. Some people don't care about grades. I've learned to care about grades." Others indicated that school had helped define their lives (e.g., "School taught me a little about life; how to get along in life"; "Showed me important things about life"; "It taught me about the world"). Chrissy felt that school had helped her decide what she wanted to be in the future, which was "either a secretary or a boss in a company." Four described positive social influences ("made me meet new people," "taught me to get along with people," "helped me to be kind"). According to Sheila: "School taught me how to meet a lot of people and deal with different people. I didn't really learn any education. There should be more vocabulary and spelling."

It was apparent that school influenced low-income adolescents' identity; they communicated an uncritical acceptance of school's portrayals of students—themselves and others. When problems existed, they tended to view themselves, not the nature of school, as their source. As Les, who had spent seventh and eighth grades in a self-contained class for emotionally disturbed youngsters, volunteered:

> School has turned me around. To start, I had a bad attitude. In sixth grade I hated school. My teacher for the past 2 years, Mr. W., really turned me around. He helped me deal with classes; helped with family problems. He showed me he cared what happened to me. He convinced me that school is there to help people.

After numerous vivid descriptions of problematic situations in school, Trent said: "School kept me out of trouble." Apparently, he believed the risks for getting into trouble were even greater in nonschool than school environments. Trent's father was in jail on abuse charges, having caused severe injury to a girlfriend's toddler.

Others felt the school environment was a catalyst for trouble. Beth was angry about "unfair discipline," and Nadia was annoyed about "rumors." Dusty complained: "The teachers don't listen to you, and the principal don't listen to you. He always sides with the teachers." Some felt they had been treated like trouble-makers without deserving that reputation. Darcy complained: "School makes me feel shy and lonely. I feel like I don't belong." Karen said:

"School makes me feel slow." Stacy confided that she "always felt stupid in school." Sheila complained: "Teachers call you names, like 'dumb,' and make you feel stupid." Annie stated simply: "School has introduced me to people I don't like." On further questioning, she replied: "Both teachers and students." Max felt that the "prejudice against blacks" had affected him, even though he was not black.

Dusty, who hated school, cynically bragged: "The best thing that school's done for me is kick me out. I got kicked out 17 times this year." Later he confessed that his "goal in life" was to "get out of special ed." Thus even the resistant Dusty revealed the importance of school in self-definition—it was essential to him that he not be perceived as a special education student.

Another sign that unsuccessful low-income students cared about school was their prizing of certain aspects of schooling. Wendy said: "School got me started in sports." Kit stated: "Track gave me the chance to excel." Dean was grateful that he had learned to make things in workshop. Sonia said she had learned how to cook in home economics and had learned to play an instrument in band. Two special education students, Jim and Teresa, were pleased about "job training" and "being taught how to work in the community." Those who could not think of positive aspects of school also had depressed outlooks on nonschool topics.

When asked about positive ways that school had influenced them, Nick and Darcy both responded: "Takes up my time." For seven others, "using up time" was a negative aspect of schooling. As Madalene, a high-achiever, grumbled: "So much work takes all my time." Time had a more positive connotation for her. With some irony, four others said they did not want to get up so early (e.g., "School messes up my sleeping habits").

Three low-income respondents listed specific subjects as having a negative impact on them—one did not like math, another fretted about being "terrible in spelling," and a third did not like "boring courses like history or social studies," saying: "What's the sense of learning about the past when you have the future to look out for?" Although 5 low-income adolescents could not think of positive influences (e.g., "Nothing. School ain't done nothing for me"), more than three times as many (17, 42.5%) could not think of ways that school had negatively affected them (e.g., "hasn't," "nothing bad," "no, no way really," "I can't think of any right now"). The resiliency of positive views of school, in spite of the pain they reported its causing, undoubtedly resulted from an inculcation of the benefits of education, rather than respondents' independent judgments. They were glib about common generalizations (i.e., myths) about schooling, whereas critical responses were more hesitant and belabored.

The social aspects of school were positive for most high-income adolescents (e.g., "Helped me associate with older people like teachers"; "I've made a lot of friends"). Libby believed: "School has helped me socially. I know kids who are taught at home and they're real bad in social situations—they don't know how to act." On the negative side, Andrew observed: "School separated everyone into cliques; it kind of makes me feel disliked." Marissa confessed: "I dislike the competitive aspects of school. We always compete with each other to do better. It makes everybody up-tight." Mario confided: "The social scene has shown me how some people don't really care about me." Jeremy maintained: "I've been exposed to some racial discrimination." It is suspected that there was more loneliness among adolescents than they chose to discuss. The interviewer got the impression that a number of adolescents—from both classes—were ashamed of being unpopular or feeling friendless.

Some high-income adolescents complained that school precipitated certain bad habits (e.g., "I get bored, then lazy"; "It has made me cynical; I see a lot that could be done that isn't"; "It made me negative about a lot of things"). On the positive side, they named what might be called "forced action," as Melissa said: "Being in school and having to do the work has built up my language and speaking skills."

SCHOOL EVALUATION

Just as other status indices, the grades reported by adolescents differentiated respondents of the two income levels: 24% of high-income students had A's and 67% had B's, whereas no low-income students had A's, only 12.5% had B's, 37.5% had C averages, and 50% had D's or below. For low-income adolescents, 11 of the 15 C averages were reported by students in special education. Three of the five low-income students with averages of B or above were black (Madalene, Scott, and Jeff).

Regarding satisfaction with grades, 25 low-income adolescents (62.5%) were not satisfied and 15 (37.5%)—10 of whom were in special education classes—were somewhat satisfied. Grades were clearly important, and all would have been pleased to have received better grades. Responses ranged from a "Well, of course, I'd like better grades" to a nonchalant "It wouldn't hurt to improve." "Keeping grades high enough to get into [a good] college" was the most common goal stated by high-income adolescents.

Nineteen low-income adolescents (47.5%) believed that their parents were not satisfied with their grades, thirteen (32.5%) felt theirs were, and eight (20%) said their parents did not care. As Max said: "They don't see my grades. They don't care." Six of these eight implied that years of negative school careers had resulted in their parents' supposed indifference; their parents had given up caring. Darcy claimed: "She doesn't care what kind of grades I get anymore, as long as I graduate." Scott said his mother was content because "she doesn't know that I'm not trying my hardest." Only Madalene reported that her mother was "proud." Dissatisfied parents had mainly verbalized unhappiness about poor school performance; however, four adolescents had been grounded and one had lost telephone privileges. Chrissy had been "yelled at everytime I bring a report card home." She added: "I always say I'll improve, but it seems like I do worse instead of better." Louann had been offered an incentive for good grades (i.e., $5 for A's, $3 for B's, and $1 for C's), but she confessed: "I earned a total of $1 during my 2 years in junior high school."

The majority of high-income parents (26, 82%) were felt to be satisfied with their children's grades, but parents were said to apply constant pressure (e.g., "They expect top grades from me"; "They would be a lot happier if I made straight A's or A plusses"; "They are satisfied with what I get, but they'd be very happy if I did better"). As Tony quipped: "I get a lecture about how smart I am and how well I *could* be doing with every report card." The eight whose parents were "not satisfied" were not necessarily the ones with the lowest grades. Nicole, who had a 3.8 grade-point average, said: "My parents would really like me to get a 4.0 like my sister. They think I'm lazy."

Most high-income respondents felt it was possible to improve their grades. In contrast, of the 36 low-income adolescents who were still in school, 16 thought their grades would stay the same in the future, 13 were unsure, and 7—mainly those who had already reported higher grades—expected to do better. Thus the majority either doubted their ability to improve their grades or suspected that they would not exert more effort in the future. Upset about his past year's grades, Randy tentatively speculated: "I hope I pass, but I don't know if I can. High school is supposed to be hard."

Low-income adolescents fretted that the grading standards of individual teachers or particular schools were "too stiff" or "too hard" but still judged the grading system to be "fair." Only Chrissy questioned the basic practice: "The grading system doesn't give some kids a chance!" Others subscribed to the concept of meritocracy in schooling and did not question the legitimacy of attaching a hierarchical, norm-referenced evaluation system—in which some students are bound to succeed and others fail—to a public education system with a compulsory attendance policy. Those with low grades blamed themselves, not the system. Randy maintained: "It's a little rough. Like if you're lazy like me this year, it's rough. But, it's fair."

Although they endorsed school evaluation as fair, responses revealed that grades had an impact on self-esteem. Since most high-income adolescents received good grades, the grading system was usually described as having a positive influence, such as "building confidence," "letting me know my strengths," "making me feel pretty good about myself," or "making me feel like I've accomplished something." There were a few distressed replies among high-income respondents. Seth said his grades made him "feel guilty for not trying harder." John ambivalently clarified: "Sometimes I'm ashamed, sometimes proud; my grades aren't terrible, they could be worse, but I know they're not as good as they should be." Sarah felt "a little guilty for not trying harder; my parents keep telling me I could get all A's." A B student, Andrew admitted: "I do a lot better on achievement tests than I do in my grades. But I don't form conclusions about myself from the grades I get." Libby, a nervous straight-A student, said: "I'm proud of myself, but sometimes I worry that I'm not going to be able to keep getting such good grades. I'm an overachiever. I study too hard. My grades are better than my real intelligence. Others can do just as well with less work."

Eleven low-income respondents claimed not to care about grades. Thomas asserted: "I'm not really embarrassed. I couldn't care less what others think." Nick stated: "I don't care. The school hassles me about them, then backs off." Chrissy expounded: "I'm bothered by them. But I don't mind showing others my report card. If they don't like them, then it's their problem; they're my grades, and they don't have to worry about it." Bret claimed: "I don't try to get good grades. I don't care what they give me." He then added: "Maybe I'll do better in high school—probably I'll like it better. Yeah, I feel kind of bad about my grades." Again, the common pattern of an initially defensive reply followed by more humble honesty might be noted.

Six low-income adolescents claimed their grades—and hence their response to grades—went up and down. Max, an 18-year-old who would enter eleventh grade in the fall, divulged: "I do better than most people. I got some bad grades and had to go to summer school; that made me feel lousy. Grades make me feel average." At another point in the interview, when asked if he was proud of anything he had done in school, Max replied: "I was proud when I got an A in sophomore English." Teresa, classified as mildly mentally handicapped, said: "Good about some, but not the F's." Celestine revealed: "Embarrassed. A little bit down. But when I accomplish something, like get a good grade in something, I say 'neat!'" Dusty said: "Not proud, not ashamed—I just don't like them." Rachel equivocally stated: "Average: not dumb, not smart." Leejohn, whose grades were D and below, tried to be nonchalant: "Bad, but I'm not embarrassed. I think I did pretty good, even though I'm repeating seventh grade."

Nineteen low-income adolescents were quite perturbed when discussing their grades. Jim moaned: "Bad. Embarrassed. Awful!" Tammy confided: "Feel awful, stupid, ashamed. I wouldn't show others." Carol's reaction was: "Disappointed. Mad at myself." Tricia said: "Ashamed—a lot!" Sheila, who usually had an air of confidence, said: "I feel sad—bad about myself, ashamed to tell others, guilty about not studying harder."

According to Festinger (1954), individuals assess their ability by comparing their performance with that of others. Within-group comparison was evident for low-income youth. For example, Sherry said: "Sometimes some of my friends think they are so much better than I am. They think that I am not as cool if I make lower grades than them." Nadia confessed: "I feel bad. My friends get better." Tammy said: "Usually I'm not ashamed or embarrassed. Some friends make better grades, and I'm embarrassed with them." Will said: "Embarrassed. But my friends aren't really that smart. Sometimes I do better, usually worse." Of the five children in his family, Will admitted that his grades were "the worst." Trent claimed: "Before I got into special education, my friends got better grades. I felt bad—embarrassed." The performance of peers was an important factor in respondents' feelings about their own grades, but even if they reported similar or worse grades for their friends, they had negative reactions to low grades.

Many low-income students attempted to save face by concealing their grades. Stacy admitted: "I hid my report cards. I was ashamed to give them to Mom. I never could understand how they done it. They put these numbers all together and came up with a grade." Wendy did not let others see her grades, but still: "Once in a while when the teacher gives you a smoke-up [i.e., midterm failure warning] in class then everybody knows, then you're embarrassed." Michael felt other forms of public disclosure of competency were also humiliating: "Like in reading, when you don't know a word, you're embarrassed."

The notion that certain students are proud of bad grades or intentionally do not make an effort in school to avoid being labeled "goody goodies" did not apply to the low-income respondents in this study. Randy's confession was typical: "I'm embarrassed. I don't tell people. I'd never brag about getting four F's." He also confided that his low grades made him feel like he was "taking after my dad," who had not done well in school and was presently in prison on a drunken driving charge. Randy seemed to be quoting teachers or parents when he speculated: "I know it's my fault. I got 142 questions right on the competency test; that's above average. Above-average kids should not be getting four F's." Louann's reaction to bad grades was: "Hey, I'm dumb. I don't like to try. I don't like school." Then, in a more somber tone, she added: "Nobody else knew about them. If they did, I would be embarrassed." Those who maintained that they did not try generally had diffusely depressed reactions to school and, more generally, to their out-of-school lives. They seemed to have given up trying out of depression, not rebellion.

PERCEPTIONS OF INTELLIGENCE

Adolescents referred to a broad range of characteristics in identifying "intelligent people" (see Table 5.1). Some were reluctant to offer observable

TABLE 5.1. Adolescents' Views of Intelligence

	Low-Income		High-Income	
	N	(%)	N	(%)
Signs of Intelligence				
Speech/talk	8	(20)	12	(36)
Actions/appearance	10*	(25)	8**	(24)
School work habits	-		6	(18)
Knowledge/ideas	-		3	(9)
School grades	13	(33)	-	
Course enrollment	1	(3)	-	
Social skills	3	(8)	-	
Unsure/noncommital	5	(13)	5	(15)
Importance of Being Intelligent				
Important	31	(78)	23	(67)
Unimportant	7	(18)	4	(12)
Uncertain	2	(5)	7	(21)
Variations in Intelligence				
Differences great	17	(43)	9	(27)
Differences small	18	(45)	12	(36)
Uncertain	5	(13)	13	(39)
Total	40		34	

*Eight school-related.
**Four school-related.
(Note: Due to rounding, percentage totals do not necessarily add to 100.)

signs, because, as May (l-i) said: "You really can't tell by looking at someone." Others felt that even actions were deceiving, as Kelly (h-i) observed: "Some people act really dingy, but they still may be intelligent." Barbara (h-i) felt: "Smart people usually cover it up. We don't like to be known as brains."

The most frequently mentioned sign of intelligence was some form of speech. Low-income respondents claimed one could identify an intelligent person by: "what they say," "more sophisticated talk than others," "the vocabulary they use," or "the way they use words." Stacy observed: "You don't have to talk to them like a child. They can carry on a conversation. They make good decisions. They think ahead." Offering a sociolinguistic hypothesis, Annie said: "The way they talk depends on the status of their parents. They say certain things the way their parents do. That makes them sound smart."

In an ethnic- or class-centered manner, several high-income adolescents mentioned ways that intelligent people "did not talk" (e.g., "They don't talk with a twang"; "They talk regular, you know, without those southern accents"). Jessica cautiously ventured:

> Most of the kids that aren't smart—you know, that aren't in the high classes, I mean, they don't do well in school—most are country kids, or maybe poor kids. They talk like country people. You know, they're the ones we . . . they call grits.

Other high-income respondents focused on the content of speech (e.g., "The way they talk and what they talk about"; "If they say something that is not very typical—that shows they know more than everybody else"; "By how they express their ideas"). Hilary said: "How interested they are in what you say when you talk to them."

Seven high- and five low-income respondents offered general actions as signs of intelligence (e.g., "People who know what they're doing"; "The way they act—mature"; "You can tell by their smartness, their decisions, their friends"). Will (l-i) volunteered: "Most preps are smart. They have control. They don't let people push them around. They're leaders." Les (l-i), classified as emotionally disturbed, said: "By the way they act toward me. If they are nice and polite, it means they're smart; they know that if you treat someone good, they'll treat you good and that means they're smart."

In spite of their problematic school careers, more low- (22, 55%) than high-income youngsters (10, 30%) gave school-related behaviors as indicators of intelligence. Low-income respondents used such school criteria as grades (e.g., "They get all A's"); effort (e.g., "You can tell how smart they are by how hard they work"); participation (e.g., "The way they act; they've always got their hands up; dumb people sleep in class"); correct responses (e.g., "They act different; they raise their hands and always get the answers right"); academic skills (e.g., "They're good readers, do good in math and stuff like that"; "They can read and spell good; they act real brainy"); curricular track (e.g., "If they go to those hard classes, you know, kinds of science"); postschool plans ("If they are going to college"); and general school behaviors (e.g., "Their actions in school"). School-related responses of high-income participants included: "Smart people pay attention during class"; "You can tell they are smart by the way they act in class—answer questions, do well; some work harder than others"; "They do their work and do it well"; "Some have a knack for figuring things out"; "They're quick at answering."

Lower-achieving high-income respondents were skeptical about the connections between school performance and intelligence. Seth said: "I don't do great in school, but I'm not dumb. Some teachers are bad. I don't catch on all the time, but the teachers aren't very clear." Audrey remarked: "You can't tell by grades. I'm not dumb, but I sometimes make bad grades." Damon analyzed: "Some students do great in school, but they're just there to impress. They always get along with teachers, and they let everyone know their grades. They will usually tell you they're smart, but I don't consider that type to be smart."

In discussing the signs of intelligence, 13 low-income teenagers (32.5%) specifically stated that grades were related to intelligence (e.g., "They get good grades and stuff"; "They get straight A's and take a lot of hard courses like biology"). Yet when directly asked about the correspondence between grades and intelligence, 34 (85%) stated that they were not closely linked, 2 (5%) were uncertain, and only 4 (10%) said there were strong connections. Effort was believed to be an important variable in the grades–intelligence equation, as Thomas conjectured: "Some people work extra hard to get good grades— they're not real smart, but they work for grades. Some just know it all. Some kids get bad grades, but they're not dumb—they don't try, don't care. Some get bad grades even when they try."

High-income adolescents also denied a very direct correspondence between grades and intelligence. John said: "Sure some people get good grades. But they work their bippies off too. Some of the people on the honor roll are basically stupid." Simon complained:

> I know a lot of people who think grades do mean you're intelligent.
> They really flash their grades around. There's one girl I hate, who rides
> our bus. When report cards come out, Polly really makes a scene.
> She says "Oh, I can't believe I got all A's again!" loud enough for the
> whole bus to hear. But she's a jerk. I refuse to believe that girl is really
> smart. I don't care what kind of grades she gets.

Theories resembling Gardner's (1983, 1987) multifaceted model of intelligence were offered by respondents as rationales for the lack of direct school success–intelligence correspondence. Low-income adolescents observed that in addition to book-learning there were other kinds of intelligence, such as common sense, social skills, or mechanical strengths. Stacy described a cousin who got "real good grades—mostly A's—but had no sense of what to say or do when she was around people." Adam observed: "Some kids get good grades and do good in school, but they're dumb at normal life things." Karen hypothesized: "Some tests are so easy. Some kids get a chance to cram. Some cheat. Some have A's and no common sense at all." These arguments were primarily used by adolescents who were not academically successful, perhaps as a rationale for still believing they were personally intelligent. In spite of being less likely to use school-related criteria in discussing signs of intelligence, high-income respondents were also less likely to offer broader (than cognition and knowledge) definitions of intelligence. Since compared to their less affluent schoolmates most did well in school, school-like definitions of intelligence were suitable.

On an abstract level, then, low-income adolescents maintained that "trying," "caring," and "working hard" were important in determining grades. They did an about-face, however, when talking about their own grades—rarely attributing low grades to not trying. Covington and Omelich (1979) contend that there is a common pattern of low effort and withdrawal on the part of students having difficulty, which they hypothesize is an attempt to protect self-image. By not exerting maximum effort in risk situations, students avoid establishing beyond a doubt that they lack ability. Yet, with local adolescents, this theory seemed more applicable to high- than low-income teenagers. High-income youths who did not receive top grades often maintained that with additional effort they could get better grades. They also offered a variety of reasons for low grades (e.g., "Me and that teacher did not get along"; "I really hate the sciences"; "I can't force myself to do the boring work"). In contrast, low-income adolescents did not claim a lack of effort; instead they implied that low grades resulted from personal intellectual inadequacies. True, they generally admitted that they did not work very hard in school, but the grounds for lack of effort tended to be attributed to a sense of futility about school. They did not contend that with more effort they could improve grades. In fact, many stated the opposite, indicating that a change in effort would not affect performance evaluations.

The overwhelming attitude of the majority of low-achieving adolescents was passive and defeatist in nature. Most indicated that low grades reflected their intellectual status, made them feel unintelligent, and would be interpreted by others as signifying that they were not smart. Thus low-income, low-achieving teenagers espoused an objective theory about grades that did not correspond to their subjective reaction to grades. External evaluation was important in providing information about achievement, intelligence, and, ultimately—since high intelligence was so valued—personal worth.

According to their own accounts, high-income respondents exemplified "smart people." As Greg (h-i) said: "It's hard to tell by the way they act. Usually smart people have confidence and don't brag. But they don't act stupid. We think before we talk. I usually think people are smart if they have my same opinions." Lynette (h-i) conjectured: "It's hard to tell about intelligence. I'm an introvert, so I think a lot of people don't know I'm smart." In talking about the signs of intelligence, only one low-income adolescent used a personal pronoun. Madalene (l-i) said: "Smart people speak up. Some people just

sit there and don't say anything—don't participate. I'm learning to speak up."
High-income adolescents typically included a personal pronoun in their judgments of the signs of intelligence.

When specifically asked about their own intelligence, fewer than half of
the low-income adolescents gave an affirmative answer (e.g., "kind of," "pretty
smart," "in some things," "in some ways," "sort of," "fairly," "average," "I guess,"
"I have common sense"). Adam qualified: "Yes, but I know things and then
forget them." May said: "Yes, I was worked with a lot when I was young."
Thomas quipped: "I like to think I am!" Although Celestine said, "I catch
on to things pretty easy," Stacy's "I just didn't understand much" was more
typical.

A third of the low-income adolescents conveyed that it was not up to
them to judge their own intelligence. Nadia, a student in a self-contained class
for the learning-disabled, said: "I don't know. People in special education aren't
really smart, but they aren't stupid either." Of the eleven low-income teenagers who claimed not to be intelligent, six were in special education placements
(i.e., three learning-disabled, three mildly mentally handicapped), three had
repeated two grades in school, and two were at grade level in school, with
one receiving low grades and the other average grades. Of the sixteen who
claimed to be intelligent, five were in special education (i.e., one emotionally
handicapped, four learning-disabled), two had been retained 2 years, six had
been retained 1 year, and three were on grade level receiving above
average grades. Thus actual success in school careers was not highly correlated with stated feelings about personal intelligence.

It became clear that for high-income adolescents, thinking themselves
"smart" was a social class–determined response. Tony speculated: "I'd say all
of the kids in college prep classes are basically smart, otherwise they wouldn't
be in those classes. The voc. ed. kids couldn't make it in those classes." Jessica felt: "Most preps are smart." Low-income students were their negative
reference group. As a class, then, they felt themselves to be—whether by
nature or by definition—intelligent. The responses of low-income adolescents
were congruent with those of their high-income counterparts: Regardless of
whether they were high or low achievers, they clearly saw preppies as intellectually superior to grits. When they did say they were smart, it was usually
within the context of "all humans are smart" or, as Madalene said: "I'm a
lot smarter than most of the kids around here." High-income adolescents
could feel smart, even if they felt less smart (i.e., not "brains" or "geniuses")
than within-group peers, because they felt others (i.e., low-income students)
were dumb.

Although more likely to see themselves as intelligent, high-income participants differentiated between being "a brain" and being "smart." Jeremy
qualified: "I'm not a brain, but I'm conscious of what's going on." Audrey

replied: "If you mean really smart, then no. But I guess I'm about as smart as most other kids. I don't think anyone has ever called me dumb." Libby recalled: "There were some real geniuses in my physics class. Like Mario knew everything before he took the class. He gets A plusses in courses at the university. I am definitely not smart like that. I have to work hard to stay on the honor roll." Nicole said: "Some kids I know got SAT scores that were 200 points higher than mine. I can make good grades, but I don't remember everything for tests. I guess that's the difference between superbright kids and regular smart kids."

Respondents estimated how their parents, friends, teachers, and schoolmates would judge their intelligence. High-income adolescents gave similar evaluations for all four groups, whereas low-income respondents ascribed more negative perceptions to those further removed from themselves. They were more likely to believe that their parents and friends (i.e., within-class people) thought they were smart than that their teachers or students in general thought they were smart.

It was clearly important to be perceived as intelligent, with slightly more low-income adolescents stressing the benefits (see Table 5.1). A defensive tone was noted among five of the seven low-income adolescents who denied the importance of intelligence (e.g., "not really," "not that important," "you don't have to be"). Those who felt unintelligent typically asserted that it was "very important" to be intelligent and to be perceived as intelligent by others.

High-income adolescents' sense that one could have ordinary high intelligence without "being a brain" allowed them to philosophically deny the importance of high intelligence, whereas for their low-income counterparts the alternative to being thought of as intelligent was being thought of as dumb. High-income adolescents rarely worried about others' perceptions of their intelligence—being stupid was not part of their social class role. Low intelligence was reserved for members of lower social classes. In fact, some said that they did not want to be perceived as "too smart." Jessica volunteered: "Sometimes I'm embarrassed about being smart. My friends see me as an airhead, and then they see that I'm on the honor roll." Apparently being an airhead (i.e., pretty and popular) was the preferred role. Hilary confessed: "I'm seen as smart. I sometimes wish it was the other way around. They only see how smart I am. They stay away from me. They don't see anything else of me." But Sarah, an average student, remarked: "I sure wouldn't want to be seen as stupid." Nicole stated: "It's not the most important thing, but I do like others to see me as intelligent."

In terms of the distribution of intelligence among people, high-income adolescents tended to be circumspect, whereas low-income respondents usually ventured an opinion, claiming that the differences were either great or small (see Table 5.1). Perhaps high-income adolescents had been taught that it was polite to verbalize similarities among people. As Greg (h-i) surmised: "There's not a big difference to start with. In the end it all depends on what an individual wants and works for." Similarly, Mario (h-i) said: "It depends upon how people apply themselves." Sarah (h-i) thought: "The differences are small but some work harder than others, so, in the end, the differences seem great." Rhonda (h-i) asserted: "All people are intelligent, but not everyone uses it." Sally (h-i) said: "I think there are a whole lot of people in the middle—most people really." Carol (l-i) vacillated: "Basically, well, usually small. But you got a low group of people that doesn't do anything at all. That makes it a big range." Dusty (l-i) said "small" then cautioned: "Just because somebody doesn't know as much as the others doesn't mean they're dumb."

BEING PART OF SCHOOL

The importance of families and students being "predisposed to participate" (Finn, 1989) in the events of school and to identify with schools has recently been emphasized (Duran & Weffer, 1992; Finn & Cox, 1992). Students who take advantage of the opportunities in school do better academically in the short and long run.

In this study, high-income adolescents were much more likely to participate in school activities than their low-income schoolmates (26 high-income, 76%, versus 18 low-income, 45%). Some high-income respondents participated in as many as 5 extracurricular activities (2.5 activities per participating adolescent; 1.9 activities for total number of high-income adolescents). It was obvious that some were consciously building their resumes. Fewer than half (i.e., 16, 40%) of the low-income respondents remembered participating in extracurricular activities at any grade level in school, and, even then, many reported activities which were not school-based. Eliminating these reduces the number of participating students to 13 (32.5%) (i.e., a mean of 0.4 activities per low-income adolescent, or 1.2 per participating student). Two of the 13 had participated in Special Olympics through their special education classes.

Several low-income respondents offered reasons—some personal, some situational—for not joining in extracurricular activities. Randy said: "I was going to run track, but I got lazy. Anyway, I found out that if you don't get good grades, they don't let you participate." Similarly, Dean claimed: "I was in too much trouble in school, like skipping and smoking, so they wouldn't let me try out." Bret admitted: "No. I like sports, but I don't like school, so I don't participate." Thomas clarified: "We don't have a car. I wouldn't have a way to get home from school. Besides, the equipment is expensive. Mom can't afford it." Similarly, Karen explained: "No. No car. We can't afford the sports clothes."

When asked if they were proud of anything they had done in school, 32 (94%) high-income adolescents offered incidents that ranged from athletic feats to the "highest score in my advanced math final" to a "lead in the annual musical." Only 18 low-income respondents (45%) were able to recall such occasions, and many of these dated back to their early elementary years. The sources of pride, however, were school-conformist in nature. As Wendy said: "In first grade they asked us all to stand up and count as high as we could. I could count the highest." Madalene was proud about "making the honor roll in junior high," and Max was happy about "getting an A in English in tenth grade." Adam was pleased when he "passed the test to get out of special education." Nick received a "most improved student" in elementary school. May and Jeff were proud of receiving "perfect attendance" awards. Unfortunately, 22 (55%) were unable to recall any source of pride.

CONCLUSION

A number of researchers (e.g., Casebolt, 1987; Sinclair & Ghory, 1987; Strahan, 1988, 1989) contend that sometime before or during middle school, marginal students become disconnected from school and separate the tasks of school from the rest of their lives. This separation supposedly happens by low-achieving students' denying the relevance of school (and school evaluation) to themselves. Adams (1978) maintained that, at least in the case of black low achievers, there was an attempt to broaden the definitions of intelligence (e.g., common sense, mechanical ability, streetwise ability) so that they could still think of themselves as smart. Although this study provides some evidence of these phenomena, a more prominent finding was that adolescents subscribed to a model of intelligence that corresponded to school-related variables and was stratified according to social class. Moreover, school-defined intelligence was reified into an important quality of individuals; that is, low achievers were considered not only unintelligent (e.g., "know-nothings," "ignoramuses") but also unworthy by both high- and low-income respondents.

Most low-income adolescents were negative about their school performance (i.e., they had internalized school evaluations), had abandoned ambition for school success, and had accepted their low achievement and subordinate standing as natural. Furthermore, few named nonschool sources of personal pride. High-income adolescents were comfortable with school's positive definition of themselves. Thus adolescents learned to perceive themselves as either more or less competent, as well as more or less worthy, in the social setting of school. Others have maintained that conceptions of self are anchored in ongoing social relationships in (recurring) social settings (Berger, Rosenholtz, & Zelditch, 1980; Faunce, 1984; Foucault, 1980; Rosenholtz & Simpson, 1984). In this study, it became clear that adolescents' perceptions of themselves as students were grounded in the social reality of inequalities of status and power in their schools and community.

Not only are institutionalized conceptions of ability reproduced in individuals during ability formation (Bourdieu, 1984), but school also socializes students to become accustomed to the differential reward structure that they eventually experience in society. In other words, ability formations socialized through both overt and covert school curricula are generalized to broader social settings. While high- and low-income adolescents learn to accept inequities in school rewards as natural consequences of human differences, they also learn to expect similar status differentials later in life. Low-income respondents worried that their lack of success in school would have a negative impact on their futures, whereas their high-income counterparts conveyed that their school competencies entitled them to privileged status both now and in the future. Thus school-based ability formations become society-based status formations.

In England, Willis (1977) described working-class youth as having strong social class identifications, equating mental labor with femininity and manual labor with masculinity; hence they rejected school achievers and school norms. As discussed in Chapters 2 and 3, there were few signs of social class loyalty, positive group identity, or psychological bonds among the low-income adolescents in this study, and the few that existed (defensive group reactions to taunting) were only erratically expressed. There was also little evidence of rejection of dominant-group norms. Ideologies more appropriate for affluent students (e.g., that success in school was due to individual merit; failure, to personal inadequacies) were echoed by low-income adolescents. There were signs of striving to conceal inferior position (i.e., pass as middle class, bright, respectable, mainstream) and of denial, which was of a fantasy nature (e.g., "headbangers don't like preppies—we really avoid them"). Low-income respondents generally had a subdued or evasive reaction to their negative school careers; they silently tolerated or psychologically withdrew from painful and humiliating school circumstances.

At the same time, almost all low-income informants expressed a certain amount of skepticism about school's negative definitions of themselves. Their posture was ambiguous, even contradictory. They partly accepted school criteria as a measure of intelligence (and worth) and partly rejected it, thus simultaneously adhering to dominant messages about the importance of (school-defined) intelligence but also denying school as a definer or enhancer. Accusing school personnel of discrimination, developing alternative definitions of intelligence, and rejecting the idea of a connection between grades and intelligence were forms of resistance to the subordinate student role. Suggestions that multiple levels of understanding be examined (Giroux, 1984; Ramsay, 1985) are particularly relevant to unraveling the contradictions and inconsistencies of low-income adolescents' feelings about themselves as students.

Evidence of multiple levels of reaction was also present in high-income adolescents' narratives. On an abstract level, many vocalized the idea that people are inherently similar in intelligence. On the surface such an ideology seems both democratic and empathic; however, the notion of basic human similarity also provides the justification for lack of sympathy for those who do not succeed and, ultimately, for an uneven distribution of rewards. If people are perceived as similar, then differences in achievement can be attributed to hard work (i.e., worthy behaviors)—not chance or bias. In other words, if differences in outcomes are felt to result from differences in effort, then stratified outcomes are likely to be seen as legitimate. On the other hand, if people are believed to be innately different then the legitimacy of the contest nature of school could be challenged.

Bourdieu's (1984) idea of the "taste of necessity" is relevant to this discussion. His theory suggests that people assume that poor people prefer the inferior circumstances of their lives; poverty, then, becomes a matter of taste. Consistent with this idea, high-income respondents implied that the lack of school success of their low-income counterparts was intentional; that is, a matter of choice. They conveyed the belief that low-income adolescents perversely choose to be unsuccessful. Ending up "dumb," then, was due to a lack of moral fortitude. With such a rationale for the others' failure, achieving students were not obliged to care about the others' lot.

CHAPTER 6

Trouble and Punishment

A widely held social construct is that the education of good kids who want to learn is often spoiled by bad kids (from bad families) who do not value education. A. K. Cohen's 1955 study of the culture of gangs was concluded by stating that delinquent boys "overreacted to" and "inverted" the middle-class values imposed by schools. Cohen described the gangs as subcultures with "non-utilitarian, negativistic, and malicious values" (p. 7). Similarly, in 1965 Cervantes described the "bipolar characteristics" of school dropouts and school achievers, claiming that "upwardly mobile" youth were affectionate, alert, goal-oriented masters of their environment, whereas dropouts were affectless, hyperactive, and thrill-oriented pawns of theirs. Both studies characterized values and actions but virtually ignored the influence of school context or the thoughts of the youth. In a later study of student groups, Castlebury and Arnold (1988) quoted a subject's description of "bullies": "These are the idiots in school. They think it is cool to bother other students. Their parents don't care about them at all. They hate school and wish they didn't have to be here" (p. 101). School-conformists, teachers, and the institution of school are viewed as innocent victims of trouble-makers' unprovoked and unjustified actions.

It is also taken for granted that students' anger is of home rather than school origin. In a study of the correlation between family structure and trouble-making, it was found that youths who lived with two parents were less likely to be disruptive than those who lived with just their mothers or who had a stepparent (Steinberg, 1987). Findings such as these suggest that children's problematic school behaviors are related to their family situations. Perhaps it is assumed that children learn negative behaviors from parents through modeling processes or that their anger results from unmet emotional needs caused by nonnurturing home lives.

Unlike home environments, school environments are usually viewed as positive and therapeutic or, at least, neutral. Rarely do school personnel, the lay public, or, for that matter, researchers attribute disruptive behavior to the nature of the school experience. Yet there is evidence that school climate is related to the amount and extent of trouble-making (Elias, 1989; Guttman, 1982:

Lightfoot, 1981; Vernberg & Medway, 1981), that school adversity produces behavioral deviance (Rutter, 1983), and that alienation is an underlying factor in school violence and vandalism (Newmann, 1981; Pink, 1982).

Over the past few years the number of children classified as learning-disabled and emotionally disturbed has steadily increased (Gerber & Levine-Donnerstein, 1989; Zill & Schoenborn, 1990). Students who experience problems in learning (i.e., those classified as learning-disabled) also exhibit more negative behaviors, fewer positive behaviors, and higher levels of anger than their classmates (Heavey, Adelman, Nelson, & Smith, 1989; Safran & Safran, 1985). Although some imply that these negative behaviors spring from the same nonschool sources as the learning problems (Lindsey, Daniels, & Rutledge, 1986), others conjecture about causal links, maintaining that the adverse school careers cause frustration and, subsequently, antisocial behaviors (Elias, 1989). Still others believe that labeling students as outsiders causes resentment, which is expressed in disruptive ways (Pink, 1982).

The interconnections among students' school experiences and their emotions and behaviors have received relatively little attention. In a 1974 study, Balch and Kelly found that students of all socioeconomic levels acknowledged that teachers avoided contact with low-status students and treated them less kindly or fairly than others. The authors further speculated that the degrading punishment students received solved immediate problems but resulted in a deterioration of their emotional commitment to school. In this chapter, adolescents' accounts of the types of trouble they had been punished for in school will be analyzed. The nature and extent of disciplinary measures they had received will also be addressed.

THE NATURE AND EXTENT OF TROUBLE-MAKING

All informants had very conventional, and very similar, views of trouble-making. When speaking generally, they disapproved of aggression, disruptiveness, and lack of effort. However, in describing personal situations, low-income respondents vacillated between condemning these behaviors and asserting that they were legitimate reactions to inequities and discrimination. This discontinuity between the general belief and specific situational reaction reverberated through low-income youths' narratives about problems in school.

More low-income adolescents than high-income adolescents reported that they had been punished for trouble-making (i.e., 31, 78%, and 11, 33%, respectively). Low-income youth also claimed more frequent and more serious infractions (see Table 6.1). Gender made some difference, with 87% of the low-income boys compared to 72% of the girls admitting to problems.

TABLE 6.1. Types and Likely Causes of Trouble in School

	Low-Income		High-Income	
	N*	(%)**	N	(%)
Hostility/Anger				
Fights	23	(58)	0	–
Sassing	15	(38)	1	(3)
Lack of Motivation				
Work-related	7	(18)	3	(9)
Tardiness	4	(10)	2	(6)
Skipping class	2	(5)	1	(3)
Truancy	4	(10)	0	–
Socially Active				
Chatting	6	(15)	3	(9)
Goofing off	4	(10)	3	(9)
Value Conflict				
Smoking	2	(5)	0	–
Total	67		13	

*Total misbehaviors reported.
**Percentage of reported misbehaviors.

Fights were the most prevalent form of trouble-making for low-income adolescents, with 67% of the boys and 52% of the girls claiming they had fought in school. Descriptions of conflict ranged from a slight push to an incident that involved a weapon (i.e., Bret's "I pulled a knife on someone"). Most fights fell into the category of scuffles. Adolescents also included threatening postures, gestures, or verbal feuds as "fights."

Adolescents who had been involved in conflicts inevitably claimed they had acted impulsively and had been on the defensive. As Randy (l-i) said: "I got into a few fights, but I never started a fight in my life!" Max (l-i) asserted: "I fought people who called me names—like grit or nigger!" Sonia (l-i) maintained: "I hit someone because they hit me first." Fights, then, were seen as legitimate attempts to defend honor or redress wrongs.

Although not all adolescents were precise about the immediate causes of fights, most alluded to name calling and teasing. It was clear that low-income adolescents were alert to signs of rejection by preppies; in fact, they were scrupulously attuned to detecting insult and were particularly sensitive to epithets that referred to social status (e.g., "scum") or intelligence (e.g., "retard"). Resentment stemming from rejection by affluent students resonated through the narratives of low-income respondents. As Chrissy (l-i) said: "I hate it when others call me names like spoiled or grit—stuff I'm not." Nick (l-i) complained: "I've been called a grit plenty of times, and a hick, too. The preps think they are hotshots and can get away with anything. They're so cool. They do what they want, and they never get in trouble."

Not only were accusations of snobbishness leveled at high-income school-mates, but low-income youth felt that they had been aggressively teased and "picked on." Celestine (l-i) fought in response to "a prep giving me the middle finger." May (l-i) fretted: "I avoid places where the preps hang out because they don't want us around them and they can get pretty nasty." Bret (l-i) insisted: "The punks and some of the preps pick on us whenever they get the chance. They call us names and push us around." Satisfaction resulted from taking a stand against abuse. Low-income respondents bragged about the bravery involved in confronting more powerful schoolmates and mean teachers who were, perhaps, perceived as "evil outsiders."

Nevertheless, it is likely that the allusions to cross-class violence, which dominated the narratives, inflated the actual rate of occurrence. Low-income adolescents certainly wanted to attack elites—perhaps fantasized about striking out—but, in reality, their detailed descriptions were mainly of within-class friction. Carol and Nadia had fought with girlfriends who had "spread rumors." Dusty admitted: "When one of my friends says something about my mom—like bitch—then I hit them. They think they can get away with it because I am in special ed." Such within-class disputes might be attributed, at least in part, to displacement of anger. The firmly established status hierarchy (i.e., pecking order) in school perhaps dictated that only other low-status students were acceptable outlets for frustration. At any rate, adolescents described fights with peers with much less enthusiasm than those with outsiders.

Conflicts with teachers (i.e., usually "sassing") were the second most frequently mentioned school offense for low-income students (see Table 6.1). The same tendency to react impulsively (i.e., what teachers might call "overreacting") to incidents with schoolmates could be detected in their accounts of relationships with school personnel. Max admitted: "Teachers say something I don't like and I get loud with them." Jim "got in trouble for backsassing the teachers." Ruth had "yelled at teachers." Only one high-income adolescent claimed to have "sassed" a teacher.

Few adolescents cited problems with schoolwork (e.g., "getting work in," "not listening," "sleeping in class," "not doing good in school") as incidents of trouble. The small number of such infractions was not consistent with low-income adolescents' poor school records. If negative performance evaluation had been judged as "trouble in school" by adolescents, the rate of school-work-related incidents would have included about 90% of the low-income respondents. Work-related problems may have been underestimated because respondents' attention was drawn to the more salient instances of interpersonal conflict. Or secondary teachers may not have treated the inadequate schoolwork of low-income adolescents as problematic, perhaps even considering failure to be endemic to their social class. However, the three high-income respondents who reported work-related problems conveyed that they had been hounded for working below their ability or, it may be more valid to say, for achieving below what teachers expected of students of their socioeconomic status. Hence it is likely that lack of motivation was more noticeable, or at least more problematic, for high- than low-income adolescents.

There were clear and substantial qualitative distinctions in the nature of the school problems reported by high- and low-income respondents. Problems with socially active behaviors and lack of motivation were the most prevalent forms of trouble-making for high-income adolescents. Both ostensibly stemmed from teenagers' creative and social energies and thus might even be considered healthy and constructive ways of dealing with sameness and boredom in school. Moreover, although seen as misbehaviors, most were fundamentally prosocial (e.g., "fooling around," "passing notes," "gabbing with my friends"). More low-income adolescents reported incidents of a socially active nature, but they were proportionately less important for them, and, even within the category, their pranks often bordered on being aggressive (e.g., throwing paper wads, practical jokes) and hence were antisocial. Thus the nature of problems differed radically, with high-income respondents being playful, even if bothersome, and low-income respondents tending to be violent or rude—behaviors that typically stem from anger. Smoking was categorized as a value conflict because adolescents implied that teachers were morally opposed to their smoking rather than simply following up on a rule infraction.

THE ANGRY IMAGE OF LOW-INCOME YOUTH

High-income adolescents caricatured their low-income counterparts as obstreperous (e.g., "short-fused," "ready to fight," "perpetually angry," "real tough"), referred to them with epithets that implied violence (e.g., "bully," "redneck"), and indicated that trouble-making was widespread among them. Polly's rendition of the other was: "Some kids—the grits—are constantly rude. They're just raised to be rude—or born rude. They get into trouble all the time. They deserve to." With disdain, John judged: "The things I do don't amount to anything. The thugs, the rednecks are always in the office or they're suspended. I'm not sure what all they do, but they act tough and they're always in trouble." When asked for specifics, John puzzled: "I really can't remember anything specific. They're not in my classes, so I don't see what they do. But I know they're trouble-makers. You can tell that by the way they act around here—the way they walk around the halls and hang out in the parking lots." Few respondents were able to provide concrete evidence of the aggressive acts they surmised.

Although none personally admitted to misdeeds, high-income adolescents' accounts of intergroup conflict, in fact, put peers in the role of transgressors. Both groups of adolescents recounted similar scenarios of encounters that had taken place in corridors or by lockers; apparently as pranks, preppies pushed one another into low-income students (i.e., contaminated students, carriers of cooties), then scurried away and left the victims to settle the situation. Low-income respondents claimed that if a tussle ensued, the pushed preppy would plead innocent to school personnel and the low-income youth (who had justifiably retaliated) would suffer the consequences.

Tony (h-i): Like one of your friends will push you into somebody and try to
    get you into a fight. These kids are always ready to jump on you.
Interviewer: Which kids?
Tony: The grits—poor kids.

Similarly, Chrissy (l-i) recalled: "Preps fought with us. They would start something and then walk away before the teacher got there or they'd lie and the teachers always believed *them*." Such borderwork between the social classes was initiated and culminated unidirectionally: only high-income students pushed and only low-income students were targets of pushed schoolmates.

Nevertheless, it was low-income youth who had the reputation for being feisty. As Greg (h-i) observed: "Grits are usually hostile to people who aren't in their groups. They pick fights, smoke." Low-income adolescents also alluded to anger and higher rates of misbehaviors among members of their own social class (e.g., "always in fights," "mean," "mad at the world"). Although this negative image can certainly be attributed to social class stereotyping by outsiders as well as insiders, it is also likely to be based on the reality of observations in school and community settings.

Part of the aggressive image of low-income youth certainly resulted from their choice of clothing and mannerisms. They were said to wear spiked boots; jackets with studs and chains; muscle shirts; and T-shirts depicting bloody scenes from movies, military emblems, heavy metal rock groups, motorcycle insignia, or other symbols of violence and death. They were also said to swagger down the halls and act macho. As Bret (l-i) said: "Headbangers wear heavy metal concert T-shirts and earrings. They look tough and they are tough." Thus many low-income youth intentionally incorporated aggressive images into their public persona.

A likely hypothesis for the intentional creation of a tough image by low-income youth was that they generally felt vulnerable and wanted to ward off the abuse to which they were so alert. This sense of being threatened was likely to be a causal factor in their wanting to portray themselves as strong and invincible and in their use of violent metaphors in discourse. Because of their low status relative to others and because of the powerlessness of adults in their environment, it is likely that they felt they had to protect themselves.

ATTENDANCE PROBLEMS

The standard pattern of more problematic school careers for low-income adolescents surfaced again in their accounts of school attendance. Although most had not listed skipping class as "trouble in school," when specifically asked, eleven high-income adolescents (33%) said they had skipped school, as had 20 low-income teenagers (50%). Of the high-income youth who had skipped school, most had done so "once," "twice," "a couple of times," or "three to four times a year." Low-income respondents who skipped had done so much more frequently. Before quitting, Dean had skipped "all the time" and Louann said "always." Bret had skipped "every other day" and Kit had been truant for "long periods of time." The latter two claimed that they were determined to graduate from high school. Kit, Louann, and Bret had all been taken to court on truancy charges, and Dean had been threatened with such a procedure before he quit school. For low-income adolescents, truancy increased with age. Few junior high students had done more than "play sick," whereas several older low-income adolescents had high rates of missing school. Eighteen-year-old Max estimated that he had skipped 30 times the previous year. Truancy was clearly a form of resistance to schooling.

For many there was a fine line between not going to school for puny reasons and skipping school. Karen (l-i) maintained: "I've not really skipped. I've played sick." But most felt that feigning illness was skipping school, and this was the most common form of truancy for high-income adolescents. John (h-i) had "stayed home when I wasn't sick." Aaron (h-i) said: "Sometimes I just don't feel like going or I miss the bus, then I tell Mom I'm sick." Max, Scott, Trent, and Dusty (all l-i) had occasionally "just slept in," as had Audrey, Simon, Vanessa, Ian, and Seth (all h-i). Others had skipped classes as a prank. Celestine (l-i) "went up on the school roof at Loring. Just for fun." Andrew (h-i) had "gone for a spin on my friend's new motorcycle. It was a kick. We got caught though." (But not punished.)

Adolescents volunteered rationales for truancy: Nick (l-i) "was bored," Rachel (l-i) "got tired of going," and Jim (l-i) "just felt like it." Leejohn (l-i) skipped "just to do it," Max and Ruth (both l-i) "to do something with friends," and Seth (h-i) "to catch up on my sleep." Dean (l-i) did not go because: "When I went to school teachers hassled me. The dean wouldn't leave us boys alone." Louann (l-i) "couldn't take the social scene at school—both teachers and students." Nicole (h-i) had "stayed home because I wasn't ready for a test."

There were also reasons for not skipping. Many high-income adolescents mentioned that skipping one day would mean more work the next. As Libby said: "What's the point? I'd just be home worrying about getting behind." John questioned: "Why do it? They take 2% off your school grades if they catch you. I'd have no place to go." Low-income adolescents often mentioned the likelihood of getting into trouble as a deterrent. Michael (l-i) asserted: "I'd get in trouble with Mom and Dad, and the police. I don't think it's right—if I skipped no telling what else I'd do." May (l-i) said: "Mom would kill me!" Tammy (l-i) replied: "A friend tried to get me to, but I wouldn't do it. I knew if I got caught there would be real trouble." Thomas (l-i) quipped: "I've been tempted, but with my luck I'd probably get caught." Les (l-i) said: "I like perfect attendance."

INTERPRETATIONS OF CONDUCT PROBLEMS

Low-income adolescents had conventional stands regarding student conduct—views identical to those of affluent students. However, in evaluating their own (mis)behaviors, they fluctuated between espousing the legitimacy of their actions and condemning themselves. When talking about specific instances of belligerent reactions to schoolmates, they maintained that their actions were provoked—and thus were retaliations for wrongs (e.g., "I hit someone because they hit me first"). Descriptions of humiliating school experiences were climaxed with declarations of having retaliated (e.g., "told off," "kept away from her") against those responsible for their pain.

Confrontative interactions with teachers were also reported as counteraggression (e.g., "backsassing," "she was mean, but I wouldn't take nothing off her") (see Figure 6.1). Low-income informants felt teachers had been rough on them first, so they had reciprocated. Kit insisted: "Teachers get a kick out of watching me go to the office—they really do." At another point she said: "They like seeing me in trouble. I lift a finger and they get on my case!" Nadia maintained: "I got mad at that teacher because she was mean." Thus they

FIGURE 6.1. Conflict with Teachers

Causes of Conflict: Frustration/resentment
                             (favoritism to affluent/advanced)
                             (failure)
                             Feelings of being under attack
                             (public humiliation)
                             (ostrasizing punishment)
                             Feelings of vulnerability
                             (powerlessness of self and family)

Nature of Reaction: Passive-aggression
                             (deliberate nonparticipation)
                             (withholding affection)
                             (withdrawing)
                             Counteraggression
                             (sassing, rudeness)

Outcomes to Reactions: Stereotyped as bad, mean, uncaring,
                             short-fused, defensive, sullen
                             Viewed as emotionally handicapped
                             Continued failure
                             Increased punishment
                             Increased anger
                             Feelings of unworthiness
                             Giving up/dropping out
                             Alienation

maintained that their behaviors were legitimate reactions to the negative attitudes they discerned in teachers.

Low-income adolescents also described passivity in school as the natural outcome of the abuse they felt they had received from teachers. After talking about a teacher who did not like him, Dusty said: "I just don't do anything she says." Chrissy reported: "I just refused to talk to most teachers because they picked on us—they were unfair." Similarly, Sheila asserted: "No, there's no way I could change my relationships with some teachers. They just do things to me, so I don't talk to them. I don't laugh when they say something funny. Why should I talk to them after class when they don't take time during class for me? They won't change!" Stubborn opposition to active participation in class was bragged about as courageous acts of resistance to those who did not mean well.

To some extent, then, low-income respondents maintained that they were on the defensive and that their aggressive actions were justified. But few were consistently confident that they were in the right. It was more typical for them to assess their own emotional reactions and behaviors as out-of-place and in need of being curbed. Will claimed: "I used to talk back; now I'm straightening up." And Kit confessed: "I couldn't get along. I'd argue with the teacher. I got mad, fought. I was a renegible [her word] child." To a certain degree, then, they believed that teachers were well meaning and preppies innocent. The general pattern was for them to accuse others of misdeeds when recounting specific incidents, but in summarizing behaviors they usually judged members of their own social class, including themselves, to be at fault. They internalized blame for school problems, apologized for their guilt, excused teachers for penalizing them, and even implied that there was cause (i.e., their own unworthiness) for others to shun or mistreat them. Thus low-income adolescents adhered to a code that endorsed passive cooperation and delegitimated anger and their own violence. Moreover, they saw their second-class status as justified because of personal inadequacies.

THE EXTENT AND NATURE OF PUNISHMENT

Given the disproportionate rate of trouble-making, it is not surprising that low-income respondents reported a greater number and variety of penalties (see Table 6.2). Even then, an undercount of milder penalties (e.g.,

TABLE 6.2. Amount and Types of Punishment Received

	Low-Income		High-Income	
	N	(%)*	N	(%)
Sent to office	19	(48)	3	(9)
Reprimanded by teacher	13	(33)	7	(21)
In-school suspension	12	(30)	2	(6)
Suspended from school	12	(30)	0	—
Put in hall	10	(25)	0	—
Received extra work	9	(23)	0	—
Stayed after school	6	(15)	0	—
Sent to court	3	(8)	0	—
Spanked	2	(5)	0	—
Total punished adolescents	32	(80)	10	(30)
Total punished incidents (mean per student)	86 (2.15)		12 (.35)	

* Percentage of group who named particular type of punishment.

lowered grades, teacher admonishments, detentions) is suspected because adolescents' attention was focused on traumatic events. It is typical for teachers and administrators to apply a hierarchy of consequences beginning with classroom reprimands, proceeding to office interventions, and finally resorting to the out-of-school solutions of suspension, expulsion, or taking an offender to court. Low-income adolescents talked about those on the more serious end of the continuum.

A number of low-income teenagers reeled off a string of outcomes for misdeeds. Without bravado, Dean confessed: "I was in trouble all the time for everything. The dean was giving me a bunch of trouble. I was suspended, sent to the office, yelled at, put in the hall. I couldn't take it. I quit." Max said: "I've been suspended, whacked, sent to the hall, the office, flunked, yelled at." Bret admitted: "I got 70 office referrals. I went everywhere: the office, suspension, court, probation." Trent recalled: "We had the pink slip system at school—I got many, many!" Leejohn said: "I had to stand in the hall a lot."

Thirteen high-income adolescents glibly announced that they had never been punished because, for example, "I don't do anything wrong," "I stay in line," or "I'm not a trouble-maker." In a matter-of-fact manner, William announced: "We don't do anything to get ourselves in that kind of a position." Similarly, Mario claimed: "I never do anything to get in trouble." Lynette said: "Why would I be punished? I don't misbehave."

When asked if they and their friends had been punished more than others, 8 low-income teenagers were fairly noncommittal, maintaining that they did not get into trouble and that they had not been observant about what went on with others in school. As Sonia replied: "I don't know. I never did anything wrong. I don't know about the others." But, the majority (32) felt they had received a disproportionate amount of punishment and, furthermore, that their penalties were undeserved, too severe, not commensurate with misdeeds, or that they had been "picked on" or "singled out." Beth maintained: "I get blamed for another person's wrongs. Like fights—they say I was in on them when I wasn't always." Stacy said: "I had a fight once. A girl called me a name and lied. I blackened her eye. I got kicked out for two days. That seemed like too much to me." Wendy claimed: "I was punished more. I got typed by my brothers' behavior. My brothers fought in school."

There were qualitative differences in the kinds of punishment received by high- and low-income adolescents (see Table 6.3); also, low-income adolescents described more severe punishment and more stringent consequences for the same infractions. Among the high-income respondents, Hilary said: "A teacher was after me about socializing. He felt I was neglecting my work." Hilary believed she was admonished because the teacher was concerned about her. Aaron's desk had been moved to curb his talking to friends, and he concluded that the teacher had done it "for my own good." Others had received

TABLE 6.3. Nature of Consequences Received

	Low-Income		High-Income	
	N	(%)*	N	(%)*
Rejecting/ostracizing	40	(47)	2	(17)
Humiliating	27	(31)	1	(8)
Illogical/counterproductive	9	(10)	1	(8)
Involved legal system	3	(4)	0	–
Physically violent	2	(3)	0	–
Civil/commensurate	5	(6)	8	(67)
Total incidents	86		12	

*Percentage of group's responses.
(Note: Due to rounding, percentage totals do not necessarily add to 100.)

the standard rule-based consequences (e.g., "I was sent to the office for being late to class"). High-income adolescents felt their punishment had been commensurate with their misdeeds.

Contrary to the dignified handling of affluent adolescents, low-income respondents reported less professional teacher behaviors. Carol said: "Teachers get mad at me. They really get mean sometimes." Their punishment often involved public humiliation (e.g., "yelled at in front of the class"), ostracism (e.g., "made to stand in the hall all day"), and rejection (e.g., "I was suspended from school all the time"). Stigmatizing and degrading punishment resulted in increased anger on the part of the recipient. The moderation, civil treatment, and respect shown to high-income teenagers did not provoke a negative reaction.

Various rationale were offered for discrepancies in punishment. Some low-income adolescents attributed the higher rate of punishment to their own behaviors. Jim said: "I was punished more because I wouldn't listen to teachers." Bret asserted: "I tried to get punished. I knifed a guy who threw a book at me." Randy felt his "personality clashed with some teachers." Trent remarked: "It just came into my head that I was punished more than some few. I think I make teachers mad."

Seventeen low-income adolescents attributed disproportionate punishment to prejudice, focusing on teacher affect as a causal factor. Sherry felt: "I was punished more than others. I was not the teachers' pet." Sheila believed: "Teachers had it in for me." Nadia bitterly recalled: "Mrs. B. could be nice, but evil too. She accused me of stealing. She wasn't being fair to me." Ruth observed: "Discipline depends on how much the teachers like the student. I got in more trouble than most. Me and all my friends don't like teachers; they don't like us. Some kids get away with more." Teresa said: "I was not treated fair. They pick on some people more." Not specific about the "we," Dusty said: "We get into fights. But when other kids fight we get blamed for it." Most left the discredited group unnamed. Will inferred intellectual factors: "I get punished more than others. Definitely. With smarter kids—those with good grades—teachers just snapped their fingers at them. We got punished."

Eleven low-income respondents specifically pinpointed social class discrimination. Sheila estimated: "More than half of the teachers have pets. Certain teachers like the preps more than anyone else. They think they have to pay more attention to them." Karen complained: "Some teachers are not really fair. They have favorites and let certain kids get away with stuff that others can't. A good teacher treats you equally. I think a lot of teachers like preps more than normal kids." Thomas, who was not a "trouble-maker" himself, observed: "Some only help kids who have real good potential. Kids they've known for a while. Most favor preppies. At times—with grits—they are watched. Someone else could get away with the same things. Grits are assumed to be trouble-makers."

Both high- and low-income adolescents, to some extent, attributed the discrepancy in penalties to manipulating and crafty behavior on the part of affluent adolescents. Chrissy (l-i) felt that: "Preps lie about stuff so they look like little angels." Jeremy (h-i) confessed: "We get away with more. We're sneaky. We stick up for each other." Aaron (h-i) admitted: "I get away with more. We always find a way to get out of trouble." Kirsten (h-i) maintained: "We don't get punished. My group doesn't stand out. We usually know what we can get away with, when to stop." Kelly (h-i) replied: "Me and my friends don't test teachers much, but occasionally we get away with bending a rule. If you're careful, teachers don't mind."

Two high-income adolescents who experienced academic problems felt they had received undeserved punishment as a result of teachers not liking them. As Seth said: "I get punished a lot because I always come in late. But the teacher has to make such a big deal of it. She doesn't like me, anyway." Vanessa, a high-achieving hippie type, complained that teachers held her to "silly little rules." She analyzed: "School is a real bureaucracy. They have regulations for everything. They're pretty illogical about punishment." With these few exceptions, high-income adolescents felt that discipline was "fair"—a more accurate interpretation might be that they were satisfied with preferential treatment.

Nineteen high-income adolescents (56%) acknowledged a personal advantage in the meting out of discipline. Libby concluded: "They don't often punish those who are good in school." Aaron believed: "They're easy on jocks." Hilary said: "We're in a popular group. I think teachers kind of respect us. We don't get punished even when we get a little wild. Some teachers think it's funny. They don't care." Marissa said: "I get away with a lot. My mother's a teacher, and my dad's well known in this town." Thus rationales for preferential treatment included a sense that teachers were more tolerant of high-income adolescents because they trusted them, were intimidated by their parents, or identified with them and so were not threatened by their behaviors.

Nine low-income respondents (23%) also felt they were punished less; some of their reasons overlapped with those of their high-income counterparts, while others differed. Nick said: "I got away with more. They knew my mother would come in and raise cane." Karen stated: "Mom goes in and yells at them if they get snobby." Jeff hypothesized: "You don't get into much trouble until you start getting a reputation. I've been mostly out of trouble." Rachel, too, concluded: "I get away with more. I don't have a bad reputation." Scott, an athlete involved in a number of school sports, said: "I got away with more. I had a good reputation, so I got away with more." Les maintained: "I got away with more. I hardly ever did anything wrong. I didn't have a bad reputation, so I got away with more." Madalene believed: "I get away with more. If teachers think you are a nice person—if you don't cuss and you get good grades—and another person isn't—cusses, gets bad grades—then if both are accused of the same thing, the teachers are more likely to blame the bad kid." She added: "The kids who were paddled deserved it—they got out of hand." High- and low-income adolescents concurred that school personnel were hard on "thugs," "bad kids," "bullies," and "rednecks." There was considerable agreement that school discipline depended on personal reputation, achievement, and social status; that is, that it was not really fair.

PARENTAL REACTION TO TROUBLE IN SCHOOL

Adolescents' perceptions of parental response to trouble in school were explored by asking who their parents blamed when they heard about problems. Most high-income adolescents (i.e., 25, 73%) felt that their parents would not immediately blame either school personnel or the adolescent, but would follow up on an ambiguous situation by finding out the truth and getting the problem resolved. Parents were felt to hold both teachers and students accountable for their actions. John said: "They would start off lecturing. Then they'd listen to me—try to find out what it's all about—try to help me. They support me. But they don't let me get away with anything. If they think it's my fault, I'm in trouble!" Andrew said: "My parents are pretty laid back usually, really too busy to get very involved. But I think my mother always worries that I'm screwing up. She's pretty quick to blame me. But I really don't like her to go to school because then she gets annoyed at the teachers. She bawls them out if she doesn't like the way they're doing things. It's embarrassing." Five felt that their parents would always assume that school problems were their fault and if they contacted school it would be to confirm problems. Tyler elaborated: "My mom is always concerned. She's strict. She's always on me about what's happening in school. How I'm doing. If there's a problem, she's on her way to school to talk about it." Four believed their parents would blame school for problems. Damon said: "My mom is pretty down on the school. She thinks a lot of teachers aren't doing their job right—don't care. She probably would sympathize with me."

Twenty-nine low-income teenagers (72.5%) said their parents generally supported school personnel and thus would assume that problems were their fault, seven (17.5%) were unsure, and four (10%) believed their parents would blame teachers; that is, they tended to take an oppositional stance regarding school personnel. The majority of parents, then, were perceived as being in agreement with the schools' interpretations of teenagers' behaviors and, perhaps, in support of the disciplinary measures enforced in school. Many said they preferred lunchtime to after-school or Saturday detention because then the school offense would not be disclosed to their parents and they would not have to suffer additional punishment at home. Low-income parents had apparently conveyed that school discipline was fair or that they wanted to avoid conflict with (school) officials; thus they chose to disregard their offsprings' claims about discriminatory practices. This finding supports Kohn and Schooler's (1983) theory that working-class parents emphasize conformity to externally imposed rules more than their middle-class counterparts.

However, in light of the results of an earlier study of local low-income parents in which most complained about social class bias in teachers' interaction with pupils (E. A. Brantlinger, 1985c), adolescents' perceptions of a high congruence between adults at school and at home is surprising. In that earlier study, low-income parents accused teachers of bias and felt that their offsprings' problems in school were not necessarily the kids' fault. In spite of what they said on an abstract level, in interaction with their own children they may have stressed conformity and cooperation regardless of the fairness of policies or the objectivity of those who enforced them—perhaps recommending passivity in the face of power as a survival tactic. Parents' own low self-esteem may have been generalized to their children; that is, they may have conveyed that their offspring were generally culpable and guilty of misdeeds. On the other hand, teenagers may have incorrectly associated the feelings of the two authority figures, especially in relationship to adversarial positions and challenges to their freedom and independence.

Teenagers were presented with the hypothetical case of having been falsely accused of an offense they had not committed or having been given a grade they did not deserve. They were asked to describe how their parents would react to their proclamations of injustice. All affluent respondents felt their parents would confront school personnel, and 25 low-income adolescents (62.5%), somewhat more hesitantly, believed theirs would. Carol (l-i) said: "My mom would say, 'Well, you better get it worked out. If you can't, tell me. I'll go to school and get it settled.'" Tammy (l-i) thought: "First my father would say it was my fault. Then he might believe me. If he thought I wasn't wrong, Dad would be mad and call school." Nadia (l-i) reminisced: "That happened once. My mom was mad. She went to talk to the teacher."

Fifteen low-income adolescents (37.5%) said their parents would do nothing. Some felt that although they would have to handle it on their own, their parents would empathize with them or offer advice. Adam said: "They would give me advice on what I should do, but they'd let me handle it." Tammy said: "Hopefully understand. Tell me how to improve the situation." Randy said: "My mom is sympathetic to my fights. She knows I wouldn't start one—I never would. But she just lets me get detention." Sonia conjectured: "They'd like to help me, but they'd probably do nothing. They'd just say 'Don't worry about it, it's not your fault.'" Stacy predicted: "She wouldn't be mad at me at all, but she wouldn't do nothing. She wouldn't go to school." In retrospect, Dean felt that his mother had believed his version of school occurrences, but "She still told me to straighten up!" Others were disgruntled and implied their parents were uncaring or cowardly. Wendy complained: "I don't think he'd do anything about it. Maybe he'd get involved if grades were concerned." Tricia grumbled: "Get mad. Do nothing." Trent said: "Grandma would be upset, but she wouldn't do nothing." Les guessed: "Let me work it out on my own. She'd tell me to work it out." Thomas predicted that "Mom might support the teachers." Scott said: "She wouldn't like it, but she'd still let it happen." Max announced: "They don't care. They wouldn't get involved."

Even the low-income adolescents who believed their parents would contact school personnel tended to be pessimistic about the outcome. They were not convinced that their parents' actions would produce the desired effects. In essence, their parents were seen as powerless in influencing school circumstances. High-income adolescents were confident that the situation would be settled in their favor—they did not doubt their parents' power to negotiate successfully in their behalf.

Depictions of parents' approach to school personnel also varied according to social class. High-income parents were usually described as interacting with school authorities in a calmly assertive manner, taking it for granted that bringing a problem to their attention would result in its correction. Low-income adolescents said their parents would be "mad" or "upset" and would go to school to express their emotions without expecting problem resolution. Annie said: "If it's school's fault, they'd raise hell!" Most had little confidence that there would be an acceptable outcome. Tammy said: "She knows damn well it won't do any good. They won't listen to her." Adolescents' interpretations of parents' reactions to a single incident were clearly embedded in the context of perceptions of parents' relationships with themselves as well as school authorities.

CONCLUSION

In analyzing adolescents' descriptions of their misbehaviors and teachers' reactions to problems, it was difficult to disentangle unique exposures from unique perceptions from unique ways of stating things. Dissimilarities in the groups' school histories meant that they did not share the same experiences, just as variations in home circumstances meant that they would tend to perceive the same events somewhat differently. A problem in taking adolescents' descriptions of trouble-making literally is that self-reports are influenced by complex motives and thinking processes. Some adolescents may have been in the habit of denying wrongdoing to adults to avoid punishment or to save face. Another problem in interpreting results was that speech idioms peculiar to each social class meant that they might not describe events in the same way. For example, when high-income adolescents said teachers "talked to" them about misbehaviors and low-income used the expression "bawled out," it is unclear whether different figures of speech were used to describe the same actions or whether members of each group had been treated uniquely. A case-by-case analysis revealed that informants who used "yelled at" in one context also used "talked to" in another, a fact that suggests a correlation between descriptions and actual events. Their accounts, then, for the most part, were taken at face value.

The misdeeds of high-income participants were minor and resulted from a lack of motivation and an active social life, whereas the acting-out and withdrawal behaviors of low-income youth were more serious and constant. They often stemmed from anger about situations connected with their subordinate status and unsuccessful school careers. Low-income respondents were frustrated by divisive, differentiating, and humbling school situations. Their vivid accounts of a variety of school circumstances revealed their feelings of vulnerability; they were alert to threat and ready to take defensive action with both students and teachers. In response to such actions, they suffered further humiliating, rejecting, and ostracizing penalties—consequences likely to fuel their rage as well as increase their feelings of impotence. It was apparent that school was a source of stress to these teenagers, not a neutral or therapeutic setting; their reactions to school were far from affect-free.

School was also not a neutral place for high-income adolescents; it was a privileging setting—a place where they learned of their own efficacy. They portrayed school as an orderly place where teachers were fair, objective, and basically on their side. They felt that good behaviors would yield rewards and that problems could be corrected. The few penalties they received were commensurate with misdeeds. In fact, most confessed to an advantage in the meting out of punishment. Similarly, the moderation, respect, and civil treatment they received from teachers did not provoke a negative reaction.

All respondents noted social class disparities in teachers' responses to misbehavior. Whereas low-income youth attributed these differences to the bias of school personnel or the manipulativeness of high-income students, affluent teenagers implied that low-income adolescents were simply getting their due. In spite of observations to the contrary, they accepted myths of the prevalence of undesirable traits among low-income teenagers—a mind-set that rationalized more severe punishment as deserved. It was clear that high-income adolescents felt that the superiority of their status entitled them to unique interpretations of their behaviors and a less stringent doling out of consequences. They took privileged treatment for granted. High-income adolescents also knew that their family's status acted as a symbolic threat that buffered teachers' emotional reactions to them; low-income students had no such back-up.

On an abstract level, all participants had conventional views of troublemaking—condemning violence, disruptiveness, and lack of effort. In discussing specific situations, however, low-income respondents were torn between condemning these behaviors and asserting their legitimacy given the widespread inequities and discrimination. In other words, they wavered between dominant ideologies that touted school as fair and beneficial for all and counterhegemonic sentiments that challenged such uncritical common wisdom.

There is growing concern about school as a source of stress for low-achieving students (e.g., Block & Gjerde, 1986; Comer, 1988; Drummond, 1982; Goodlad & Oakes, 1988; Lightfoot, 1987; Rutter, 1983; Schunk, 1989; Strauss, Frame, & Forehand, 1987). Elias (1989) described students' pervasive sense of failure and of being thwarted in the search for acceptable identities. Wynne and Walberg (1985) pinpointed the negative psychosocial influence of unsuccessful school careers. Studies of school dropouts indicate that school climate has an impact on dropout rates (Fine, 1986, 1991; Hahn, 1987). Some look further and assert that societal circumstances, rather than families, are at the root of children's emotional states (e.g., Carrier, 1986; Drummond, 1982; Skrtic, 1988).

Although passive resignation appeared to be the most common reaction to schooling, such quiescence was periodically interrupted by outbursts of anger. Low-income adolescents' anger was erratic and individualistic rather than systematic and collective. Such expressions of wrath would tend to be viewed by school personnel as indications of personal pathology rather than a legitimate response to unfair circumstances or signs of social class action. According to Schostak (1986), context and political implications need to be considered when analyzing violence, yet it is more typical for school personnel to decontextualize violence and see it as abnormal. Instead of perceiving expressions of anger as legitimate and appropriate, teachers and school administrators postulate that certain students have a predisposition for violence.

A popular intervention for disruptive students is to directly teach prosocial behaviors and consistently reward their use (Goldstein, 1987). This approach, however, treats the symptoms, or surface behaviors, and does not address the affective underpinnings of behaviors. Newmann (1981) suggested that episodic violence by acting-out students be dealt with by attempting to reduce alienation, promote integration, improve the quality of schools, increase student participation in school governance, and encourage a sense of belonging by creating schools within schools. Although such ideas address the origins of anger, they have not been widely used. The results of this study indicate that these approaches should be given more serious attention. It is important to take a close look at underlying factors in understanding the behaviors of students before selecting remedies.

CHAPTER 7

Family and Friends

Other chapters in this book have dealt with adolescents in the context of school. This chapter covers adolescents' social relations in their homes and neighborhoods. The first part addresses adolescents' views of intimate social settings and social interactions by exploring feelings about home lives, relationships with families, and intentions to emulate or reject family lifestyles. Additionally, adolescents' perceptions of their family's ability to meet their needs and their parents' support for their school careers will be examined. The second part focuses on adolescents' descriptions of their friends and the nature of their friendships. As usual, perceptions of the social class influences on family life and friendships were of particular interest.

FAMILY

Goodnow, Knight, and Cashmore (1986) have theorized that parenting behaviors—that is, styles of socialization—involve schemas, or interrelated patterns of perceptions, values, and behaviors, that vary according to socio-economic status. Kohn (1983) showed how parents' socialization styles were integrally related to the particulars of their economic roles in society. Apparently, parents from management classes were likely to encourage independence and creativity in their children, whereas working-class parents emphasized conformity. Many (e.g., Bugetal, 1985; Henderson, 1981; Hess & Shipman, 1973; Laosa, 1982; Maccoby & Martin, 1983; Morgan, Alwin, & Griffin, 1979; Rodman & Voydanoff, 1978) have hypothesized that early in childhood, individuals are socialized (by families) to behaviors that lead to poverty.

Family's Way of Life

Although the question was phrased very generally (i.e., "How do you feel about your family's way of life?"), respondents inevitably focused on material well-being. Barbara (h-i) enthusiastically replied: "I love it. It's great. I couldn't ask for more. We have everything that we want." An ambivalent Will (l-i) said:

"We are a good family, but the economic side could be better." Kit (l-i) bluntly declared: "We're underprivileged. Mom has a lot of physical and emotional problems. Dad is better off, but he can't keep me right now."

With the emphasis on family funds, it is not surprising that there were social class distinctions in adolescents' contentment with their family's lifestyle (see Table 7.1). High-income adolescents were mainly satisfied (e.g., "We have a nice house, good cars"; "I'm rich and I like it"; "I'm satisfied; I don't want more money; I like their lifestyle"; "It's a lot better than other people's way of life; I don't look down on them though"). In contrast, 29 low-income adolescents were dissatisfied, ambivalent, or noncommittal. They were bitter that their families lacked sufficient funds or that their parents were out of work or had low-paying jobs or jobs that lacked prestige (e.g., "We need more funds and all that goes with the money"; "Things could be better—a lot better; my parents don't have real jobs").

The ambivalent low-income respondents were concerned about family finances but still found strengths in their families. As May said: "They don't have good jobs. But we're not dirt poor that we have to live in a box. We do all right." Madalene reported: "We're not rich. We need more money, but we've got decency." The nine ambivalent high-income adolescents focused mainly on negative interpersonal relationships. Nicole wavered:

> We've got a good family. Most of the time we get along. I guess my parents are annoyed at the kids a lot. They want my older sister to be more social and me and my brother to be less social. They spoil my little sister. They get pissed when the older kids don't want to do things with the family. But we basically get along.

Insecure about his parents' recent divorce, Seth, the only high-income respondent who was negative, said: "I'm not satisfied—well, they aren't really either. They want more for me." In a unique perspective, Andrew judged: "It's okay. Sometimes I feel we're too wealthy. I don't like conspicuous consumption."

Several low-income respondents were frustrated about multiple family problems and difficult living situations. Teresa accused her father of sexist attitudes: "Dad says a woman's place is in the home. She wants to work, but he won't let her. We'd be better off if she could work." Stacy elaborated:

> My life could be a lot more straightened out. My half-brothers' dad keeps causing trouble. He's burned my clothes, Mom's clothes, the Christmas presents. He keeps getting put in prison. She has left him and has another boyfriend, a construction worker. I guess she's happy with him, but he's the jealous type. When he's off work, he wants all

TABLE 7.1. Feelings About Family's Life

	Low-Income		High-Income	
	N	(%)	N	(%)
Satisfaction with Present Circumstances				
Satisfied	11	(28)	22	(64)
Ambivalent	8	(20)	9	(27)
Dissatisfied	16	(40)	1	(3)
Uncertain/noncommital	5	(13)	2	(6)
Evaluations of Family Relationships				
Positive	8	(20)	33	(97)
Mixed	26	(65)	1	(3)
Negative	6	(15)	0	
Causes of Friction with Parents				
Control/independence	9	(23)	13	(39)
Adolescent's attitude	8	(20)	6	(18)
Adolescent's behavior	8	(20)	3	(9)
Money	5	(13)	0	
School performance	5	(13)	9	(27)
Types of friends	3	(8)	3	(9)
Uncertain/noncommital	2	(5)	0	
Desire to Emulate Parents				
Want to be similar	4	(10)	23	(67)
Want to be different	34	(85)	11	(33)
Uncertain/noncommital	2	(5)	0	
Expect to be Similar to Parents				
Expect to be similar	11	(28)	27	(79)
Expect to be different	24	(60)	7	(21)
Uncertain/noncommital	5	(13)	0	
Total	40		34	

(Note: Due to rounding, percentage totals do not necessarily add to 100.)

her time. I really want to do my own thing. All this stuff is hard on a person.

As indicated in Chapter 1, and similar to findings elsewhere (e.g., Edelman, 1987; Ehrenreich & Piven, 1984), 27 low-income adolescents had little or no contact with one (or both) of their parents—usually fathers. Nevertheless, many of these adolescents did not mention the absence of fathers as a problem, perhaps because single-parent families were so commonplace in their neighborhoods. Those who were unhappy were usually the ones whose fathers had lived with them at an earlier point. Although it might be assumed that adolescents would attribute family problems to absent fathers, on the contrary, most blamed mothers for negative circumstances (e.g., "Mom's sick and can't find good jobs"; "Mom should work—make money—support us!"; "We need more money; I want Mom to earn it"; "It could be better if Mom worked; I guess she can't find a job"; "I don't like it; Mom should have done better"). The subsidized-housing ghetto had perhaps become so matriarchal that mothers were seen as solely in control, hence responsible for the adequacy of conditions—fathers were not present to be blamed. The 4 teenagers who had been abandoned by mothers were vocal about their bitterness, whereas annoyance at absent fathers was either not expressed or substantially less intense.

Desire to Emulate Parents

In discussing whether they wanted to be like their parents, the materialism again surfaced. Thirty-four (85%) low-income teenagers saw their parents as models to be avoided, stressing a desire to be more vocationally and financially successful. Adam stated simply: "No. I don't want to be like them. I don't want to be poor." May clarified: "My parents did not know what they were doing. They didn't think ahead. They can't get good jobs. I want to find a better job and marry somebody with more money." Celestine said: "I want to work, maybe. I don't like telling people we're poor." Madalene responded: "I want more financial security and a house." Tracy vowed: "My parents are poor. They didn't get enough education. I am going to finish school if it kills me." Jim claimed: "They have trouble with jobs. I'd better be different, otherwise I'll never be able to pay the bills." Scott quipped: "Hell, no. She's not even got enough money to support us. I want to be rich!"

Embarrassed that the family lived in subsidized housing or in the slums, many low-income respondents were determined to "get off The Hill" or "get out of the projects." Wendy said: "I'd like to move out of our apartment. I hate The Hill. The people around here are mainly dopeheads." Similarly, Teresa said: "I'd like to be different. Richer. Live someplace else. I don't like where we live." Beth expounded: "I want things to be different. I'd like to be a good mom like my mom, but I want things better. I don't want to live on The Hill. I try to get my mom to move off The Hill. Both our lives would be better if we moved." Jeff said: "This part of town is seedy. I'd like to live somewhere nicer, maybe out there by Kinder school. I like it out there." Madalene dreamed: "I'd like to move to a house with land and have some horses."

Low-income parents were offered as negative role models related to family planning (e.g., "I'm not going to start a family so early"; "I would not have five kids"; "I would not have children so young"); childrearing and housekeeping (e.g., "My mom neglects the children; I won't be like that"; "I'll stay with my family"; "I would not yell at my kids"; "I'd be more open with my kids; give them more freedom; pay attention to them; not just watch TV"; "I hope not; I want to be different; I'll keep my house clean"); marital relations (e.g., "I will not argue so much like my mom and dad"; "I will marry someone I like—not lazy like my stepdad"); substance abuse (e.g., "I don't want to be like my mom; she drinks a lot—she's an alcoholic"; "My brother never comes home—he's on the streets at night; my sisters are druggies; I would change the way I am—not do pot or drink"; "I hope not like my dad; I don't want to drink and live like that"); and educational attainment (e.g., "I'm not going to drop out of school like my mom did"). Others spoke generally (e.g., "I want to be somebody bigger"; "I don't want to bum off people"; "Not like them— they are jerks"). Annie said: "I'd do more to experience things in life—be more involved in what's going on in the world. I'd be more carefree and energetic." In contrast, Leejohn declared: "I don't mind being like my mom—I wouldn't want to be like no prep and think I'm better than everybody else."

High-income adolescents were mainly satisfied with their lives; hence they were generally eager to follow in their parents' footsteps (see Table 7.1). Sarah said: "I want to have all that they have and be happy." Kirsten said: "My dad has more money than my mom. I like them both, but I guess I'd rather be like my dad." Those who rejected parents as models focused on personal traits. A negative Lynette wavered: "Not exactly. Some qualities are nice. I want to reach all my goals. I don't want to settle for the mediocre." Andrew criticized: "They sit around too much. They're depressed at times. I'd like to do more. Not be so selfish." Nicole planned: "I want to be more active." Greg asserted: "No, I don't want to work so much. I want to get rich young, then hang out and travel most of the time." Many felt their parents were tense and pressured. Tony wanted "to be more easy-going." Marissa said: "I wouldn't mind being like them. Their life is pretty good, but they need to loosen up." Kirsten, whose parents were in the midst of a divorce at the time of the interviews, said: "I'd like to be somewhat like them. They are practical. But they need to be more relaxed. Right now they're both unhappy and dissatisfied. They're confused—in the middle of a midlife crisis. They have good values, though."

When high-income adolescents discussed the work ethic, they claimed parents worked too hard or led stressful lives; low-income adolescents criticized from an opposite direction (e.g., "They need to work harder"; "She should try to be more successful"; "She needs to get a better job"; "She should not be so lazy").

Respondents were more likely to expect to be like their parents than to want to be like them (see Table 7.1). When asked if she expected to be similar to her parents, Libby (h-i) asserted: "I expect so. They've thrown values into my head that have influenced me." Similarly, Hilary (h-i) said: "Most kids usually end up like their parents because of the influence of all those years." Stacy (l-i) related: "My mom's afraid I will grow up to be like her and have a baby when she did. But I want to be my own self. I'll never have a kid that soon. All the kids my age around here are pregnant—not me!" Randy (l-i) poignantly confessed: "When I saw my report card I thought, Jesus, I'm going to be just like my dad. Then I said, 'No way.' I hope not!" The majority of low-income adolescents optimistically—but often defensively—asserted that they would be different as adults.

Adolescents' feelings about families and family circumstances were also reflected in their conjecturing about their own futures. The majority of adolescents planned to get married, with high-income youth slightly more positive than low-income respondents (79% compared to 73%). In terms of having children, high-income girls were the most negative; 37% said they probably would not have children, whereas only 20% of high-income boys felt they might not have children. These high-income girls felt that children might interfere with career goals. High-income males did not see children as a hindering factor. In contrast, low-income boys were less positive about children than low-income girls (i.e., 58% compared to 76%, respectively).

Relationships with Family Members

There were clear social class differences in adolescents' evaluations of their relationships with their families (see Table 7.1). Most respondents mentioned some problems within the family, but low-income adolescents usually summarized the relationship as mixed (or negative) and high-income adolescents as positive. Even the "mixed" count is likely to be unrealistically high for low-income adolescents because of their seeming hesitancy to, as one said, "come down hard on your family." Many of those who complained the most about family situations throughout their interviews still felt compelled to put on a positive face when asked directly. Kit said: "I think it's fine. I come and go as I please. I get along with my mom and stepdad, although I'd prefer to live with my dad." Thomas summarized: "I like it. I'm raised in a decent family with people who care." Those who revealed more tended to whisper when discussing disgraceful aspects of their family's lives.

Low-income respondents discussed family relationships with a good deal of emotion (e.g., "I don't live with my parents; I don't get along with my dad; I live with my grandparents"; "I don't like it; my parents just got a divorce; my dad is in prison—he's an alcoholic and has been arrested five times for drunken driving; my mother only makes minimum wage"; "I hate my stepdad!"; "My mom hates my stepdad; she shouldn't have married him; he doesn't work—won't help Mom; it makes me upset—me and Mom aren't as close as we should be"; "I want Mom to come back!"; "Mom wants me to go back to school so that she can have my baby to herself"). Although they conveyed that family business was private business, they seemed relieved to have a sympathetic listener with whom they could discuss concerns.

Adolescents described a variety of sources of friction with their parents (see Table 7.1). Conflict revolved mostly around issues of control and independence for both low- (e.g., "I get mad at them when I want to go out and they won't let me"; "They don't let me do all the things I want; I can't go out late"; "She won't let me go into town"; "My staying out late with friends, my independence") and high-income adolescents (e.g., "My freedom"; "Going over to friends—they won't let me go"; "Minor things like coming in late"; "There's friction from my being a teenager; I don't like my curfew; they always have to know where I am; I think they're overprotective because I'm the only girl").

Problems involving the teenagers' personalities or attitudes toward parents also frequently caused problems. Libby (h-i) said: "Talking back makes them mad. But we are all Christians, and that makes us close and together." Nicole (h-i) reported that her parents got upset at her "not showing respect for them" and added: "My father and I are too stubborn." Vanessa (h-i) said: "There's conflict over opinions. They don't like my personal opinions." Dusty (l-i) argued: "My dad gets mad at the way I treat my stepbrother, but he deserves it. He is a real pain in the butt." Audrey (h-i) said: "They bug me about cleaning, picking up. I hate it." Scott (l-i) complained: "Like blaming me for something I didn't do." Jessica (h-i) confessed trouble resulted from "being caught in a lie." Kirsten (h-i) believed her parents were bothered by "my friends and the way I dress."

Accusations of behaviors such as drug and alcohol abuse were cited as causing friction. Hilary (h-i) claimed: "They accuse me of drinking or being on drugs." Seth (h-i) discreetly said: "They get mad at . . . well, I'm not going to say anything that would incriminate me." From the opposite perspective, Tricia (l-i) "was mad at" her mother for "being a drunk—for just not caring about anything or anybody."

Friction arising from school situations was more common among affluent youth. They claimed their parents pressured them and criticized them about school performance. Seth (h-i) maintained: "The thing that they get most upset about is my bad grades." Greg (h-i) stated: "They are after me about homework. They think I should be a perfect student." Low-income adolescents, however, got in trouble when school officials called to report a disciplinary infraction. Will said: "The principal called Mom about something I did. I got grounded for a month." Dean recalled: "Dr. B. called my mom all the time. She got me in trouble."

Parents' Roles Related to Schooling

The increasing dependence of educational attainment on social origin is generally acknowledged (e.g., Mare, 1981; Scott-Jones, 1984). Considerable research has focused on the link between parental values regarding schooling and children's achievement behavior (Cockburn, 1989; St. John, 1972). Beliefs and aspirations are said to be cognitive mediators that influence parents' responses to their children's school-related behaviors (Harkness & Super, 1985; Hess, 1981; Kohn, 1983). Communication involves verbal statements of value meant to be acted on by offspring, messages derived from parents' actions (i.e., parents as models of achievement), and parents' achievement-supporting behaviors (Seginer, 1983).

The connection between parental achievement and offspring achievement is demonstrated by the finding that the educational attainment of parents has the highest relationship of all socioeconomic-status subvariables to offspring aspirations and achievement (Henderson, 1981; Laosa, 1982). The best predictor of educational attainment for adolescents is their beliefs about their parents' positions on education, and parental assumptions about college attendance are positively associated with actual attendance (J. Cashmore & Goodnow, 1985). Parents, in general, have high aspirations for their children, but lower socioeconomic status is associated with a wider range of aspirations and a difference in the floor for acceptable occupations or education attainment (Rodman & Voydanoff, 1978). In other words, all parents would be happy to have their children obtain high-status educational degrees and occupations, but low-income parents are also satisfied with lower levels of educational attainment and less prestigious jobs for their offspring. Parents' aspirations for their offspring are affected by their children's educational careers, and they modify their initial aspirations in response to evaluative information received from schools (E. A. Brantlinger, 1985b; Rosenholtz & Simpson, 1984; Seginer, 1983; St. John, 1972).

Other studies have found that economic hardship and the stress of such hardship affect parent–child interaction (Elder & Liker, 1982); the lower the socioeconomic status of a student, the lower the perceived parental support, control, and consistency (Scheck & Emerick, 1976). Adolescents from intact families have been found to be more optimistic about the future than those from homes in which there has been a separation, divorce, or parental death (Saucier & Ambert, 1982).

The intent of including questions on family support for education in this study was to examine intergenerational values related to education from the adolescent's perspective. The focus on families represents an attempt to delve into the origins and underpinnings of adolescents' attitudes and incentives related to school.

There were a number of class-related differences in adolescents' descriptions of their parents' belief systems as well as ways their parents had been involved with their education through the years (see Table 7.2). Although all

TABLE 7.2. Parental Participation with Schooling

	Low-Income		High-Income	
	N	(%)	N	(%)
Parents Attend Conferences				
Usually attend	10	(25)	31	(91)
Sometimes attend	10	(25)	–	
Never attend	20	(50)	3	(9)
Parents Help with Schoolwork				
Parents help	18	(45)	23	(67)
(used to help)	16		9	
(still help)	2		14	
Parents do not help	22	(55)	11*	(33)
Parents Attend Social Events				
Attend often	12	(30)	27	(79)
Attend sometimes	4	(10)	1	(3)
Never attend	24	(60)	6	(18)
Parents Have Contact with School Officials				
Have had contact	24	(60)	11	(33)
(parent-initiated)	8		8	
(school-initiated)	16		3	
Parents have not had contact	16	(40)	23	(67)
Total	40		34	

*Students claimed not to need help.

adolescents recalled that their parents attended conferences when they were in elementary school, high-income adolescents maintained that their parents attended conferences and open-houses regularly through junior high and high school, whereas low-income adolescents indicated that their parents' attendance dropped sharply during the middle school years (e.g., "I don't think she's set foot in Loring, but when I was at Southside she used to go all the time").

A number of reasons were offered for their parents' lack of visits to secondary schools, including circumstances such as "The school's too far away; she has no way to get there" and "She works nights, so she can't go." But more frequently heard were such comments as "I think she got tired of hearing them teachers complain" and "Why should she go? It wouldn't do any good." Parents had conveyed that they anticipated hearing negative things at conferences or they did not believe an effort to attend conferences would prove efficacious.

Adolescents in special education classes reported more frequent conference attendance for their parents. Parental involvement is mandated by law (PL 94-142), so parents are routinely contacted about case conferences or annual reviews. But even special education students indicated that parental participation decreased over time. As Dusty said: "What's the use? They [school personnel] don't have anything new to tell."

High-income adolescents were also more likely than their low-income counterparts to report that their parents had helped them with schoolwork (see Table 7.2). They indicated that they made use of technical assistance on homework, such as parents' typing and editing their written assignments. Some were grateful for parental support, whereas others implied it was imposed on them. According to Andrew: "I really avoid asking them anything. My father launches into a long lecture for every simple question, and my mother gets mad when she thinks I'm doing sloppy work."

The different rate of parental help with schoolwork is likely to result both from differences in parents' competencies—or perceived competencies—and the nature of adolescents' school careers. Low-income parents had dropped out of school prior to graduation, and high-income parents had high levels of educational attainment. Moreover, high-income teenagers were in advanced tracks, while low-income teenagers were in basic or general classes; the difficulty of schoolwork, hence adolescents' need for help, would presumably differ for these tracks. Low-income adolescents were likely to be in classes where academic demands were geared down; thus they did not ask parents for help because they did not need it. By the time low-income adolescents reached high school, their parents may have been resigned to the low grades they received and efforts to help may have seemed fruitless.

High-income adolescents also reported more active parental participation in social events (see Table 7.2). Yet when low-income adolescents participated in extracurricular activities, they claimed their parents were enthusiastic audiences. Others believed that if they had "been on a team" or "in a show," their parents would have been proud to attend. Thus the social class differences in parents' participation mirrored the uneven student involvement in activities.

There were social class differences in the rate and direction of contacts between parents and school personnel (see Table 7.2). High-income parents initiated more contact with school personnel, while low-income parents tended to be involved in school-initiated interactions. When parent-initiated, the focus was likely to be on track placement, clarification of assignments, disputes over performance evaluations, or requests for reports of student progress. When school-initiated, the issues tended to be grade retention, special education referral, or disciplinary infractions such as fighting, truancy, or friction with a teacher or schoolmate. High-income adolescents claimed parents had seen teachers or guidance counselors, whereas low-income adolescents' parents had been contacted by deans, administrators, or special education personnel.

A cautious interpretation of differences in parent–school contacts is necessary for a number of reasons. Parental actions paralleled the different school careers of high- and low-income students. Thus student roles dictated the types of roles parents were called on to play. If school careers had been similar, parental response might have been similar. Of course, the opposite might also be true; that is, if low-income parents had done more pressuring and been more assertive in their offsprings' behalf, their children might have done better in school. Their own cognitive appraisal of the situation (e.g., regarding school, themselves, their offspring) is likely to have prevented them from taking a more active stance.

FRIENDS

Research indicates that peer relationship styles are consistent across an individual's lifespan (Sroufe & Fleeson, 1986); that is, individual differences in friendship patterns transcend developmental changes (Bukowski, Newcomb, & Hoza, 1987). During adolescence, however, all friendships are said to increase in intensity and volatility (Douvan, 1983). The roles of gender, developmental, and individual characteristics in friendships have been explored, but, with few exceptions (e.g., Bichard, Alden, Walker, & McMahon, 1988; Coleman, 1974; Eder & Stanford, 1986), there is a dearth of information about social class influences on friendships or about the differences in friendship patterns among members of different social classes. In this study, the nature of high- and low-income adolescents' friendships were explored. These explorations focused on the types of interactions, the personal qualities of friends, and ways of making friends. Through the examination of friendships, considerable information was revealed about the needs, tastes, and feelings of adolescents. Just as student groupings and classifications engendered animated narratives, friendships were obviously of fervent interest to respondents.

Characteristics of Friends

Adolescents claimed that their friends usually were in the same curricular tracks, that they participated in the same school activities, that they dressed similarly, and that they liked the same musical groups or films; that is, they selected friends from familiar circles and often ended up with mirror images of themselves. But aside from these similarities in friendships, descriptions of the characteristics of friends varied in a number of significant ways for high- and low-income respondents (see Table 7.3).

Altruism and kindness have consistently been found to be important in maintaining relationships (Leahy, 1983). Even very young children show distress when observing friction between people (Zahn-Waxler, Radke-Yarrow, & King, 1979). But affective qualities in friends and the affective bonds of friendships were mentioned much more frequently by low- than high-income respondents. The characteristics "friendly," "nice," "kind," "supportive," and "helpful" echoed throughout low-income adolescents' narratives about friends. For example, Louann described a friend (i.e., a nonboyfriend neighbor): "He is nice. A real sweet kid. He claims me as a big sister and my baby as his niece."

Just as low-income adolescents were more attuned to teachers' attitudes and affect, these same attributes were important in friends. Over a third of the low-income adolescents named friends' attitudes toward themselves as an important feature of friendships for both males (e.g., "He is very loving to me"; "He really enjoys being with me"; "Doesn't make fun of you or anything"; "He respects you even if you say you can't do something") and females ("She'll help me out; a lot of friends I had just used me;" She doesn't care that I'm in special education; she doesn't hold it against me"; "My best friend is 23; she treats me like I'm a daughter"; "She doesn't put me down"; "She likes doing stuff with me"). Low-income adolescents were grateful for others' affection and acceptance, perhaps because they generally felt vulnerable, unworthy, and rejected in so many of their social interactions. It may be that high-income adolescents believed that they were likable and worthy of respect. More

TABLE 7.3. The Nature of Adolescents' Friendships

	Low-Income		High-Income	
	N	(%)	N	(%)
Characteristics of Best Friends				
Affect	33	(83)	9	(27)
Attitude toward respondent	15	(38)	1	(3)
Personality	11	(28)	11	(33)
Intelligence	4	(10)	16	(48)
Appearance	4	(10)	4	(12)
Family status	3	(8)	4	(12)
Peer social status	0		7	(21)
Talent	0		4	(12)
Problems with Friends or Friendships				
Friend has no flaws	20	(50)	5	(15)
Relationship problems	12	(30)	10	(35)
Personal annoyances	8	(20)	19	(56)
Reasons for Friendships				
Companionship/affiliation	33	(83)	30	(90)
Mutual tastes/interests	25	(63)	28	(84)
Supportive relationship	19	(48)	9	(27)

sure of themselves, affection from friends was expected and not notable. Or it could be that friendships served another function for them; being seen with high-status peers seemed a critical factor in establishing and maintaining their own status.

High-income adolescents were more likely to name status attributes, such as friends' brand of clothes or popularity, as relevant to their friendships (e.g., "My best friend is pretty and popular—it makes me a little jealous!"; "He is very well-dressed; he always has the most expensive brand-name clothes"; "My friends are popular students"; "She's free-spirited, very nice"; "She is popular, but she doesn't flaunt her popularity"). High-income adolescents also talked about their friends' family status (e.g., "My friends are good kids from good families"; "He wears nothing but Polos; his parents are filthy rich"; "He's very smart (4.0), musical, and from a very wealthy family"; "She's pretty, popular, very wealthy"; "She's from a good family—our parents are friends; they've got more money than us").

Mention of peer social status was virtually absent in low-income adolescents' discussions of friends. Of the three who mentioned family variables, only Madalene said that her friend's parents were "well-educated." The other two referred to problematic situations. Max elaborated:

> I've known my friend for about 8 years. I met him in the neighborhood. He ran away about 2 weeks ago. We talked about it. He asked me if I wanted to go and I said no. His dad hates me. He don't like the way I talk and am. Says I get his son in trouble—which I don't. His dad is prejudiced. They think they are higher-class. It don't make sense because his dad came from The Hill, too, but they've lived in Eadsville for awhile now. They have a boat and a new car. His mom is rich because she is a nurse. The dad works at a lumberyard.

Nick described his friend as: "Fat, a little self-centered, pretty open-minded, underprivileged—lives in a problem home, but he's friendly and good company."

Intertwined with social-status descriptions, high-income adolescents frequently referred to the intelligence and talents of their friends (e.g., "My friends are musicians"; "My friends are intelligent, liberal"; "They are good students"; "She's really smart"; "He is quiet, intelligent, not really outgoing"; "He's a top athlete, great musician, straight-A student and he doesn't have an enemy in the world"; "The kids I hang around with are usually good students and are trying to stay out of trouble"; "Most of my friends are good students, but they don't really enjoy school"; "They are pretty popular, smart, basically nice kids"; "The majority are smart, athletic"; "My friend is someone I could look up to—very intelligent, on the baseball team, goes to a lot of parties"). Four times as many high-income adolescents mentioned intelligence when discussing friends' attributes; in fact, two of the four low-income teenagers who talked about intelligence stated that their friend was *not* smart (i.e., "My friend is a low-income philanderer; Not as smart as me, but pretty"; "He's pretty dumb").

Personality characteristics of friends appeared at equivalent rates in high- and low-income adolescents' narratives. Some form of "sense of humor" was the most frequent attribute mentioned by high-income adolescents (e.g., "fun personality," "likes to joke around," "has a sense of humor," "she's funny," "she makes me laugh a lot"). Two high-income males focused on conformist characteristics ("My friends are regular guys"; "We're all just ordinary kids"), whereas nonconformity was valued by other high-income youth (e.g., "They are themselves; they know what they want; they don't try to be like the others"; "She's down to earth—not trivial like most kids"; "She's out of the ordinary") and their low-income counterparts (e.g., "Willing to consider doing something different"; "He is goofy"; "He is a go-atter; he tries interesting things"; "She is a tomboy—a real tomboy"; "My friends are quiet—not like others"). Adolescents also talked about the absence of negative traits in friends (e.g., "She's not a show-off"; "He doesn't bug me"). Low-income respondents brought up choosing friends who avoided substance abuse (e.g., "He doesn't smoke or drink or do drugs"; "She don't cause no trouble; she don't do drugs").

Low-income respondents were less likely to be critical of their friends (see Table 7.3). When they talked about flaws, the flaws had more to do with the nature of the relationship than with personal attributes. Randy said: "Sometimes he aggravates me. He does stupid stuff. Tries to get back at me. It is easy to get on my nerves." Trent offered: "Sometimes he shoves me. Teases me." According to Teresa: "She gets mad at me about her boyfriend. She thinks I'm trying to steal him—I'm not. I never get mad at her. She is nice. I can get along with her better than any other friend." Louann complained: "He picks on me, and it makes me mad. I pick on him, and he just laughs. I also don't like his attitude—the way he talks to his mom, the way he treats her. I gripe at him. I used to yell at my mom, but I decided I would be good to her while I can." Will mentioned: "Sometimes they joke around too much. I get mad. Sometimes I don't really feel like horsing around." According to Annie: "I don't like her attitude toward people. I don't stereotype people and she does."

High-income adolescents were frequently critical of friends' personalities or personal characteristics. Such defects included: "She's not punctual; It bugs me"; "She's prejudiced"; "I don't like her boyfriend; he's a barbarian"; "It bugs me when they joke about something I'm serious about"; "He acts stupid once in a while"; "He's too uptight"; "He's too goody-goody; he's skeptical of doing things like overdrinking"; "He's not really responsible"; "I don't like his political views"; "She's too judgmental"; "She's immature"; "She's sort of selfish"; "She is too tomboy, too rough; She is more shy than anything else." Themes of competition and jealousy were prevalent among the responses of high-income adolescents (e.g., "She gets jealous sometimes"; "Sometimes he's a little stuck-up"; "Sometimes he's bigheaded—brags—but it's no problem"; "I don't like her other friends"). Libby said: "A friend of my friend manipulates her. Turns her against me." Lynette complained: "One friend has low self-esteem. One is too perfect, too popular. It seems like my friends and I are mad at each other a lot of the time." Jessica was bothered that: "She's always on the phone—takes me for granted. She always waits for me to call her." Kirsten was annoyed because: "She's really smart and she always does better than me and she lets me know it whenever she can. Like she says, 'That test was real easy' when she knows I thought it was hard." Greg confessed: "I don't trust him." Marissa admitted: "Sometimes we plan to do something, and she gets something better to do and changes her mind. She ignores me when her boyfriend's around. I wouldn't care so much if he wasn't such a jerk!"

According to adolescents, friendships had originated in neighborhoods or elementary schools. This was particularly the case for low-income respondents. As Dean stated: "My friends are like me. Live in the neighborhood. I've known them 2 or 3 years—some all my life." Will said: "I hang around mainly with Downing kids." Teresa responded: "Most friends live close and like to do the same kind of thing." Tammy claimed: "I mixed with kids from other schools, but my best friends were from Hillview and were neighbors." Jeff revealed: "You stick with elementary school friends—they're the only people you know. As the year goes by you break up a little bit." Nick hypothesized: "Elementary school kids keep together to insure having friends."

Although the majority of high-income adolescents had met their friends in their neighborhoods and had known them since elementary school, a greater proportion of high- than low-income adolescents had met friend(s) through citywide or secondary school–based activities (e.g., marching band, plays, academic contests, ballet, tennis, church). Some announced that after leaving elementary school they had little to do with peers in their immediate neighborhood, often claiming "little in common" or competitive relationships with neighbors. As Damon said: "Tom used to be my best friend when we were at Kinder. We don't do much anymore. I'm pissed off at him 'cause he acts like a jerk."

High-income respondents talked about spending nonschool time with friends who lived outside their neighborhoods. Lack of transportation was usually not an obstacle. Four brought up out-of-town contacts as friends. Polly asserted: "I have many best friends in different areas of the world, but not in Hillsdale—and we don't hang out at the mall!" Low-income adolescents had friends with whom they "hung around" only at school. For instance, when asked if she had a best friend, a lonely Darcy replied: "No. Not really. Last year I did. We would meet in the lunchroom and in classes, but this year I had no classes with her. I only saw her in school, and when we weren't in classes we lost contact." Similarly, Teresa clarified: "My best friend is a girl with a baby. We can't do much anymore. She moved off The Hill—lives on the south side now. I go to see the baby at her house sometimes. She's not in school anymore. She quit to take care of her baby. I don't see her much. I can't get down there." Randy complained: "One friend lives 2 or 3 miles away. I used to ride my bike to his trailer court; but my bike was stolen, so I don't see him."

Rationale for Friendships

People are social beings and like to do things with others (Berndt, 1986); sharing common interests and activities are major links between individuals in forming friendships (Kandel, 1978). The importance of peer support has also been emphasized in the literature on children's friendships (Berndt, 1986; East, Hess, & Lerner, 1987); by adolescence, help and support evolve as the most important aspects of friendship in conjunction with a decreased emphasis on commonality of interests and activities (Bukowski et al., 1987).

In this study, the most salient rationale for friendships mentioned by both high- and low-income respondents was some form of companionship (e.g., "Fun to be with"; "He'll go with me to the mall and stuff") (see Table 7.3). "Having someone to do things with" was a universal need. In some ways, both groups did similar things (e.g., "mostly hang out," "talk on the phone," "go to the mall," "get together at my house or her house," "sit around and talk," "run around"), although high-income respondents were more likely to be engaged in expensive (e.g., "go skiing," "skateboard," "go to the lake," "go to movies") or school-organized pursuits (e.g., "We're in marching band together; we have a blast at contest, especially the overnighters"). Only 2 low-income partici-pants mentioned "going to parties" (i.e., social events at people's homes) as something they did with friends, whereas 20 high-income respondents (59%) supposedly "partied" with their friends.

Friends were company for social activities, but companionship had another dimension. It was important to have a friend to avoid social isolation, to guard against being perceived as rejected or ostracized. Apparently, it was difficult to face the peer social scene in school without allies. Adolescents were also fearful of looking as if they were socially unacceptable if they did things alone. Thus a friend was a stamp of social acceptability. Kit (l-i) called her-self "brave" for being a "by-myself kind of person." Respondents who had just completed junior high and were heading to high school, particularly low-income respondents, often discussed deliberate plans for whom they would hang around with when they got there. It was clear that they were worried about the social scene and wanted at least one reliable sidekick in the new setting.

Sharing interests and having tastes in common closely followed the com-panionship role in importance in friendships for low-income youth (e.g., "We share the same interests"; "He likes the same stuff"; "We agree on things"; "He likes to do what I like to do"; "She likes the same kind of rock groups that I do: Bon Jovi, Cinderella"). Sheila (l-i) elaborated:

> Ruth, she's nice. We're a lot alike. We're crazy. We don't want to grow up too fast! Other kids wouldn't want to do the things we do. We used to go [roller]skating, swimming, go to each other's house. Some kids like to do drugs. I used to go along with them, then I thought about my health, career, future—so I don't hang around with them anymore. One thing that Ruth and I have in common is that we're antidrug. Me and her get along real good. If she moved, I'd die!

High-income respondents also talked about personal similarities (e.g., "He's just like me; we're both here to have fun"; "We're very similar; we agree a lot"; "My friends are mature, serious—like me"; "We dress similar and do the same things, like play tennis, go to the mall, to movies").

The shared-taste aspect of friendships served to firmly establish class identity. Many of the commonalities in high-income adolescents' friendships were simply inaccessible to low-income adolescents because of a lack of funds. As Carol (l-i) asserted: "I don't wear mall clothes; we can't afford it. K-Mart stuff is the same except for the label and the price." Low-income adolescents often described things they were not: "I don't dress like no prep!"; "We don't act stuck-up like the popular group"; "We wear jeans, 'cycle boots, T-shirts— no brand names." A friend reflected one's own taste and standing.

Social support has been found to rank first in importance in friendships (e.g., Bukowski et al., 1987), but in this study it was mentioned less than companionship or shared interests and tastes by both groups of adolescents. Low-income respondents, however, were more likely to talk about the importance of mutual support, loyalty, trust, and even nurturing in friendships (e.g., "He is there when I need him"; "When he needs something, I give it to him; when I need something, he gives it to me"; "He is a good listener"; "He is loyal and likes to do the same things"; "He ain't a friend that would turn on me even if he got to be friends with someone else"; "Friends stick together"; "We talk about problems"; "I can confide in him and he won't tell my secrets"). Rachel said: "My friend is nice, loyal. I wouldn't have any friends without her. I have friends at school, but I don't see them that much." Max described: "He is like a brother. Whenever I need something, I can go to him and get it. He'd give me anything I needed." Trent elaborated: "You like people because they don't shove you around, don't tell you what to do. They don't sit around when people are pushing on you. They help you." Only one high-income adolescent mentioned the "mutual-defense" aspect of friendship. As Jeremy said: "We stick up for each other."

Not having someone to "be with" (i.e., affiliation need) or "do things with" (i.e., companionship need) was a source of stress for adolescents. A number claimed to be lonely and depressed. Darcy (l-i) said: "I feel lonely. I'd like more friends." Tricia (l-i) complained: "I don't really have any close friends." Then she added: "I'd like to be better looking, smarter, and more popular." Similarly, Andrew (h-i) said: "I'm kind of an introvert. I'd like to be better looking." Libby (h-i) admitted: "I envy kids with lots of friends, those who make friends easily." An exception, although it is likely that her response was defensive, Kit (l-i) claimed she chose to be friendless: "I don't have friends. I have associates. I learned lessons about people—they take advantage. I'm a by-myself person. I'm not scared to do things by myself."

Low-income respondents' discussions of losing friends revealed the importance of friendships. Tammy said: "My friend moved. It makes me feel depressed, kind of lost." Jeff divulged: "I had a best friend, but as the year went by we broke up a little bit. I feel kind of bummed out about it. We should keep in touch." Tracy confessed: "She's gone. The only thing I do is sit around. Oh, God, I might go crazy." Bret flatly stated: "I had a friend who shot himself in the head 2 months ago. He told me about his life. The kid did drugs. His parents didn't care. It really makes me feel awful." The adolescents who seemed happiest with their social lives were those who named one close, dependable friend and a broader circle of companions. Adolescents who described a number of friends, but no particular friend, were more insecure and hesitant in talking about friendships.

Academic achievement influenced friendships, with high achievers among the high-income group and low achievers among the low-income adolescents being the most likely to feel socially isolated. In other words, of the total group, students at both ends of an academic-achievement continuum were most likely to feel that they lacked friendship ties with peers. High-income high achievers often indicated that they did not have time for friends, that they were too busy with their various pursuits (e.g., taking classes at the university, studying for their high school classes), whereas low-income low achievers felt shunned by others.

Gender was important in friendships; only three respondents (i.e., two l-i, one h-i) named persons of the opposite sex as best friends, and two stated that these were "boyfriends." All three were comparatively less satisfied with their friendships, admitting to loneliness and isolation. Others discussed having "boyfriends" or "girlfriends"—that is, romantic interests—but the expression "best friend" was usually reserved for someone of the same sex with whom one had a nonromantic relationship. Several more, especially older high-income adolescents, named persons of the other gender as belonging to a circle of immediate friends, but they usually also had a best friend of the same gender.

Friendships were inevitably bound within social classes. Friendship dyads, or even clusters, rarely cut across social class lines except in the case of African-American low-income adolescents; four of the six appeared to have some fairly close social ties to high-income schoolmates. Will and Scott, both athletes in college preparatory classes, claimed "friends from all over town" whom they had met through either sports or classes. Junior high student Jeff occasionally hung around with some high-income boys he had met through Junior League baseball. Eighth-grade Madalene had been best friends with an Iranian girl, whom she had met in school. Unlike the three African-American males, who appeared to be open to friendships with others of all social classes and who "hung around" mainly with "kids from the neighborhood," Madalene was scornful of most of the neighborhood girls and rejected them on the grounds of their tastes (i.e., "tacky clothes"), attitudes (i.e., "not caring about school"), and behaviors (i.e., "acting sleazy"). In contrast, Will and Scott said their best friends lived in their neighborhoods and had gone to elementary school with them.

CONCLUSION

Social class differences in attitudes toward and relationships with parents were related to the conditions of adolescents' lives. Comfortably satisfied with their present circumstances, high-income adolescents, for the most part, hoped to emulate their parents. In contrast, the lack of family funds was troublesome for low-income adolescents—in terms of income, parents were models to be avoided. Low-income teenagers discussed dissatisfactions with the financial circumstances of their lives, their stigmatizing neighborhoods, and their own low prestige in relationship to high-income schoolmates.

School personnel have standardized views of the proper role of parents related to schooling (Lareau, 1987). In this study, adolescents of both social classes expressed views concerning what parents should do in relationship to schooling that were mainly consistent with those attributed to professionals. By adopting a dominant-culture perspective, many low-income adolescents' evaluated their parents' parenting behaviors as inadequate. The tendency to blame (or credit) parents for family circumstances fits into the general pattern of personalizing situations and internalizing causes found in this study. People, rather than societal conditions, were held accountable for negative outcomes.

High-income parents are reputed to fulfill parental roles better than their low-income counterparts, but it would be hasty to jump to the conclusion that low-income parents are not aware of an idealized role. Unfortunately, many do not have the wherewithal or the confidence in their own power to attempt to realize their goals related to schooling (E. A. Brantlinger, 1985c). Moreover, since their offsprings' status in school varied from that of high-income students, the incentive to interact with school personnel in a manner similar to high-income parents was clearly missing. For instance, results indicate that low-income adolescents believed that their parents would attend school social events if they were involved in activities or would attend conferences if they believed there would be constructive outcomes. Parents were described as realists—albeit negative realists—in terms of what they expected from themselves, their offspring, and school.

Nevertheless, regardless of their own educational attainment, low-income parents are not apathetic about their children's schooling (E. A. Brantlinger, 1985b; Johnson & Ransom, 1980). They even express ambition for their children in terms of dissatisfaction with their own lot and use themselves as models to be avoided (E. A. Brantlinger, 1986; Newson, Newson, & Barnes, 1977). Furthermore, in spite of differences in family structure, children's socioeconomic status accounts for more variance in school performance than does family configuration (Henderson, 1981; Maccoby & Martin, 1983; Morgan et al., 1979). One explanation for this might be that the complexity of communication patterns results in parents intending to convey messages that children do not receive (Bugetal, 1985). Another might be that the obstacles to improving one's lot are too great for many to overcome regardless of their efforts.

Regarding friendships, adolescents were animated in discussing positive relationships, sad and embarrassed in confessing loneliness, and emotional in describing friction with friends. In terms of satisfaction with social relationships, having one close, reliable friend appeared to be more important than having a broader circle of friends (i.e., acquaintances). Friendships served the functions of companionship and support, but peer associations were clearly important in establishing identity and adding the stamp of approval to personal worth. In other words, having friends not only prevented isolation but also signified status and social acceptance. According to Bourdieu (1984), tastes are closely linked to habitus (social surroundings) and define different classes and class factions: "Social subjects, classified by their classifications, distinguish themselves by the distinctions they make" (p. 13). Adolescents' descriptions of the tastes they and their friends had in common were consistent with Bourdieu's theory that perception of the social world is a product of internalization of social class divisions.

CHAPTER 8

Futures

The gap between the income levels of rich and poor Americans has been expanding, and a growing proportion of Americans fall within the poverty range (Gladstone, 1990; Harrison, Tilley, & Bluestone, 1986). Negative conditions for the poor have been exacerbated by the loss of job mobility, a proliferation of low-paying service jobs, and an intensification of job competition (Bastian & Fruchter, 1985). These social and economic trends are bound to have an impact on students; for schools to be responsive to all constituencies, the nature of that impact should be understood.

This chapter addresses adolescents' aspirations and expectations for their remaining school as well as their postschool years. It includes their opinions about the value of the high school diploma and the importance of college attendance. It also covers their knowledge of the requirements for college admission, plans for college attendance, and expectations of college success. Respondents' perceptions of their parents' aspirations and expectations related to schooling were also examined in order to provide insight into the messages adolescents receive about educational pursuits from their parents.

Interconnections among aspirations, expectations, motivation for achievement, performance, performance evaluation, and self-concept have been the focus of considerable speculation and research (Gamoran, 1987; Seginer, 1983). The direction and degree of influence are not easy to discern, yet mutuality of influence is not disputed. In this chapter, aspirations (ideal expectations, desires) are distinguished from (realistic) expectations. Others have found that ideal goals for educational attainment and perceptions of occupational status are fairly similar for all social classes (Laosa, 1982), but actual expectations decrease as the amount of parental schooling decreases (Seginer, 1983). All parents want their offspring to achieve high status, but, apparently, lower social status is correlated with a wider range of aspirations (Frieze & Snyder, 1980; Gottfredson, 1981). Youngsters see those in their social class as their reference group, orienting to class norms and adopting class standards of success (Rodman & Voydanoff, 1978). Thus definitions of success vary across individuals and situations, and perceptions of the relationship between schooling and success vary as well.

Covington and Beery (1976) found that achievement behavior was motivated by the desire to maintain a high self-image of ability or, conversely, to avoid the shame and distress of seeming to lack ability. Faunce (1984) hypothesized that students' self-investment in academic achievement is a selective process through which activities become differentially imbued with significance for the maintenance of self-esteem. When attempts at high achievement result in failure, students engage in the face-saving strategy of attributing failure to insufficient effort, bad luck, or task difficulty (Weiner, 1979). Or they cope with negative evaluation by withdrawing self-investment in achievement (Good et al., 1987).

Olneck and Bills (1980) found that social class background and the educational attainment of parents affected persistence in school. Conklin and Daily (1981) reported that when students' parents have gone to college, it is taken for granted that they also will attend—moreover, when college attendance is taken for granted, students usually go (Hoelter, 1982). By definition, high-income parents are better able to pay for college than low-income parents; thus taking college attendance for granted and having rational plans for attendance (i.e., parents will pay) are naturally more likely among children of high-income families.

One factor that has been found to affect aspirations is the perceived accessibility of occupations (Gottfredson, 1981). For a variety of class-related reasons, low-income students have fewer educational and occupational options. Rather than seeing differential attainment as due to variations in learned motives and skills, as in a socialization model, Kerckhoff (1976) offered an allocation model in which attainment is viewed as due to application of structural limitations and the selection criteria of society. From this standpoint, schools and teachers are targeted for blame for inferior pupil outcomes. Interpersonal interaction patterns, as well as school and classroom conditions, vary according to social class; these differences have an impact on the school careers of children (Good et al., 1987; Rohrkemper, 1984; Rosenholtz & Simpson, 1984).

The nationwide dropout rate increased from 22.8% in 1972 to 29.1% in 1984 (Rumberger, 1987), and it has been projected that this rate will continue to grow (McDill et al., 1986). In a study of factors associated with dropping out, Rumberger (1987) found that 29% gave their reason as disliking school, 26% cited marriage and/or pregnancy, 20% named economic reasons, 7% mentioned poor school performance, 7% had been expelled or suspended, and the remaining 11% gave various other reasons. Fine (1986, 1991) concluded that dropouts are generally skeptical of the benefits of schooling and are more politically astute than their counterparts who remain in school.

ASPIRATIONS AND EXPECTATIONS
FOR HIGH SCHOOL COMPLETION

Aspirations and expectations for high school graduation were uniformly high for all adolescents (see Table 8.1). All 34 high-income adolescents and the 36 low-income respondents who had not already dropped out wanted to graduate from high school. All high-income adolescents and 32 low-income respondents (89% of those still in school) expected to earn a high school diploma. Four low-income teenagers (11%) were "not sure." Related to high school graduation, then, there was a match between aspirations and expectations.

TABLE 8.1. Educational Aspirations and Expectations

	Low-Income N	Low-Income (%)	High-Income N	High-Income (%)
Aspirations/Expectations for High School Graduation				
Aspire to high school diploma	36*	(100)	34	(100)
Expect high school diploma	32	(89)	34	(100)
Aspirations/Expectations for College				
Aspire to college attendance	26	(65)	32	(94)
Expect college attendance	14	(35)	31	(91)
Expect college success	7	(18)	33	(97)
Parents' Aspirations/Expectations for College for Student				
Parents talked about college	16	(40)	34	(100)
Parents want college for student	24	(60)	33	(97)
Parents expect college for student	9	(23)	32	(94)
Parents will pay for college	1	(3)	34	(100)
School Performance Compared to Parents				
Adolescent's performance better	11	(28)	6	(18)
Similar performance	17	(43)	13	(39)
Mixed performance	4	(10)	5	(15)
Adolescent's performance worse	4	(10)	5	(15)
Uncertain	4	(10)	5	(15)
Total	40		34	

*Only in-school adolescents.
(Note: Due to rounding, percentage totals do not necessarily add to 100.)

Thirty-one low-income respondents (77.5%), including two who had already dropped out, felt that high school graduation would benefit them in the future; two (5%) felt that it "would not make any difference"; and seven (17.5%), including the other two who had dropped out, were uncertain about benefits the diploma might bring. In general, these latter nine were among the more discouraged and cynical of the adolescents. In contrast to the teenagers in Willis's (1977) and Fine's (1991) studies and the white youths in MacLeod's (1987) study who "did not buy into" the achievement ideology, the majority of teenagers in this study talked about the importance of success in school and graduation. When they mentioned barriers to their own successful completion of school, their tone reflected frustration and depression. However, endurance (i.e., "sticking it out," "just getting through") was emphasized more than achievement (i.e., "doing well").

All high-income respondents gave a perfunctory "sure the diploma is important" answer—they knew it was a prerequisite for college. Although there were some emphatically positive replies among low-income respondents, the majority gave fairly tentative answers that seemed neither genuine nor deeply felt, but rather mechanical articulations of well-indoctrinated messages about the importance of school. Although most did not specifically quote either parents or teachers, their replies echoed advice often heard from these sources. The majority of low-income teenagers were critical of the quality and goal-directedness of the school curriculum, and only a few claimed to be actually learning things that would help them in the future. But staying in school and earning the diploma had symbolic value; that is, it signified literacy and respectability. As Kit stressed: "I've got to get that diploma—if not, I'll be real left out. It will make a difference in how I feel about myself."

Other rationales supporting the importance of graduation included improved chances of obtaining a job—particularly a "good" or "decent" job—and getting into college. Chrissy cautioned: "You don't want to quit school because you won't get that good a job." Louann, a dropout, said: "You need an education in the world these days." Although she had contemplated returning to school, Louann admitted that the chances were small because she was "hooked on the daytime soaps."

When asked to think of plausible reasons for dropping out of school (i.e., "If you were to drop out of school, what would your reasons be for that decision?"), high-income adolescents were reluctant to offer conditions—the thought seemed too far-fetched. They gave circumstances that were extremely dire (e.g., "If I were dying"; "If I were hooked on drugs"). Similarly, some low-income adolescents had strong reactions to the idea of quitting. As May forcefully asserted: "I'm smart enough to know better; I'd never quit school—I don't like it, but I won't quit." Sonia said: "I would quit if the world ended, but that's the only thing that would stop me." Tammy replied: "Stupidity. It would be dumb to quit school after so many years."

Yet the idea was not so foreign to others; 32 (80%) low-income respondents readily supplied reasons for quitting. Bret maintained: "My reason would be that I don't like it." Trent figured: "I might just get tired of going to school every morning and just quit." Similarly, Celestine responded: "I might just not want to go no more. Felt lazy, tired of it." Darcy revealed: "If I just sat and did nothing in school and felt like it was not doing any good anyway. If I could quit, I just would." Annie predicted: "The school system might get me down." High-income Lynette gave a similar response: "I'm tired of school. I could imagine myself becoming lazy and just not going back." But she added a disclaimer: "That's not likely because my parents would be horribly upset."

Two low-income respondents said "the right job" could lure them away from school—both had repeatedly expressed concern about family finances. Enticing careers listed by three high-income adolescents were more of a fantasy nature. Sarah dreamed: "If I got a chance to become a highly paid fashion model, I'd do it." If John were "elected president," he figured he "would have to drop out of school." Nathan said: "If I was offered a job as executive director of a multinational company, I would take it." Two high-income high achievers, Vanessa and Mario, were considering the possibility of entering college prior to high school graduation.

Low-income respondents claimed that continuing negative evaluation and repeated course failures gave them a sense of futility about the possibility of graduation and might result in their dropping out of school. Carol hypothesized: "I might quit if I was failing too many classes and felt like I'd never make it to twelfth grade. If I felt hopeless." Chrissy said: "Maybe because I wouldn't be doing well and felt it was too late to raise my grades." Less hypothetically, Tricia revealed: "I'd drop out because it's tough and I'm making F's." Michael said: "Maybe if I thought I couldn't make it or felt I didn't belong." Five high-income adolescents also gave "if I were failing" responses; however, unlike low-income respondents, none were presently having school problems.

Problematic relationships with teachers were cited by five low-income adolescents (e.g., "teachers not being nice," "because I didn't like the teachers," "discipline of the teachers—unfairness," "teachers—getting into trouble with them"). Sherry complained: "A particular teacher rides me. I don't like it. It might make me quit." Only Max mentioned peer influence: "If my friends quit, like everyone quit—I'd quit."

Family problems were posed by three high-income adolescents. Mario said: "If something happened to my parents—that would be the only reason that I can think of." Marissa figured: "If I got pregnant, I'd be too embarrassed to keep going to school." Family reasons were also offered in nine of the low-income cases—three involving pregnancy, three involving financial support for family, and three involving family friction. Scott conjectured: "Problems around the house. If me and Mom got into it really bad. Then I'd leave." Tracy revealed: "I might get mad at Mom and Dad and leave home." Kit asserted: "Revenge. Get back at Mom!" Two males offered support for a pregnant girlfriend as their most likely reason for quitting.

The four adolescents who had already quit described school as a site of much displeasure. Dean clarified:

> I never did like school. Me and teachers didn't get along. If you didn't understand, some teachers treated you like a piece of trash. The preps smart off—call us grits and stuff like that. The preps ran the school. I never had much part in school. Didn't bother. Miss B. (the high school dean), she don't like me. She was giving me a bunch of trouble. She was always hard on us boys. She was giving me problems about everything. I just quit when I got to be 16.

According to Stacy:

> It made me angry to have to be there when I didn't want to be there. I never skipped—never, ever—not like everyone else. I just sat there and waited it out, trying to listen. I didn't feel like school was helping. I didn't like school. I had nothing to look forward to. Then I flunked seventh grade. I had already repeated kindergarten and one other grade. That put me behind. I thought, Oh God! So there I was with a lot of really young people. I was stuck with a lot of sixth graders in eighth grade. School seemed to me like a problem—something I had to get off my mind. I just had to get out, you know . . . face the real world. I couldn't wait. I just had to do it right then.

Louann confided:

> I could have stayed in school pregnant. I thought about it—other people do it. I was afraid people would laugh at me because I was pregnant, but also I'd been in so much trouble in school—before the pregnancy, in the past. Mrs. R. [dean of her high school] took me to court for truancy. I had to go to court not knowing if they were going to send me to girls' school. It was terrible. I got put on probation. It felt awful. It felt good to skip school but not to go to court and everything. I hated school—hated the stuck-up teachers, stuck-up students. Really, I just couldn't stand the social scene. Pregnancy was just an excuse for quitting. I skipped so much that, really, I had quit school long before I got pregnant.

Theories of human rationality postulate that humans weigh their present effort and pain against future rewards (Burr, Hill, Nye, & Reiss, 1979). Many local low-income teenagers were skeptical that what they described as suffering in school would be worth it.

High-income adolescents were sure their parents wanted them to finish high school, except for one of the two who wanted to start college early. Most low-income teenagers (37, 92.5%), including those who had already quit, believed their parents wanted them to graduate from high school. Social class differences surfaced, however, in adolescents' perceptions of their parents' reaction to their quitting school. High-income adolescents conveyed that their parents "would be very upset" and "would not let them." For example, Lynette said: "Kill me. Be mad. I joked about it once with my dad and he gave me a big lecture." Marissa quipped: "Early death. Make me move out. Make me go back." Libby elaborated: "They'd be real shocked. They'd ask me why. They'd say it was a stupid reason and would persuade me to go back." In fact, the majority named a violent response and indicated that they would be "disowned" or "kicked out" if they did not follow their parents' advice and go back. They also believed that, regardless of their own wishes, their parents had the power to make them attend school. Some high-income adolescents indicated that the possibility was so unlikely that they could not predict their parents' response, and a few even refused to discuss the question. Polly said: "That's an unrealistic situation. It's not worth talking about."

Low-income adolescents' responses ranged from "they don't care" (3, 7.5%), to mild censure (6, 15%), to passive opposition (10, 25%), to assertive opposition (21, 52.5%). Max stated flatly: "They wouldn't care. They're weird." With resignation, Leejohn shrugged and said: "She wouldn't be surprised. She wouldn't encourage me to stay in school." Tricia felt that her mother did not care about anything that happened to her, and that included her school attendance. All three were critical of their parents' attitudes, conveying that it was the role of parents "to care" about school.

The "mild censure" category included three distinct types of perceptions. First, it included parents who felt that dropping out was a viable alternative to staying in school under adverse circumstances. Louann's mother worried about trouble with school and legal authorities. "Mom twisted my arm—made me quit. She didn't want me in more trouble." But Louann felt that under more positive conditions her mother would have preferred that she remain in school. Dean stated: "Mom didn't want me to quit, but said if that's what I want to do—do it. She would rather see me quit than in trouble." The choice, then, was not between "doing well in school" or dropping out, but between "doing poorly in school" or "being in trouble" and quitting.

"Mild censure" also included parents who had communicated that it was the adolescent's decision. As Les claimed: "She wouldn't like it, but she wouldn't make me go back because it's my decision." Some parents had con-veyed—or adolescents had surmised—that, since parents or other family members had quit school, it was unfair to make the teenager continue. As Tammy said: "They wasn't too happy, but both my sisters quit and it wouldn't be fair to make me go." Bret said: "My brother quit, so they can't make me go if I don't want to."

In a study of low-income parents (E. A. Brantlinger, 1985b), similar rationales were offered for the lack of intervention when offspring dropped out of school. Parents communicated that their opinions on the matter were no more valid than their offsprings'. It was hypothesized that this sense that they lacked justification to intervene stemmed from deeply entrenched feel-ings of inadequacy combined with ambivalent attitudes toward school. Yet other parents who had dropped out of school had convinced their children that it was important not to follow in their footsteps. Randy stated: "They wouldn't approve of it. They quit at 16 or 17, and they know what it is to quit." Such parents used themselves as negative examples or models to be avoided, blaming their lack of occupational success on their inadequate education and stressing the importance of their children's taking another course of action.

Responses categorized "passive opposition" included 10 (25%) who claimed their parents would verbalize opposition but do nothing to prevent them. Ruth believed: "Mom would be mad but she wouldn't say anything to me." Michael hypothesized: "Surprised, disappointed—wouldn't kill me." Stacy, who had already quit, said: "Mother, oh God, she didn't want me to, but she couldn't take me by the hair and take me back." In contrast, 21 low-income adolescents (52.5%) believed that their parents would vigorously oppose any notions they had of quitting and would take action to prevent them. With picturesque details (e.g., "shock," "fire and brimstone," "pick up a base-ball bat and hit me across the room," "I'd be dead," "get killed," "get all over me," "dangerous thought," "surprised and very, very angry," "really, really mad," "kick me out of the house") similar to those of their high-income coun-terparts, such respondents indicated that they really did not have a choice.

ASPIRATIONS AND EXPECTATIONS FOR COLLEGE

High-income adolescents not only wanted to attend college but also expected to attend and judged that they would do well in college (see Table 8.1). Of the three who did not expect to go, Audrey said she would not go "until or unless I make up my mind about what I want to do with my life." Lynette did not know what she wanted to do after high school but was "pretty sure" she would not go to college: "At least not right away. I'm tired of school. I need a break." Seth wanted to go to college but was worried about both his grades and finances since his parents' recent divorce. His parents had assured him they would give him some support, but he knew they worried about money.

Among low-income respondents, college attendance was perceived as vocationally advantageous and prestigious—campus life had an idyllic image. Yet unlike the convergence of desires and expectations regarding high school completion, almost twice as many (i.e., 26, 65%) wanted to go to college as expected (i.e., 14, 35%) to go. First, they perceived college as hard and, particularly, as too hard for them (see Table 8.1). Only 7 judged their chances for success in college to be good. Shakier replies (e.g., "College is supposed to be hard, harder than high school—I'm not sure if I would do well") were provided by 17 (42.5%); 11 (27.5%) felt that college would definitely be too hard for them; and 5 (12.5%) were uncertain. Often respondents with the most problematic school careers (i.e., special education placement, low grade-point average, multiple grade repetition) glibly alleged "no problem," whereas those who seemed better prepared doubted their abilities. Kit, classified as learning disabled, exclaimed: "With flying colors!" Louann, who had repeated two grades before dropping out, with seeming confidence announced, "pretty good," then added: "If I go to high school first."

Others had more pessimistic "no chance for success" attitudes. Adam said: "Not good. I think it would be too hard for me." Bret responded with a resigned: "Probably bad. I wouldn't know what to do in college. It would be a waste of my money, as much as I hate school." Randy confided: "College seems kind of scary. I don't think I could do it." Sherry predicted: "I don't think I'd do well," although she claimed to get A's and B's in school. Thus there was a bimodal split among low-achieving students; those who were unrealistically positive and those who were unremittingly negative. The few teenagers with cautious expectations for success seemed most attuned to reality. Will estimated: "I'm afraid it's going to be real hard, but if I try and really listen in classes, I'll do pretty good."

PERCEPTIONS OF THE REQUIREMENTS
FOR COLLEGE ATTENDANCE

Adolescents were asked what they would have to do if they wanted to attend college. Responses were judged to be realistic if adolescents mentioned both a source of funds and an acceptable level of school performance. Realistic plans were easier for high-income adolescents: Their parents could and would pay for at least part of their college fees. Five indicated that they would be expected to contribute to the expenses, and all but one of these claimed to be currently "saving toward college." Interestingly, none of the high-income adolescents mentioned pursuing scholarships.

Since most of the high-income adolescents were fairly high achievers, school performance was not of much concern. They still discussed improving their performance, broadening their activities, and doing well on the SATs—but in the context of getting into the college of their choice rather than just getting into college. Many worried that they would not get into the caliber of institution that they (or their parents) desired. As Polly said: "I'm ambitious. I want to go to a prestigious college. If I don't make it, I'll have to go to [the local university]. I don't want to do that. I'm ready to get out of here!" A few indicated that their parents were pressuring them to apply to colleges with very competitive admission standards, and they were concerned about disappointing them if they did not get in or about succeeding in such places.

The majority of low-income teenagers did not have a clear understanding of the requirements for college admission, even though they indicated that it was probably beyond their reach on a number of counts. Twenty-four (60%) did know that it depended on high school achievement and completion. They made such comments as "to go I'd have to get better grades," "go back to high school," or "work hard(er)." Dusty said: "I think I would have to get out of special education." And, he admitted: "I would have to attend school more." Only two teenagers, Will and Scott, both athletes and black, mentioned the need to think about SATs.

When low-income respondents talked about college, most noted that they would need a source of funds. "Lots" was added or eyebrows were raised to accentuate the cost of college. Many said that college attendance was not likely because their parents could not afford it. Only Will named a family member as a source of financial help, yet the father who "would pay" had been out of contact for many years. Six said that they would have to "earn money" and five of these—all African-American—mentioned athletic and/or minority scholarships as a way to pay for college.

The six low-income adolescents (15%) who named both school performance and finances were judged to have an accurate idea about the requirements for college attendance. Seventeen-year-old Scott elaborated: "Take college prep courses. Keep my grades up. Do well on SATs. Keep getting athletic letters so that I get an athletic scholarship. Get a job and save money." Yet even these realistic low-income teenagers did not go on to state specific personal plans to meet financial and academic requirements. One exception, eighth-grader Madalene, was currently working (i.e., babysitting) and putting money in the bank for college. Others mentioned "earning" and "saving" as future undertakings. Of the respondents who said that they hoped to obtain scholarships, only three claimed to be maintaining good grade-point averages in college preparatory courses. Thus the fourteen who expected to go to college could not be judged to have rational plans for college attendance. "Rational plans" for most teenagers with college aspirations usually means the assurance that parents would pay the expenses—a luxury not available to low-income teenagers.

Adolescents were asked if they had discussed college with their parents, if their parents would like to have them attend college, and if their parents expected them to attend (see Table 8.1). All high-income respondents recalled conversations about college with their parents. As freshman Simon said: "We talk about college all the time." They also felt their parents wanted and expected them to attend. John said: "I want to go, but I really don't think I have any choice. My parents have never mentioned my not going." One exception, Audrey's father, said he would only be willing to pay for college if she had definite career goals that depended on a college degree. Audrey's parents had gone to college; in fact, her father had done some graduate school work. Both parents were artists; as Audrey said: "My sister wants to be an actress, and she did not go to college. She moved to Hollywood and tries out for parts." All the other high-income adolescents claimed that their parents had always conveyed that they were expected to attend. Several volunteered that their parents expected them to get advanced degrees.

Most low-income adolescents had not discussed the possibility of college attendance with their parents. Louann "did not even know what college was until our church worked at a basketball game." Even those who had discussed college were not necessarily being encouraged by their parents to attend. Chrissy explained: "Mom told me that they can't send me. We don't have that kind of money." Others who had not specifically discussed college plans with their parents still felt their parents would be pleased if they were to attend. Sheila said: "Mom hasn't talked about it, but she'd be happy if I went. They'd brag on me. Most of my relatives don't usually go to college." Many had received rather mixed messages from their parents about college. Tracy confided: "They said they don't expect me to go, but somehow I think they want me to." Darcy said: "I guess if I wanted to go, she'd let me go. She doesn't care." Four claimed that their parents "pushed college." Thomas joked: "Yes, since I was about 7 or 8. Mom started in early. She really wants me to go." Madalene responded: "Yes, all the time." The discrepancy between perceived parental desires (24, 60%) and parental expectations (9, 22.5%) mirrored that of adolescents.

POST-HIGH SCHOOL PLANS

Since adolescents are expected to make general career decisions prior to leaving high school, it was conjectured that they would be actively thinking about their futures. For low-income respondents, that did not turn out to be the case. When asked what they planned to do when they finished high school,

31 high-income adolescents said they would attend college—a feasible plan for them. Even the 2 who were classified as learning-disabled received resource room support for their college preparatory classes and maintained at least average grades.

In contrast, most low-income adolescents were vague or unrealistic in describing their postschool plans. Fifteen (37.5%) named "going to college" as what they would do after high school, and an additional 8 (20%) named professions that require college degrees. Thus, although when they were directly asked if they expected to go to college only 14 (35%) responded affirmatively, 23 (57.5%) offered college or professions requiring college as postschool plans. (It might be noted that only 6 low-income adolescents were judged to be making realistic progress toward college attendance.) Five others named skilled or semiskilled labor or service jobs (i.e., truck driver, car repair, beautician, secretary, emergency technician), which might seem feasible; however, the one who wanted to be a secretary was attending classes for students classified as mildly mentally handicapped, so it might be assumed that her literacy skills were too low for secretarial work. Three low-income adolescents simply "wanted a job," and 9 (22.5%) "did not know" what they were going to do.

When asked about the probability of their expectations being realized, most of the high-income adolescents confidently judged their plans to be attainable. Of the low-income adolescents who named postschool intentions, most were skeptical about whether their plans would materialize, with 12 (30%) thinking that their chances were above average; four (10%), average; 11 (27.5%), below average; and four (10%), saying, in effect, no chance.

In addition to discussing realistic postschool intentions, teenagers were also encouraged to describe ideal or fantasy (i.e., "anything you want to be") plans for the future. As might be expected, the largest category for both high- and low-income adolescents was entertainment. Adolescents wanted to be models, soap opera stars, film actors, heavy metal and rock musicians, and singers. Two low-income boys named basketball, one named baseball, and one named boxing; three girls wanted to be track stars. Five high-income adolescents wanted to be famous scientists. Some members of both groups emphasized making money in some kind of business. One high-income adolescent wanted to be a "famous chef."

Six low-income respondents' fantasies involved having a professional career (e.g., social worker, oceanographer, doctor, teacher, engineer); six involved getting blue-collar jobs (e.g., truck driver, mechanic, cook, cosmetologist); and two just wanted "a job." Unemployed Dean set higher sights and wanted "a job with a good income." Madalene elaborated: "I don't know—be something. I don't want to be filthy rich, just comfortable. I want a good-looking husband with a good job, and a couple of kids, a nice house, and a good job for me." Teresa hoped to "get married" and be a "housewife." Four dreams of low-income adolescents were related to leisure rather than vocational pursuits (e.g., "millionaires," "rich and lie on a beach in Hawaii," "rich kid").

The most interesting "anything you want to be" dreams were what others might see as ordinary or "fall back on" plans. Apparently, from their impoverished positions, such low-status or nonspecific jobs seemed like real improvements to low-income youths. Perhaps their lives were not comfortable or secure enough for them to have real fantasies or dreams.

OPINIONS ABOUT EQUAL OPPORTUNITY

Both high- and low-income adolescents challenged the concept of equal opportunity (see Table 8.2), but they offered different rationales for barriers. The reasons for dissimilar chances most frequently mentioned by low-income respondents can be categorized as related to family financial circumstances (e.g., "Preppies have more chances; they have rich parents to help them"; "Some kids don't have the advantages of others—like money!"; "Those with better lives and better education have more money; with more money, they have even more chances in the future"; "Things are unfair—some people are poor"; "There's seldom any mobility; if you were born low-class, you'll be low-class"; "Some people are pulled, others have to climb"). Darcy observed: "They say you have the same chances, but you don't."

Besides family finances, low-income adolescents felt that family stability was an advantage and family problems, a hindrance (e.g., "People with close families that aren't in poverty have more chances"). They also offered personal effort (e.g., "Poor people and people who don't try don't have very good chances"), disabilities (e.g., "Poor people, street people, and handicapped people have fewer chances"), and intelligence (e.g., "The smarts have more chances than kids with low intelligence") as reasons for differences in children's chances.

Low-income adolescents also associated life chances with school performance and educational attainment (e.g., "Poor people with low educational levels have fewer chances"; "Some low-education people who don't try don't have chances"; "Some really poor people can't afford to send their kids to school"). The quality (i.e., social class character) of schools attended was felt to affect life chances, as Carol said: "All kids don't really have the same chances, some quit school, some go to Kinder [high-income school], and some go to schools like Southside."

Although high-income adolescents offered a similar range of conditions likely to deter social mobility (e.g., "Poor people can't get ahead because they

TABLE 8.2. Adolescents' Feelings About the Future

	Low-Income		High-Income	
	N	(%)	N	(%)
All Students' Chances				
Unequal opportunity	32	(80)	33	(97)
Equal opportunity	8	(20)	1	(3)
Personal Chances Compared to Average Adolescent				
Better than average	10	(25)	32	(94)
Same chances	16	(40)	2	(6)
Worse than average	14	(35)	–	
Personal Opportunity to Get Ahead				
Have opportunity	26	(65)	34	(100)
Have limited opportunity	14	(35)	–	
Feelings About the Future				
Optimistic	25	(64)	30	(88)
Pessimistic	15	(37)	4	(12)
Chances Compared to Parents				
Better than parents	23	(58)	21	(61)
Same as parents	6	(15)	9	(27)
Worse than parents	11	(28)	4	(12)
Total	40		34	

(Note: Due to rounding, percentage totals do not necessarily add to 100.)

don't have the money to go to college"; "The poor are victims of their environment"; "There just aren't that many good jobs"), the majority blamed poor people, usually focusing on their lack of school success. Lynette maintained: "The poor usually aren't motivated. If they are willing to work hard enough, there are plenty of opportunities to get ahead." Hilary emphasized the importance of parental efforts: "Children's futures mainly depend on how they grew up—on how their parents built for themselves." Two alluded to the effects of social class reproduction. Greg asserted: "Advantages are handed down through the family." Andrew believed:

Rich people control things in ways that make it hard for the poor to get ahead. Like, the owners of companies make big profits and still pay low wages to their workers. They send their own kids to private schools where they get even more advantages. It's all circular. It's hard to fail if you're rich and hard to get ahead if you're poor.

PERSONAL CHANCES TO GET AHEAD

Attitudes about chances for personal social mobility were explored by asking three similar questions at different stages of the interview:

1. "How do your chances in life compare to those of other children?"
2. "What opportunities do you have for getting ahead?"
3. "How do you feel about your future?"

Results indicate congruence for all three items (see Table 8.2). Family financial support and personal achievement were the main reasons given for optimism by high-income adolescents. They glibly asserted that educational achievement and attainment were essential for success, and most felt that their own school careers were positive enough for them to be on the success track. The four high-income respondents who were pessimistic discussed pollution and natural- or human-made disasters—circumstances not mentioned by their low-income counterparts.

In spite of the fact that the school careers of most low-income participants were remarkably unsuccessful, they were only slightly more hesitant than their affluent schoolmates in stressing the importance of educational attainment. Those who were optimistic referred to personal attributes (e.g., "I'm in the best classes—those that get you ready for college"; "I'm willing to try hard"). Those who were less optimistic cited conditions (e.g., "My family has no money to help"; "There are no good jobs nowadays") and occasionally personal attributes (e.g., "I have not done well in school"). Social comparison influenced the response (e.g., "Well, I have fewer chances than a lot of people because we're poor, and I'll have to work hard to get ahead, but I do better in school than a lot of kids from around here, so my chances are pretty good").

Many low-income adolescents who described multiple family and school problems still verbalized optimism. Les, a 15-year-old whose mother was physically disabled and whose unemployed father was in mandatory treatment for abusing him, had been in classes for the emotionally disturbed for a number of years. Nevertheless, he stated: "Well, I'm not physically handicapped. I have about the same chances because almost everyone has about the same chance. I have even more opportunities than most because I'm intelligent."

Similarly, Randy, whose father was in prison, whose mother earned minimum wage, and who had received "mainly F's" on his last report card, explained: "Most kids don't know that they need school. Some parents don't care about what their kids do. Mine do care, so I have better chances. I also have a dream. You've got to have a dream. My chances are better than average." Thus the importance of attitudes—which are under personal control—was stressed. Dusty said: "Well, sort of good. I've got my mind set on what I want to do— be a boxer—and that helps." Carol believed: "If people want things bad enough, they can get them."

Adolescents who were pessimistic were also extremely depressed. Trent (l-i), who had been abandoned by his mother and whose father was in prison, lived with his ailing grandmother. Several times during the interview he voiced concern about what would happen to him if his grandmother had to go to the hospital. Anxious and angry, he had little hope that things would get better in the future. Dusty (l-i), classified as learning-disabled, said: "I don't have many chances. School is the only way to get ahead and I haven't done well in school." Tracy (l-i) said: "The way Mom talks makes me worried about what's ahead." Wendy (l-i) confessed to being "very worried" because her father told her that computers were taking over jobs. Celestine (l-i) summarized: "Me and a lot of my friends feel we don't have opportunities. I'm not really optimistic. I'm upset and worried about the future. It seems unfair. I envy kids with more opportunities." Similar to Leahy's (1983) findings, older adolescents were generally more negative and fatalistic about life chances than younger ones.

In spite of the fact that 80% of the low-income respondents believed that children's life chances were unequal and saw poverty as an inhibiting factor, only 35% judged their own chances to be worse than average. There was also no clear correlation between perceived personal chances and self-identification as being poor. Only 4 of the 11 teenagers who called themselves poor stated that their chances of getting ahead were not good.

Intergenerational patterns of poverty were very evident as respondents mentioned grandparents and other extended family members who lived in their low-income neighborhoods. Yet when asked how their chances compared to their parents, the responses of low-income teens resembled those of their high-income schoolmates: both believed that they had better opportunities than their parents (see Table 8.2). Adolescents alluded to historical circumstances and comparative personal attributes in their discussions. Scott (l-i), a 16-year-old who lived with his single mother and his college freshman sister, said:

> My chances are pretty good. I started school well. I'm not handicapped and I'm a good athlete, so I can get scholarships that way. There are more minority scholarships now. Mom got pregnant with my sister

when she was a senior. I know I won't get pregnant, and I'm not
planning to get someone pregnant so that I have to get married.

Responses to questions about intergenerational mobility were fairly automatic, reflecting the widespread faith in progress. Respondents who said their
chances were worse seemed to resist coming to that conclusion. They verbalized pessimism in an apologetic manner, as if it were running against the grain
of acceptable sentiment. Of the four high-income adolescents who felt they
had fewer chances, three perceived their parents as more competent (e.g.,
"He's a lot smarter than I am") and one cited worsening economic conditions.

Adolescents compared their school performance to that of their parents
(see Table 8.2). Although it was suspected that respondents might not have
thought about such comparisons and would have trouble answering, this sup-
position turned out to be inaccurate. With the exception of four who "did not
know," low-income adolescents readily responded.

It was interesting to note that even with the high percentage of low-
income students receiving special education services, having repeated one or
two grades, and with fairly low grade-point averages, the majority of the
respondents (28, 70%) felt that they were doing as well or better than their
parents, and an additional 4 felt they had done better than at least one parent. The "mixed" responses indicated that each parent differed or that over
time their own performance had fluctuated. As Ruth said: "I usually do better, but this year I did worse." Sheila vacillated: "Same as Mom—well, maybe
a little worse. Worse than Dad." Among the four who believed that their school
performance was worse than their parents, Louann said: "Dad did better—a
whole lot better!" Michael felt that his parents "did a little better."

Many low-income adolescents who struggled in school still believed themselves to be doing better than their parents. Randy, who had received mainly
F's on his last report card, asserted: "They were worse students. From what
they tell me, I'm an angel." Max recalled: "I think I'm better. I never heard
Mom read. She says she does, but I don't know. Dad can read. He is almost
as smart as me. He knows enough to get where he's going." Stacy claimed: "I
saw some papers back when she was little that were just like mine. It was
weird. It seems like maybe she did go through school like me." A more hesitant Bret said: "They never told. I don't talk much about school with them.
I'd guess I do about the same as my dad."

In making comparisons, others focused solely on the fact that they
planned to graduate from high school. Chrissy said: "Better. I want to graduate. They didn't. I respect what Mom says, she wants me to graduate." Similarly, Tammy confided: "Mine is probably better because I plan to finish
school. I'm the reason Mom quit, and Grandma dropped out in eighth grade
to get married."

High-income adolescents bragged about their parents' academic careers. It was clear that they identified with their academic prowess, and some indicated that their own school careers were similarly brilliant. Polly, an adolescent who had performed in many theatricals, enthusiastically replied: "My mother has a national reputation in her field. I'm good in humanities—like my mother—but I don't want to teach. I want to be a famous actress." Mario believed that: "My father and I are pretty equivalent academically, but he has a talent in languages and I am strong in science."

Adolescents usually compared themselves to the parent they lived with or the same-gender parent. The high-income adolescents who felt they would do better than their parents were mainly female. Marissa hypothesized: "My mother gets on me about my grades. When I challenge her about how well she did in high school, she says she did better. But I'm not sure. I'd guess I do a little better." Libby said: "My mother finished college, but she never went further, I guess, because of me and my brother. I'd like to have more of a career." High-income males were likely to think that their school careers were less accomplished than those of their fathers. This gender difference is probably the result of unique educational and occupational careers for high-income male and female parents; fathers were considerably more accomplished in those domains (see Table 1.1).

ADULT SUPPORT FOR POSTSCHOOL PLANS

Information gleaned from the general responses revealed large class-related discrepancies in adolescents' sources of help in planning and preparing for the future. Since high-income adolescents were going to college, their chore was mainly deciding on an appropriate postsecondary institution and continuing to accrue the necessary credentials to achieve their goals. Although most had not settled on vocations, they seemed confident that career paths would emerge as they furthered their education.

Discussions with school counselors indicate that besides making track placements and dealing with individual schedules, a major part of their job is getting information about colleges to students planning to attend college, arranging for college representatives to visit the high schools, helping students get references from teachers, and getting information about tests used for college admission to students, as well as signing them up for the tests. In other words, most of their time is spent making arrangements for students who plan to attend college.

With the exception of three teenagers labeled mildly mentally handicapped, who were involved in transition-to-adulthood programs, low-income respondents had not received help in planning for the future from school personnel. Two had seen counselors about friction with teachers, but as Celestine said: "It didn't make no difference." Both felt that the counselors had taken the teachers' side and that they had been discouraged from making return visits. Both high schools employ four or five counselors, yet low-income teenagers, even those in their junior or senior years, could not recall conversations with counselors about college, vocational training, or securing employment.

High-income adolescents frequently quoted conversations with their parents about college and possible careers. Parents had the expert knowledge that adolescents needed. Low-income adolescents rarely referred to advice from their parents. Those who did often quoted pessimistic information about the availability of jobs or discouraging advice about their own chances. Wendy's father had told her that computers were taking over most jobs. Dean's unemployed older brothers had informed him that there were "no good jobs in the area."

Working-class parents are likely to be able to provide their offspring with job information and may even have the contacts to help them secure positions. Parents who are unemployed, marginally employed, or erratically employed are unlikely to have such information to share, nor do they have the influence to help their children get good jobs. Regardless of their intentions, low-income parents had little to offer their children as vocational models or sources of help. The nonexistent plans and unrealistic views of low-income respondents reflected the absence of attention to career development plans from adults.

CONCLUSION

High-income adolescents' lives were very much laid out in front of them: They would go on to college and in the meantime they would exert energy to get good grades and do the other things needed to build their resumes so that they would be able to get into the college of their choice. Most portrayed their parents in strong authoritative roles and rarely challenged the wisdom or the legitimacy of their parents' goals for them. This is not to say that their paths were free of friction. Many worried about their status relative to peers—they were competitive and striving—or about disappointing their parents because they could not measure up to parental expectations. A few were also counterculture in style, criticizing their parents or their parents' generation for environmental and social problems. But even these critics had very conventional plans for the future—they would go to college, but to Berkeley or Oberlin or someplace where they believed their ideals would be the mode.

Although low-income adolescents had high aspirations and expectations regarding high school graduation, they also readily listed numerous reasons for quitting school—reasons that matched their present circumstances (e.g., not making progress toward graduation because of failing courses, not seeing the purpose of school, being tired of school). Four (24%) of the seventeen 16- to 18-year-olds in the sample had already dropped out. In general, school dropout rates are substantially higher for low-income adolescents (Toles, Schulz, & Rice, 1986), clearly reflecting the nature of their school experiences. Dropouts, in fact, represent a large proportion of non-college-bound students.

Low-income adolescents were less likely than their affluent counterparts to either hold their parents in high-esteem or perceive them as having much authority. Because their parents were poor, or perhaps because they were primarily female and held low-status jobs, low-income adolescents did not defer to their parents' opinions in the same manner as did high-income adolescents. Their evaluations of their parents were similar to the negative attitudes held about such groups by society in general. They did, however, express affection toward various family members as well as strong feelings about the importance of family. But without the influential and enabling support of parents, low-income adolescents floundered in making future plans.

Regardless of poverty, poor school records, discontent with present circumstances, and skepticism about equal opportunity, low-income adolescents still verbalized optimism about their own chances and implied that the future was somewhat under their control. This optimism might have been based on blind hope tacked onto the widespread, well-ingrained American belief in progress. Or the vocalized faith in the future might have been done for face-saving purposes—low-income respondents might have withheld their worries about following in their parents' footsteps into a life of poverty. This unrealistic optimism has been found in a number of other studies (Fischer & Leitenberg, 1986; Kluegel & Smith, 1986; Simmons & Rosenberg, 1971; Stipek, Lamb, & Zigler, 1981). On the other hand, when given the opportunity to truly fantasize about the future, many seemed too insecure to have real fantasies. Although some wished for well-paying jobs and rich husbands, others simply said "I'd like to find a job" or "I want to get married some day."

Messages about futures from school personnel seemed mainly to encourage unrealistic plans. It is likely that the aspirations about college expressed by low-income adolescents trickled down from the diffuse messages about the importance of college intended for more affluent students or were garnered from the fact that most of schooling is structured around acquiring prerequisites for more and more advanced educational pursuits. School was linked to a "preparation for college" function, even for those with few chances to attend. Lacking viable dreams of their own, low-income adolescents verbalized watered-down dreams of their high-income schoolmates. At the same time, the college-bound–vocational divisions that structured the high schools emphasized who was to go to college: There was a mutual consensus that low-income adolescents were not going and hence would not need preparation.

School has evolved from a common school established for the purpose of educating citizens to be participants in a democratic society to a preparatory school where students advance their personal ambitions when they have the opportunity. Such a transformation might not be of concern if all pupils received comparable services to facilitate a good life. This study indicates that secondary school personnel do not devote equal time and effort to all adolescents. High-income adolescents recalled having received a large (i.e., disproportionate) amount of counselors' time, even though they had less need of adult support; that is, their futures were fairly set in advance and mainly details needed attention. Moreover, their own parents were also in a position to facilitate their goals. Apparently, affluent patrons had communicated their sense of entitlement to school personnel, who responded by instituting policies or perpetuating practices partial to them.

Several reasons for the silence among adults about the futures of low-income teenagers are plausible. Although they may want to be fair, counselors are likely to be intimidated by high-income clientele who impose their needs to such an extent that there is little time left for less-influential students. Their job descriptions may even define their role as helping with the college preparation and application process, therefore limiting their focus to certain types of students. Or middle-class school personnel may be elitist, scorning nonprofessional jobs or failing to differentiate between various types of blue-collar jobs, seeing them mainly as fall-back-on jobs not worth mentioning or preparing for. Another reason may be that, due to a lack of exposure to the working-class world, counselors are unaware of postschool possibilities for students without college plans.

On the other hand, perhaps cognizant of the scarcity of decent working-class job opportunities, counselors and teachers may choose to remain silent rather than pass on pessimistic views to low-income adolescents. There are growing numbers of people for whom survival without steady work or without hope for more than minimum-wage jobs has become a way of life (Ehrenreich & Piven, 1984; Kornblum, 1984; W. J. Wilson, 1987). Sensitive to school and societal disparities for rich and poor children, school personnel may—through embarrassment or feelings of guilt about their roles in maintaining inequities—simply avoid low-income students. So regardless of a compulsory attendance policy, the school's role in enabling students to attain future goals—or even have future goals—appears to be limited to students destined for college. "Destined" aptly connotes the importance of "one's lot" or family status in determining school careers and planning for the future.

Perhaps because they generally felt undeserving and unworthy, low-income adolescents did not blame others for not helping them develop constructive plans for a future. They apologized for their confusion about the future, just as they expressed guilt feelings about their lack of success in school. Thus low-income teenagers expect and tolerate second-class status—a position they are likely to maintain throughout their lives. School is clearly one of the places where adolescents learn their position as a surplus population. The dark side of the meritocratic system is that those who do not succeed believe that their subordinate position results from their own inadequacies; thus they echo the ideologies of winners in the system.

Equitable school policies might result in more social mobility for poor children on an individual basis, but since our society is stratified and there is not enough room for everybody at the top, it seems fatuous for public schools to be based on ideologies that postulate such possibilities. Perpetuating myths or veiling reality is unlikely to result in improved conditions for poor people. To change their situations, attention must be focused on societal conditions and the just distribution of resources (Rawls, 1972; Reitman, 1981). But, as educators, we must also examine our roles in enabling certain students' goal attainment while neglecting others. Leaving low-income students' futures in the realm of the unmentionable is certainly not an equitable practice for public schools.

CHAPTER 9

Problematizing Meritocracies

The field is rife with theories about the nature of social class influences on schooling, but this study documents the reality of schooling as perceived by high- and low-income adolescents. It demonstrates the significance of social class standing on students' thinking about schools and themselves as students and as members of families and communities. But before the results are summarized and the implications of the study discussed, it is important to review the limitations to interpretating results.

LIMITATIONS OF STUDY

First, it might again be noted that participants were from particular subsets of standard socioeconomic divisions; high-income adolescents were similar to Anyon's (1980) affluent professional class but did not include her executive-elite (i.e., the highest-income families with significant economic, political, and social power) or middle-class (i.e., white-collar workers with stable but relatively low salaries) divisions. Because the study took place in a town dominated by a large university, high-income adolescents' parents were highly educated. Low-income participants were largely from single-parent homes in which parents were unemployed or marginally employed. They lived in subsidized housing, thus in isolation from other social classes. The study did not include children from working-class families in which parents have stable jobs and moderate salaries and who live in areas with more mixed incomes and occupations.

In examining the adolescents' views, it was impossible to completely distinguish their situations from their perceptions. Dissimilarities in the groups' school (and family) histories meant that they did not share the same experiences. Although studying the two groups' perceptions of the same experiences would be possible in the short run (e.g., in a controlled experimental situation), in the long run it would not be; that is, distinct social classes exist only because people have distinct experiences. Although experiences could not be distinguished from perceptions in the adolescent study, the more inclusive community study, which included both my personal observations of schools and community as well as those of parents and school personnel, revealed considerable congruence in adult and adolescent perceptions. The implication is that perceptions are highly correlated with reality in all cases.

Another potentially confounding factor is the speech idioms peculiar to each social class. What were assumed to be differences in respondents' descriptions of their perceptions and realities might simply have been differences in participants' figures of speech (Witt, Moe, Gutkin, & Andrews, 1984). One indication that there was a high correlation between what happened and how it was described, regardless of dialect, is the fact that the same respondents used a broad range of terminology in discussing the events in school. For example, they might complain that a teacher "yelled at" them in one instance, but they also told about a teacher "talking to" them at another point. In general, I took what adolescents said very literally.

Perhaps a more serious problem is the fact that the interviews relied on the validity of self-reports, and self-reports are influenced by complex motives and thinking processes. They are, by nature, retrospective, so actual events and occurrences are likely to be unintentionally distorted by incomplete or selective recall. Moreover, adolescents are likely to have intentionally constructed their narratives to portray themselves and others in a certain manner. For example, respondents may have attempted to control their images by deliberately avoiding certain topics and embellishing on others. Humans, in general, like to construe events to present a favorable personal image. Teenagers may also have been in the habit of denying wrongdoing to adults to avoid punishment or to save face.

It was obvious that high-income adolescents had been taught the niceties of talking about social class. Perhaps in order to avoid being seen as prejudiced, they were cautious about being openly critical of low-income schoolmates and avoided disparaging epithets in referring to them; that is, they spoke within the parameters of political correctness. At the same time, however, they accused their peers of being biased against low-income students and of using terms like "grit"—a term they only whispered or used in the midst of animated discussions with interviewers. The body language, facial expressions, and voice intonations discernible in personal interviews helped cut through some of the image-building and posture-maintaining of participants. The length of the interviews also mitigated against deceit and facades; adolescents seemed to grow tired of controlling their images and eventually slipped into more sincere discourses. As respondents became more comfortable and trusting, they tended to blurt out more negative, and probably truer, feelings.

Finally, it was difficult to distinguish between genuine, deeply felt ideas and commonsense, generalized beliefs. I made a deliberate attempt to get beyond pure mental associations in my manner of asking questions, but this effort was not entirely successful. By pushing and prodding adolescents to clarify their responses and provide examples and rationales for answers, it did seem that, eventually, adolescents gave more authentic replies. A common pattern was for adolescents to initially verbalize dominant-culture messages (e.g., that high-income adolescents are better behaved, that school facilitates social mobility, that teachers are impartial). And, although such ideologies continued to weave through high-income adolescents' discourses (i.e., they worked for them), low-income respondents tended to attach more critical, reality-based conclusions to their glib, positive beginnings. This trend occurred with more frequency as the interviews progressed, perhaps because, by being supportive and encouraging the expression of true feelings, the interviewers gave respondents permission to vocalize dissent against sacrosanct American beliefs.

SUMMARY

In designing this study, I was motivated to explore several major theoretical assumptions about social cognitions, social interactions, and schooling. Whitty (1985) suggested that only by bringing the theoretical exploration of the dynamics of capitalist societies and the situational analysis of curricular practices together in an empirical manner could strategies of pedagogic and political intervention be developed. To this end, I attempted to explore how such dynamics play themselves out in the imaginings of adolescents. Since discourse involves constant reproductions and reconstitutions of texts (Hodge & Kress, 1988), the narratives were deconstructed with the intent of finding evidence related to the theoretical assumptions.

The narratives of adolescents in this study confirm a number of propositions of critical theory pertaining to social class influences on schooling. These include:

1. Social class conflict is ubiquitous (in schools).
2. School is not a neutral setting.
3. Adolescents bring their social class-determined subjectivities to school.
4. Social perceptions are shaped through school discourse.
5. Human thought is heteroglossic and dynamic.

1. Social Class Conflict Is Ubiquitous (in Schools). Friction between members of different social classes was a theme that laced tales of school. High-income adolescents pronounced disgust at behaviors (e.g., smoking, doing drugs, acting sleazy, being dumb, not caring about school, being tough) they claimed were typical of low-income youth (i.e., "grits," "rednecks," "bullies," "hicks"). They construed the "other" as negative and contaminated and communicated that they had to avoid—even protect themselves from—these outsiders (see P. M. Brantlinger, 1990). Low-income adolescents enumerated details of being rejected, humiliated, and ostracized by their high-income schoolmates as well as by teachers, whom they associated with the "other" class. Talking about social class in animated and emotional ways, both groups indicated that class distinctions and conflict were ever-present in the ongoing life in school. The narratives also revealed a dominant–subordinate delineation between social classes in adolescents' thinking.

2. School Is Not a Neutral Setting. Low-income adolescents complained about divisive, differentiating, and humiliating school practices such as receiving low grades, tracking, special education, and harsh or humiliating discipline. They were frustrated by their unsuccessful school careers and inequitable relationships with teachers. They felt shunned by high-income adolescents, whom they simultaneously envied and resented. Although their negative emotions were directed at high-income students and school personnel, their aggressive behaviors were directed mainly toward other low-income students. Their (mis)behaviors were punished in ways likely to increase anger toward school authority. Low-income adolescents' anger appeared to be of school origin—the result of their experiences as subordinates.

School was not described as a neutral or therapeutic environment, but rather as a source of stress for low-income participants. School was also not neutral for high-income adolescents—it was a privileging setting. The sense of self as superior and deserving was enhanced in school.

3. Adolescents Bring Their Social Class-Determined Subjectivities to School. The fact that human thought is neither neutral nor ahistorical, but rather historically (hence social class) determined, was apparent in the myths, perceptions, interpretations, and biases embedded in the narratives. The legends of adolescents' cognitive maps were replete with social class markers that obviously guided their interpretations of others' behaviors. Respondents detailed how members of the other class felt about members of their class. If teachers were not friendly, they were perceived as snobbish and rejecting by low-income adolescents. If high-income adolescents observed teachers punishing low-income adolescents, their accounts included the notion that these students were culpable and the consequences deserved. Low-income adolescents constantly gave social class explanations for school phenomena, while high-income respondents' allusions to social class were circumspect—they rarely made directly elitist statements, but an elitist perspective governed their stands. Although it was clear that they were aware that their social class was a force in their favor, high-income youth were more likely to pinpoint factors such as exemplary achievement or admirable behavior as influential in school.

Metaphors related to social class (e.g., "preppies are good kids," "grits are dumb") guided the mental sorting of events observed in school. The groups responded from clear within-class positions.

4. Social Perceptions Are Shaped Through School Discourse. Students not only are "taught" a formal academic knowledge and skill base in school but also are socialized by covert curricula—their epistemologies develop through various levels of discourse within the context of school. Adolescents' perceptions of the social world continued to be molded by interactions with others and observations of social class distinctions. Views of high-income students as talented and worthy and low-income students as inferior were given credence by such school practices as tracking, special education, extracurricular participation, and school evaluations and rewards.

One of the lessons low-income adolescents learned was that they were less competent and less deserving than others. They echoed school personnel and upper-income schoolmates in negatively evaluating their own participation and performance. Adolescents also learned about their families' control of school circumstances—for low-income adolescents this meant that, with their influence on schooling as a model, they had to face their family's impotence in altering a major societal institution. High-income teenagers gained confidence that difficulties could be resolved—that school personnel would respond to family pressure (whether actual or symbolic)—and that they and their parents had an integral role to play in the functioning of such institutions.

Bourdieu (1984) contends that institutionalized conceptions of ability are reproduced in individuals during ability formation. Students accept the intellectual status defined for them by the social structure and separate their ability from their control during schooling. They further reify such conceptions as intelligence so that it is seen as an important quality of individuals; hence, when they feel unintelligent they feel unworthy. Others have found that failure impacts on children early in their school careers and subsequently perpetuates a cycle of behaviors and school practices that undermine their educational and personal development (Good et al., 1987; Oakes, 1985). A complex of psychological attributes related to subordinate status, such as "alienation" (Seeman, 1959), "learned helplessness" (Diener & Dweck, 1978), and "passivity" (Good et al., 1987), were apparent in low-income adolescents in this study. Low achievers have been found to withdraw self-investment in school and learning (Switzky & Schultz, 1988) and exit from school with diminished sense of self-efficacy (Schunk, 1989). Moreover, the phenomena resulting in ability formation extend to "status formation"; that is, while socialized to accept inequities in school, students are also conditioned to expect similar disparate circumstances later in life.

The narratives of all adolescents revealed a mind-set that linked failure in school with poverty in society; both were seen as outcomes of (negative) personal attributes. The flip side of attributing success to personal factors, then, is that failure, or lack of accomplishment, is similarly linked to (negative) personal qualities. Reflecting the constant pattern in the daily life of classrooms, adolescents are socialized to believe that competence should be rewarded. Hence the sorting function of school is seen as legitimate even if it results in stratifying students according to social class. The result was a certain amount of loyalty by low-income adolescents to a system that did not work well for them.

5. Human Thought Is Heteroglossic and Dynamic. Suggestions that multiple levels of understanding be examined (Giroux, 1984) seem particularly relevant to unraveling the contradictions and inconsistencies of adolescents' feelings about school and self in this study. Although the study focused on social class influences on adolescents' thinking—hence the questions were designed to stimulate narratives about social class issues—adolescents provided various other positional explanations to interpret events in school. Sometimes narratives were tinted by gender or race; sometimes by lower-track, retained, or special education status. Respondents quoted relatives and friends or reasoned out what seemed to be very personal interpretations of school circumstances. Idiosyncrasies in all narratives lend support to the importance of human agency in actively constructing meaning out of the myriad of social signs and symbols of social settings.

Related to this theory of multiple levels of cognition, the existence of a number of dichotomies in adolescents' thinking surfaced during the analysis of results. The demonstration of these conflicted perceptions may be among the most important tasks of this book. Adolescents wavered between:

• *Social class allegiance and rejection.* Low-income adolescents' perceptions of social class, personal status, and future opportunities revealed conflicts and dilemmas. By all objective standards they were poor; however, the majority did not identify themselves as such. There was a pattern of denial of their own social class standing as well as signs of striving to pass as "respectable" or middle class. Given their negative feelings about the poor and their directing blame at low-income people, it is not surprising that they were reluctant to be affiliated with such a discredited and devalued group. Adolescents equated high-income status with intelligence, school success, admirable behaviors, and, ultimately, worthiness—a mental conglomerate neither group really challenged. These positive attitudes toward wealthy people provided the rationale for the uneven distributions of rewards. Negative feelings toward their own social class certainly strained class loyalty and obstructed collective class action for low-income adolescents. But they were united in their reaction to being shunned, ridiculed, and ostracized by high-income people. They reacted angrily to terms such as "grit"—there was consensus about the inappropriateness of such negative epithets.

High-income adolescents' discourses revealed that their low-income schoolmates were largely invisible to them. But when their paths crossed, the individual reactions of high-income youth ranged from scorn and smugness to pity and a guilty acceptance of the status quo. The more political or empathetic among them were critical of blatant elitist acts and stratifying practices, but, ultimately, they made no attempts to rectify inequities and were willing to thrive under present circumstances. They felt entitled to elite positions and accepted privilege as "natural."

• *Passive and acting out reactions.* Anger about their status and tales of resistance interspersed low-income adolescents' narratives about the rituals of schooling. Although overwhelmed and frustrated by problems they felt powerless to change, low-income respondents mainly portrayed themselves as passive and conforming students. But their subdued reaction was periodically interrupted by outbursts of anger (e.g., "sassed teachers," "fought preps")—impulsive episodes that might have cathartic value but that, because of their erratic and individualistic nature, were likely to be perceived by others as signs of pathology (i.e., emotional disturbance) or moral lassitude rather than as justified reactions to discrimination and unfairness. School was clearly an arena where social class contest was integral to social discourse; but, although expressions of anger were widespread among low-income youth, there were few signs of effective collective or systematic acts of resistance.

• *Abstracting and personalizing situations.* Another type of dichotomy in the narratives was respondents' tendency to personalize and humanize experiences. Adolescents rarely found fault with school as an institution, nor did they challenge the fairness of stratifying practices. Instead they targeted particular teachers, or teachers as a group, and held them personally responsible for the stratified system they operationalized. It was teachers who gave grades, assigned students to tracks, referred students for special education, and meted out punishment. They responded to teachers as members of a social class but also as personifications of the institution of school. This meant that teachers took on multifaceted and complex persona, perhaps even bearing much of the burden of a collective history of class relationships.

Adolescents also personalized by blaming (or congratulating) themselves for school circumstances. High-income adolescents attributed their success to their own merits. When low-income respondents were not projecting the evils of the institution onto teachers, they were internalizing blame. Ultimately, most low-income adolescents vacillated between embellishing on teacher or high-income schoolmates' transgressions and apologizing for their own inability to meet dominant standards. Feelings of unworthiness meant that they did not feel deserving of equal status with their affluent schoolmates and that they tolerated school practices not personally beneficial. They also generalized what happened to them (e.g., "My mom dropped out of school, so she can't find a good job") to broader levels (e.g., "Poor people are undereducated; that is why they are unemployed"). Their abstract theories about the world conformed to the dynamics of their personal situations.

• *Hegemonic and counterhegemonic sentiments.* Dominant-culture messages were apparent in adolescents' strong beliefs that achievement and graduation are essential to success in life—that education plays a major role in social mobility. Acceptance of the meritocratic model was widespread and ran deep; success in school was attributed to individual merit and failure, to personal inadequacies. Ultimately, both high- and low-income adolescents subscribed to a model of intelligence and achievement that stratified according to social class.

Although such ideologies did not work to the advantage of low-income adolescents and their concrete experiences were contrary to the ideal, they were still inclined to perceive schools as rewarding students fairly and objectively. Even the most belligerent teenagers, who vehemently cursed all aspects of schools, and the most belittled, who poignantly described their emotional turmoil in response to inequities, inevitably assumed some blame for their inferior status, confessing to "moods," "tempers," "laziness," and even "slowness." They detached their actions (passivity and aggression) from their incentives (not complying with unfair circumstances, correcting wrongs) and accepted blame for "bad" behaviors.

But, to varying degrees, most low-income respondents were skeptical about the validity of dominant ideologies, and many responded in ways that revealed considerable insight into the social class nature of schooling. They often began a discussion by glibly vocalizing dominant sentiments, then turned around to challenge such contentions. For example, they might start off by saying that all children have equal chances for the good life, then complain that students from influential families monopolize power and prevent significant participation by others. They expressed indignation about being punished for what they felt to be justified retaliation to others' transgressions and were annoyed that preppies were rarely blamed.

To some extent, then, students' insight penetrated the myths of school as neutral territory. Although subliminally wooed by dominant messages, on a case-by-case basis low-income adolescents dissected the veiled reality of social class relationships in school. Critical consciousness (i.e., an awareness of the reality of one's life circumstances) did not, however, completely per-

meate their perceptions of school and society; dominant messages were inter-
mittently challenged but not consistently disputed and laid to rest. Furthermore, adolescents did not generalize criticism of school relations to societal
situations. The right of the wealthy to wield disproportionate economic and
political power went unchallenged by teenagers. They straddled an ambiguous position with some insight, but substantial clouding of reality. In the end,
glimmers of awareness seemed mostly overshadowed by ideologies that facilitate the agendas of dominant classes. A well-formed critical consciousness is
seen as essential to any collective movement to change conditions for the
oppressed (Freire, 1985).

• *Rhetoric and true feeling.* The anti-establishment behaviors of low-
income adolescents often convey that they do not care about school or their
relationships with others in school. In contrast, it may be assumed that high-
income adolescents share the values associated with school personnel. It is
important to delve below the surface of students' immediate behaviors and
rhetoric in order to understand true feelings. In this study, low-income teenagers spoke in animated ways about their school experiences and their interactions with teachers. The pretense of not caring by some respondents
appeared to be a defensive reaction to anticipated rejection. Their animated
narratives about school and the tone and intensity of their response belied
their claims of indifference—school was clearly an important setting for them.
If anything, they cared too much. At the same time, a certain strand in high-
income adolescents' discourse revealed cynicism and indifference. They played
the game (i.e., conformed to rituals) to prevail in the system without really
identifying with the elevated purposes of schooling.

• *Civil and self-centered ideas.* Adolescents made it clear that school was
a setting of social class tension, but they also professed elements of utopian
ideals for human relationships and for societal institutions (see Figure 9.1).
Low-income adolescents mentioned both wanting to avoid the painful interactions with prejudiced teachers and snobby schoolmates and wanting to
improve relationships by getting others to see their common humanity. They
waxed eloquent on the value of integrated schools even as they poignantly
recalled the pain of not being full-fledged members in mixed settings. Pessimism about the inevitability of their subordinate status only infrequently shat-
tered their enduring optimism.

On an abstract level, affluent youth glibly vocalized democratic sentiments,
talking about equity and criticizing teachers who favored others or discriminated against certain groups. But, as Mickelson (1990) found, much of the
idealism expressed by high-income adolescents had little impact on the concrete happenings in school. Although they preached fairness, they enjoyed

FIGURE 9.1. How Schools Should Be/How Schools Are

Civil Ideal (abstract)	Dominant Message (normative)	Reality (concrete)
schools are equitable	with some exceptions schools are fair	schools stratify, inherently unfair
opportunity equal for all	opportunity for diligent, worthy	opportunity for the privileged
student voices equivalent	competent voices heard	voices deliberately silenced
power equally distributed	power accessible to all	power held by elites
enhances all students' futures	facilitates willing students' aspirations	privileges elites, thwarts others

their elite status in school, expected it (maybe even gloated about it), and seemed likely to oppose any reform that would threaten their own advantage. Thus the rhetoric of idealism had little effect on day-to-day behaviors. Just as Olson (1983) and Sieber (1982) found, in spite of the idealism about democratic principles, high-income school patrons expect preferential treatment in school and act in ways to secure it. This finding reinforces Freire's (1985) contention that subordinate groups cannot depend on the good intentions of elite groups to change conditions.

CONCLUSION

There are those who believe that American schools are reformist and egalitarian, that they reward students according to their abilities and achievement, not their social origin. According to this position, student successes are due to personal accomplishments, and failures result from individual inadequacies. This school structure is said to reward merit and thus to facilitate social mobility and prevent the development of a rigid, caste-based society.

But historically, the actual working of such a meritocracy has been disputed. Critics claim that there are unequal influences among citizens in school matters as in other political affairs (D. Cohen & Lazerson, 1977; Reitman, 1981; Tinney, 1983). According to theories of social class reproduction, schools reflect the social structure of the larger society (Tyack, 1974), serving as gatekeepers to entrance into power positions (McLaren, 1987; Oakes, 1988) and sorting students to fit into a hierarchical socioeconomic class structure. Bowles and Gintis (1976) wrote that class inequities in education are intentional and result from deliberate efforts on the part of a power elite to maintain advantage. Middle-class interests rather than subordinate-class inadequacies, then, are responsible for the persistence of inequalities in educational opportunities and outcomes (Farber, Wilson, & Holm, 1989; Olson, 1983; Sieber, 1982).

This study lends support to critical theorists' assertions about the social class influences on schooling by graphically illustrating the dark side of the meritocracy. Results indicate that in order to achieve an effective, democratic education for a broad range of students, it is important to understand and deal with the individualized achievement ideology (Giroux, 1986; Willis, 1977) and its accompanying phenomenon, which might be called an internalized failure–personal inadequacy syndrome. Examining how failure is institutionalized into educational policy and practice, in spite of its profound negative effect on great numbers of children and adults in our society, and attempting to prevent this from happening in the future is pivotal. In order to intervene and disassemble the social class–reproductive nature of schools it is necessary to problematize the basic assumptions underlying the views of schools as meritocracies.

Assumptions Underlying Meritocracies

Various perceptions, assumptions, and values underlie segregating, differentiating, and humiliating patterns of schooling:

- School is a meritocracy in which rewards and penalties are fairly and objectively distributed.
- Merit is adequately and efficaciously defined by schools.
- Merit is innate and unevenly distributed among students.
- An unequal distribution of school rewards is legitimate because of the disparities in student attributes. (The corollary to this is that an unequal distribution of societal rewards is legitimate because of disparities in human attributes.)
- Efficacious learning consists of a series of finite and discrete curricular entities that can be delineated and evaluated.
- Current measures of student performance focus on valid, important, and desired attributes.
- Norm-referenced performance evaluation is legitimate.
- Students should all achieve at the same level.

- The statistical mean or modal student is a real person, or, what all children should be.
- Children who diverge from the hypothetical modal child (perform below or above the norm) are lacking (e.g., handicapped) or gifted.
- Individualized and separated academic programs meet needs of students better than a common curriculum.
- Differentiated administrative arrangements reverse inadequacies and reduce student differences.
- Reducing human diversity is a beneficial undertaking.
- Human worthiness is tied to intelligence or school performance.
- Individual achievement is more important than communal goals, such as the development of empathy, cooperativeness, social consciousness, feelings of equal status, or equal access to (school) life.

In order to deal with divisive and stigmatizing practices it is essential for schools and the public to systematically, and openly, scrutinize these assumptions and the policies and practices that follow from them.

There is universal recognition among academics, professionals, and the general public that students from various social class, ethnic, and racial backgrounds differ markedly in the extent to which their performance in school meets the standards set by schools. The preponderant belief seems to be that genetic or home conditions are at the root of differences in achievement. Yet overwhelming evidence that school conditions are not equal for poor and rich children means that an equally plausible explanation is that differential outcomes are due to inequities in schooling. As Edmonds (1982) wrote:

> We happen to live in a society that values some of its people more than it values others. Educators, like all social servants, serve those they think they must and when they need not, they do not. Unfortunately, most of the children who do not get these services, in general and in education in particular, happen to be members of politically impotent groups—children who are either poor, of color, or both. (p. 272)

Newmann (1981) suggested that school personnel improve school climate for alienated youth by promoting integration, by increasing student participation in school governance, and by encouraging a sense of belonging by creating schools within schools. Although the implementation of such ideas would seem likely to alleviate the problems and improve the circumstances of low-income youth in this study, their narratives gave no reason to believe that Newmann's idea are being implemented locally.

It is essential that we also think about nonschool variables, such as the nature and state of the economy or the generally unequal opportunities available for individuals from different social classes on graduation. By setting arbitrary standards, defining narrow fields of competence, allocating resources inequitably, and overemphasizing egocentric pursuits (Bastian, 1988; Bastian et al., 1986; Newmann & Kelly, 1985), school (and societal) reforms have focused on material and social rewards for some at the expense of equity for a broader population. Those who care about social justice should take an active stand in confronting these practices.

References

Adams, B. D. (1978). Inferiorization and self-esteem. *School Psychology, 4,* 47–53.

Alexander, P. A., Schallert, D. L., & Hare, V. C. (1991). Coming to terms: How researchers in learning and literacy talk about knowledge. *Review of Educational Research, 61,* 315–343

Alpert, G., & Dunham, R. (1986). Keeping academically marginal youths in school: A prediction model. *Youth and Society, 17,* 346–361.

Alvarado, M., & Ferguson, B. (1983). The curriculum, media studies, and discursivity. *Screen, 24,* 8–21.

Amato, J. (1980). Social class discrimination in the schooling process: Myth and reality. *Urban Review, 12,* 121–130.

Anyon, J. (1980). Social class and the hidden curriculum of work. *Journal of Education, 162,* 67–92.

Anyon, J. (1981). Elementary schooling and distinctions of social class. *Interchange, 12,* 118–132.

Apple, M. W. (1982a). *Education and power.* Boston: Routledge & Kegan Paul.

Apple, M. W. (1982b). *Ideology and curriculum.* London: Routledge & Kegan Paul.

Apple, M. W. (1987). *Teachers and texts: A political economy of class and gender relations in education.* New York: Routledge & Kegan Paul.

Apple, M., & Beyer, L. (1983). Social evaluation of curriculum. *Educational evaluation and policy analysis, 5,* 425–434.

Aronowitz, S. (1980). Science and ideology. *Current Perspectives in Social Theory, 1,* 75–101.

Aronowitz, S. (1992). *The politics of identity: Class, culture, social movements.* New York: Routledge.

Bakhtin, M. (1981). *The dialogic imagination* (C. Emerson & M. Holquist, Trans.). Austin: University of Texas Press.

Bakhtin, M. (1984). *Rabelais and his world.* Bloomington: Indiana University Press.

Balch, R. W., & Kelly, D. H. (1974). Reactions to deviance in a junior high school: Student views of the labeling process. *Instructional Psychology, 1,* 23–28.

Baron, S. W. (1989). Resistance and its consequences: The street culture of punks. *Youth and Society, 21,* 207–237.

Bastian, A. (1988). Educating for democracy: Raising expectations. *NEA Today, 6,* 28–33.

Bastian, A., & Fruchter, N. (1985). *Report of the New York hearing on the crisis in public education.* New York: Advocates for Children.

Bastian, A., Fruchter, N., Gittell, M., Greer, G., & Haskins, K. (1986). *Choosing equality: The case for democratic schooling*. Philadelphia: Temple University Press.

Bayer, A. (1981). Social status hierarchy: Reading groups. *Viewpoints in Teaching and Learning, 57,* 49–57.

Beckerman, T., & Good, T. (1981). The classroom ratio of high- and low-aptitude students and its effect on achievement. *American Educational Research Journal, 18,* 317–327.

Beckman, L. J. (1976). Causal attributions of teachers and parents regarding children's performance. *Psychology in the Schools, 13,* 212–218.

Bender, W. N. (1988). The other side of placement decisions: Assessment of the mainstream learning environment. *Remedial and Special Education, 9,* 28–33.

Berger, J., Rosenholtz, S. J., & Zelditch, M., Jr. (1980). Status organizing processes. *Annual Review of Sociology, 6,* 479–508.

Berman, E. H. (1984). State hegemony and the schooling process. *Journal of Education, 166,* 239–253.

Berndt, T. J. (1986). Children's comments about their friendships. In M. Perlmutter (Ed.), *Cognitive perspectives on children's social and behavioral development* (pp. 189–212). Hillsdale, NJ: Erlbaum.

Bichard, S. L., Alden, L., Walker, L. J., & McMahon, R. J. (1988). Friendship understanding in socially accepted, rejected, and neglected children. *Merrill-Palmer Quarterly, 34,* 33–46.

Birksted, I. K. (1976). School performance viewed from the boys. In G. Rose (Ed.), *Deciphering sociological research* (pp. 265–275). London: Macmillan.

Block, J., & Gjerde, P. F. (1986). Distinguishing between antisocial behavior and undercontrol. In D. Olweus, J. Block, & M. Radke-Yarrow (Eds.), *Development of antisocial and prosocial behavior: Research, theories, and issues* (pp. 177–204). New York: Academic Press.

Blumenfeld, P. C., Pintrich, P. R., & Hamilton, U. L. (1986). Children's concepts of ability, effort, and conduct. *American Educational Research Journal, 23,* 95–104.

Bourdieu, P. (1977). *Outline of a theory of practice*. Cambridge, UK: Cambridge University Press.

Bourdieu, P. (1984). *Distinction: A social critique of the judgement of taste*. Cambridge, MA: Harvard University Press.

Bourdieu, P., & Passeron, J. C. (1977). *Reproduction in education, society and culture*. Beverly Hills: Sage.

Bowers, C. A. (1987). *Elements of a post-liberal theory of education*. New York: Teachers College Press.

Bowles, S., & Gintis, H. (1976). *Schooling in capitalist America*. New York: Basic Books.

Brady, P. M., Manni, J. L., & Winikur, D. W. (1983). Implications of ethnic disproportions in programs for the educable mentally retarded. *The Journal of Special Education, 17,* 295–302.

Brantlinger, E. A. (1985a). Low-income parents' opinions about the social class composition of school. *American Journal of Education, 93,* 389–408.

Brantlinger, E. A. (1985b). What low-income parents want from schools: A different view of aspirations. *Interchange, 16,* 14–28.

Brantlinger, E. A. (1985c). Low-income parents' perceptions of favoritism in the schools. *Urban Education, 20,* 82–102.

Brantlinger, E. A. (1986). Aspirations, expectations, and reality: Response to Olson and Weir. *Interchange, 17,* 85–87.

Brantlinger, E. A. (1987). Making decisions about special education placement: Do low-income parents have the information they need? *Journal of Learning Disabilities, 20,* 95–101

Brantlinger, E. A., & Guskin, S. L. (1985). Implications of social and cultural differences for special education with specific recommendations. *Focus on Exceptional Children, 18,* 1–12.

Brantlinger, E. A., & Guskin, S. L. (1987). Ethnocultural and social–psychological effects on learning characteristics of handicapped children. In M. C. Wang, M. C. Reynolds, & H. J. Walberg (Eds.), *Handbook of special education: Research and practice* (Vol. 1; pp. 7–34). Oxford, UK: Pergamon.

Brantlinger, P. M. (1990). *Crusoe's footprints: Cultural studies in Britain and America.* New York: Routledge.

Breakwell, G. (1978). Some effects of marginal social identity. In H. Tajfel (Ed.), *Differentiation between social groups* (pp. 301–333). London: Academic Press.

Brookover, W. G., Thomas, S., & Patterson, A. (1964). Self concept of ability and school achievement. *Sociology of Education, 37,* 271–278.

Bugetal, D. B. (1985). Unresponsive children and powerless adults: Cocreators of affectively uncertain caregiving environments. In M. Lewis & C. Saarni (Eds.), *The socialization of emotion* (pp. 67–84). New York: Plenum.

Bukowski, W. M., Newcomb, A. F., & Hoza, B. (1987). Friendship conceptions among early adolescents: A longitudinal study of stability and change. *Journal of Early Adolescence, 7,* 143–152.

Bullough, R. V., Jr. (1987). School knowledge, power and human experience. *The Educational Forum, 51,* 259–274.

Bullough, R. V., Jr. (1989). *First-year teacher: A case study.* New York: Teachers College Press.

Burr, W. R., Hill, R., Nye, F. E., & Reiss, I. L. (1979). *Contemporary theories about the family: General theories/theoretical orientations.* New York: The Free Press.

Cairns, R. B., & Cairns, B. D. (1986). The developmental interactional view of social behavior: Four issues of aggression. In D. Olweus, J. Block, & M. Radke-Yarrow (Eds.), *Development of antisocial and prosocial behavior: Research, theories and issues* (pp. 315–342). New York: Academic Press.

Calhoun, C. J., & Ianni, F. A. (1979). Notes on the social organization of high schools. In R. Barnhardt, J. H. Chilcott, & H. F. Wolcott (Eds.), *Anthropology and educational administration* (pp. 107–114). Tucson, AZ: Impresora Sahuaro.

Carlberg, C. P., & Kavale, K. (1980). The efficacy of special versus regular class placement for exceptional children: A meta analysis. *The Journal of Special Education, 14,* 295–309.

Carlson, D. (1987). Teachers as political actors: From reproductive theory to the crisis of schooling. *Harvard Educational Review, 57,* 283–307.

Carnoy, M., & Levin, H. M. (1985). *Schooling and work in the democratic state.* Stanford, CA: Stanford University Press.

Carrier, J. G. (1986). Sociology and special education: Differentiation and allocation in mass education. *American Journal of Education, 94,* 281–312.

Carter, J., & Sugai, G. (1989). Survey on prereferral practices: Responses from state departments of education. *Exceptional Children, 55,* 298–302.

Casebolt, H. (1987). *Affecting change in alienated students utilizing and adapting the FOCUS model in dropout prevention.* Unpublished doctoral dissertation, University of North Carolina, Greensboro.

Cashmore, E. E. (1984). *No future: Youth and society.* London: Heinemann.

Cashmore, J., & Goodnow, J. J. (1985). Agreement across generations: A two-process model. *Child Development, 56,* 493–501.

Castlebury, S., & Arnold, J. (1988). Early adolescent perceptions of informal groups in a middle school. *Journal of Early Adolescence, 8,* 97–107.

Cervantes, L. (1965). *The dropout: Causes and cures.* Ann Arbor: University of Michigan Press.

Clark, C. M., & Peterson, P. L. (1985). Teachers' thought processes. In M. C. Wittrock (Ed.), *Handbook of research on teaching* (3rd ed.; pp. 255–296). New York: Macmillan.

Cockburn, A. (1989). All in their family. *The Nation, 249,* 113–114.

Cohen, A. K. (1955). *Delinquent boys: The culture of the gang.* New York: The Free Press.

Cohen, D., & Lazerson, M. (1977). Education and the corporate order: Merit and equality. In J. Karabel & A. H. Halsey (Eds.), *Power and ideology in education* (pp. 393–585). New York: Oxford University Press.

Coleman, J. S. (1974). *Relationships in adolescence.* London: Routledge & Kegan Paul.

Coleman, J. S. (1976). Liberty and equality in school desegregation. *Social Policy, 6,* 9–13.

Coleman, J. S., Campbell, E. Q., Hobson, C. J., McPartland, J., Mood, A. M., Weinfeld, F. D., & York, R. L. (1966). *Equality of educational opportunity.* Cambridge, MA: Harvard University Press.

Comer, J. P. (1988). Is "parenting" essential to good teaching? *National Education Association, 6,* 34–40.

Conklin, M. E., & Daily, A. R. (1981). Does consistency of parent educational encouragement matter for secondary school students? *Sociology of Education, 54,* 254–267.

Cooper, H., & Good, T. (1983). *Pygmalion grows up: Studies in the expectation communication process.* New York: Longman.

Covington, M. V., & Beery, R. G. (1976). *Self-worth as school learning.* New York: Holt, Rinehart, & Winston.

Covington, M. V., & Omelich, C. L. (1979). Effort: The double-edged sword in school achievement. *Journal of Educational Psychology, 71,* 160–182.

Dahrendorf, R. (1959). *Class and class conflict in industrial society.* Stanford, CA: Stanford University Press.

Dale, R., Esland, G., & MacDonald, M. (1976). *Schooling and capitalism: A sociological reader.* London: Routledge & Kegan Paul.

Damon, W. (1975). Early conceptions of positive justice as related to the development of logical operations. *Child Development, 46,* 301–312.

Damon, W. (1980). Patterns of change in children's social reasoning: A two-year lon-gitudinal study. *Child Development, 51,* 1010–1017.

deBettencourt, L. U., Zigmond, N., & Thornton, H. (1989). Follow-up of postsecondary-age rural learning disabled graduates and dropouts. *Exceptional Children, 56,* 40–49.

Diener, C. I., & Dweck, C. S. (1978). An analysis of learned helplessness: Continuous changes in performance, strategy, and achievement cognitions following failure. *Journal of Personality and Social Psychology, 36,* 451–462.

Dodge, K. (1980). Social competition and children's aggressive behavior. *Child Development, 51,* 162–170.

Douvan, E. (1983). Commentary: Theoretical perspectives on peer association. In J. L. Epstein & N. Karweit (Eds.), *Friends in school* (pp. 63–69). New York: Academic Press.

Drummond, H. (1982). Power, madness, and poverty. *Behavioral Disorders, 7,* 101–109.

Dupont, H. (1989). The emotional development of exceptional students. *Focus on Exceptional Children, 21,* 1–10.

Duran, B. J., & Weffer, R. E. (1992). Immigrants' aspirations, high school process, and academic outcomes. *American Educational Research Journal, 29,* 163–181.

East, P. L., Hess, L. E., & Lerner, R. M. (1987). Peer social support and adjustment of early adolescent peer groups. *Journal of Early Adolescence, 7,* 153–163.

Eckert, P. (1989). *Jocks and burnouts: Social categories and identity in the high school.* New York: Teachers College Press.

Edelman, M. W. (1987). *Families in peril: An agenda for social change.* Cambridge, MA: Harvard University Press.

Eder, D. (1981). Ability grouping as a self-fulfilling prophecy: A microanalysis of teacher–student interaction. *Sociology of Education, 57,* 151–162.

Eder, D. (1985). The cycle of popularity: Interpersonal relations among female adolescents. *Sociology of Education, 58,* 154–165.

Eder, D., & Stanford, S. (1986). The development and maintenance of interactional norms among early adolescents. In P. Adler (Ed.), *Sociological studies of child development* (Vol. I; pp. 283–300). Greenwich, CT: JAI Press.

Edgar, E. (1988). Employment as an outcome for mildly handicapped students: Current status and future directions. *Focus on Exceptional Children, 21,* 1–8.

Edmonds, R. (1982). The last obstacle to equity in education: Social class. *Theory Into Practice, 20,* 269–272.

Ehrenreich, B., & Piven, F. F. (1984). The feminization of poverty. *Dissent, 31,* 162–170.

Ekstrom, R., Goerts, M., Pollack, J., & Rock, D. (1986). Who drops out of high school and why? Findings from a national study. *Teachers College Record, 87,* 356–373.

Elder, G. H., & Liker, J. K. (1982). Hard times in women's lives: Historical influences across forty years. *American Journal of Socioloy, 88,* 241–269.

Elias, M. J. (1989). Schools as a source of stress to children: An analysis of causal and ameliorative influences. *Journal of School Psychology, 27,* 393–407.

Enright, R. D., Enright, W. F., Manheim, L. A., & Harris, B. E. (1980). Distributive justice development and social class. *Developmental Psychology, 16,* 555–563.

Erickson, F. (1986). Qualitative methods in research on teaching. In M. C. Wittrock (Ed.), *Handbook of research on teaching* (3rd ed.; pp. 119–161). New York: Macmillan.

Esquivel, G. B., & Yoshida, R. K. (1985). Special education for language minority students. *Focus on Exceptional Students, 18,* 1–8.

Everhart, R. B. (1983). *Reading, writing, and resistance: Adolescence and labor in a junior high school.* New York: Routledge & Kegan Paul.

Evertson, C. E. (1982). Differences in instructional activities in average- and low-achieving junior high English and mathematics classes. *Elementary School Journal, 82,* 329–350.

Ewert, G. D. (1991). Habermas and education: A comprehensive overview of the influence of Habermas in educational literature. *Review of Educational Research, 61,* 345–378.

Farber, P., Wilson, P., & Holm, G. (1989). From innocence to inquiry: A social reproduction framework. *Journal of Teacher Education, 40,* 45–50.

Faunce, W. A. (1984). School achievement, social status, and self-esteem. *Social Psychology Quarterly, 47,* 3–14.

Fay, B. (1987). *Critical social science.* Ithaca, NY: Cornell University Press.

Fenstermacher, G. D. (1988). The place of science and epistemology in Schon's concept of reflective practice. In P. Grimmett & G. Erickson (Eds.), *Reflection in teacher education* (pp. 39–46). New York: Teachers College Press.

Festinger, L. (1954). A theory of social comparison processes. *Human Relations, 7,* 117–140.

Fine, M. (1986). Why urban adolescents drop into and out of public high school. *Teachers College Record, 87,* 393–409.

Fine, M. (1991). *Framing dropouts: Notes on the politics of an urban public high school.* Albany: State University of New York Press.

Fine, M., & Rosenberg, P. (1983). Dropping out of high school: The ideology of school and work. *Journal of Education, 165,* 257–272.

Fine, M., & Zane, N. (1989). Bein' wrapped too tight: When low-income women drop out of high school. In L. Weis, E. Farrar, & H. G. Petrie (Eds.), *Dropouts from school: Issues, dilemmas, and solutions* (pp. 25–53). Albany: State University of New York Press.

Finn, J. D. (1989). Withdrawing from school. *Review of Educational Research, 59,* 117–142.

Finn, J. D., & Cox, D. (1992). Participation and withdrawal among fourth-grade pupils. *American Educational Research Journal, 29,* 141–162.

Fischer, M., & Leitenberg, H. (1986). Optimism and pessimism in elementary school–aged children. *Child Development, 57,* 241–248.

Florio-Ruane, S. (1987). Sociolinguistics for educational researchers. *American Educational Research Journal, 24,* 185–197.

Forgas, J. P. (Ed.). (1981). *Social cognition: Perspectives on everyday understanding.* London: Academic Press.

Foucault, M. (1980). *Power/knowledge: Selected interviews and other writings, 1972–1977.* New York: Pantheon.

Fox, C. L. (1989). Peer acceptance of learning disabled children in the regular classroom. *Exceptional Children, 56*, 50–59.

Freire, P. (1985). *The politics of education: Culture, power, and liberation*. South Hadley, MA: Bergin & Garvey.

Frieze, I., & Snyder, H. (1980). Children's beliefs about the causes of success and failure in school settings. *Journal of Educational Psychology, 76*, 186–196.

Fuchs, E. (1973). How teachers learn to help children fail. In N. Keddie (Ed.), *The myth of cultural deprivation* (pp. 75–85). London: Penguin.

Furnham, A., & Gunter, B. (1989). *The anatomy of adolescence: Young people's social attitudes in Britain*. London: Routledge.

Gamoran, A. (1987). The stratification of high school learning opportunities. *Sociology of Education, 60*, 135–155.

Gardner, H. (1983). *Frames of mind: The theory of multiple intelligences*. New York: Basic Books.

Gardner, H. (1987). Beyond the IQ: Education and human development. Developing the spectrum of human intelligences. *Harvard Educational Review, 57*, 187–193.

Gartner, A., & Lipsky, D. K. (1987). Beyond special education: Toward a quality system for all students. *Harvard Educational Review, 57*, 367–395.

Garvar-Pinhas, A., & Schmelkin, L. P. (1989). Administrators' and teachers' attitudes toward mainstreaming. *Remedial and Special Education, 10*, 38–43.

Geertz, C. (1973). *The interpretation of cultures*. New York: Basic Books.

Gerber, M. M. (1984). The Department of Education's Sixth Annual Report to Congress on PL 94-142: Is Congress getting the full story? *Exceptional Children, 51*, 209–224.

Gerber, M. M., & Levine-Donnerstein, D. (1989). Educating all children: Ten years later. *Exceptional Children, 56*, 17–27.

Giroux, H. A. (1983). *Theory and resistance in education: A pedagogy for the opposition*. South Hadley, MA: Bergin & Garvey.

Giroux, H. (1984). Marxism and schooling: The limits of radical discourse. *Educational Theory, 34*, 113–135.

Giroux, H. A. (1986). Radical pedagogy and the politics of student voice. *Interchange, 17*, 48–69.

Giroux, H. A. (1992). Educational leadership and the crisis of democratic government. *Educational Researcher, 21*, 4–11.

Gladstone, W. E. (1990, October). *The future: Juvenile justice, education, and mental health services for youth*. Keynote Address at the National Adolescent Conference, Miami, FL.

Glaser, B., & Strauss, A. (1965). *Awareness of dying: A study of social interaction*. Chicago: Aldine.

Glaser, B. G., & Strauss, A. L. (1967). *The discovery of grounded theory: Strategies for qualitative research*. Chicago: Aldine.

Goffman, E. (1969). *Where the action is*. London: Penguin.

Goldstein, A. (1987, September 25). Teaching prosocial skills to antisocial youth. Presentation sponsored by the Indiana University Psychology Department, Bloomington, IN.

Good, T. L., & Brophy, J. E. (1991). *Looking in classrooms*. New York: Harper & Row.

Good, T. L., Slavings, R. L., Harel, K. H., & Emerson, H. (1987). Student passivity: A study of question asking in K–12 classrooms. *Sociology of Education, 60,* 181–199.

Goodlad, J. I. (1983). *A place called school*. New York: McGraw-Hill.

Goodlad, J., & Oakes, J. (1988). We must offer equal access to knowledge. *Educational Leadership, 45,* 16–22.

Goodman, J. (1988). The political tactics and teaching strategies of reflective, active preservice teachers. *Elementary School Journal, 89,* 23–41.

Goodnow, J., Knight, R., & Cashmore, J. (1986). Adult social cognitions: Implications of parents' ideas for approaches to development. In M. Perlmutter (Ed.), *Cognitive perspectives on children's social and behavioral development* (pp. 287–384). Hillsdale, NJ: Erlbaum.

Gordon, N. J. (1981). Social cognition. In F. H. Farley & & N. J. Gordon (Eds.), *Psychology and education: The state of the union* (pp. 29–56). Berkeley, CA: McCutchan.

Gottfredson, L. S. (1981). Circumscription and compromise: A developmental theory of occupational aspirations. *Journal of Counseling Psychology, 28,* 545–579.

Gramsci, A. (1971). *Selections from the prison notebooks* (Q. Hoare & G. N. Smith, Eds.). New York: International Publishers.

Granovetter, M. (1986). The micro-structure of school desegregation. In J. Prager, D. Longshore, & M. Seeman (Eds.), *School desegregation research: New directions in situational analysis* (pp. 81–110). New York: Plenum.

Grant, C. A., & Sleeter, C. E. (1988). Race, class, and gender and abandoned dreams. *Teachers College Record, 90,* 19–40.

Greer, J. V. (1989). Another perspective and some immoderate proposals on "teacher empowerment." *Exceptional Children, 55,* 294–297.

Gronlund, N. E. (1979). *Sociometry in the classroom*. New York: Harper & Row.

Guttman, J. (1982). Pupils', teachers', and parents' causal attributions for problem behavior in school. *Journal of Educational Research, 76,* 14–21.

Habermas, J. (1984). *The theory of communicative action: Reason and the rationalization of society* (Vol. 1). Boston: Beacon.

Hahn, A. (1987). Reaching out to America's dropouts: What to do? *Phi Delta Kappan, 69,* 256–263.

Hall, S., & Jefferson, T. (1976). *Resistance through rituals: Youth subcultures in postwar Britain*. London: Hutchison University Library.

Hallinan, M. T., & Sorensen, A. B. (1985). Ability grouping and student friendships. *American Educational Research Journal, 22,* 485–499.

Harkness, S., & Super, C. M. (1985). Child-environment interactions in the socialization of affect. In M. Lewis & C. Saarni (Eds.), *The socialization of emotions* (pp. 21–53). New York: Plenum.

Harrison, B., Tilley, C., & Bluestone, B. (1986). *The great U-turn*. Washington, DC: Congressional Joint Economic Committee.

Hartup, W. (1979). The social worlds of childhood. *American Psychologist, 34,* 944–950.

Havighurst, R. (1966). *Education in metropolitan areas*. Boston: Allyn & Bacon.

Heavey, C. L., Adelman, H. S., Nelson, P., & Smith, D. C. (1989). Learning problems, anger, perceived control, and misbehavior. *Journal of Learning Disabilities, 22*, 46–50.

Hebdige, D. (1979). *Subculture: The meaning of style*. London: Methuen.

Henderson, R. W. (1981). Home environment and intellectual performance. In R. W. Henderson (Ed.), *Parent–child interaction* (pp. 3–29). New York: Academic Press.

Hess, R. D. (1981). Approaches to the measurement and interpretation of parent–child interaction. In R. W. Henderson (Ed.), *Parent–child interaction* (pp. 207–230). New York: Academic Press.

Hess, R., & Shipman, V. (1973). Early experience and the socialization of cognitive modes in children. *Child Development, 36*, 869–886.

Hodge, R., & Kress, G. (1988). *Social semiotics*. Ithaca, NY: Cornell University Press.

Hoelter, J. W. (1982). Segregation and rationality in black status aspiration processes. *Sociology of Education, 55*, 31–39.

Holland, D. C., & Eisenhart, M. A. (1988). Women's ways of going to school: Cultural reproduction of women's identities as workers. In L. Weis (Ed.), *Class, race, and gender in American education* (pp. 266–301). Albany: State University of New York Press.

Hollingshead, A. B. (1961). *Elmtown's youth*. New York: Science Editions.

Hollingshead, A. B. (1975). *Elmtown's youth and Elmtown revisited*. New York: Wiley.

Howe, H. (1988). America's forgotten half: The plight of non-college youth. *Harvard Graduate School of Education Bulletin, 32*, 13–16.

Hutson, H. M. (1978). *Who controls the curriculum in the local community? A case study of community power and curriculum decision-making*. Doctoral Dissertation, School of Education, Indiana University, Bloomington.

Ide, J. K., Parkerson, J., Haertel, G. D., & Walberg, H. J. (1981). Peer group influence on educational outcomes: A qualitative synthesis. *Journal of Educational Psychology, 73*, 472–484.

Jackman, M. R., & Jackman, R. W. (1983). *Class awareness in the United States*. Berkeley: University of California Press.

Jackson, B., & Marsden, D. (1986). *Education and the working class*. London: Ark.

Jeffrey, J. R. (1978). *Education for children of the poor: A study of the origins and implementation of the ESEA of 1965*. Columbus: Ohio State University Press.

Jencks, C. (1972). *Inequality: A reassessment of the effect of family and schooling in America*. New York: Harper & Row.

Jenkins, R. (1983). *Lads, citizens, and ordinary kids*. London: Routledge & Kegan Paul.

Johnson, D., & Ransom, E. (1980). Parents' perceptions of secondary schools. In M. Craft, J. Raynor, & L. Cohen (Eds.), *Linking home and school: A new review* (pp. 177–189). London: Harper & Row.

Jones, J. D., Erickson, E. L., & Crowell, R. (1972). Increasing the gap between whites and blacks: Tracking as a contributory source. *Education and Urban Society, 4*, 339–349.

Kagan, D. M. (1990). Ways of evaluating teacher cognition: Inferences concerning the Goldilocks Principle. *Review of Educational Research, 60*, 419–469.

Kandel, D. B. (1978). Similarity in real life adolescent friendship pairs. *Journal of Personality and Social Psychology, 36,* 306–312.

Katz, P. A. (1983). Developmental foundations of gender and racial attitudes. In R. L. Leahy (Ed.), *The child's construction of social inequality* (pp. 41–78). New York: Academic Press.

Keddie, N. (1971). Classroom knowledge. In M. F. D. Young (Ed.), *Knowledge and control* (pp. 133–150). New York: Collier-Macmillan.

Kerckhoff, A. C. (1976). The status attainment process: Socialization or allocation? *Social Forces, 55,* 368–381.

Kickbusch, K. W., & Everhart, R. B. (1985). Curriculum, practical ideology, and class contradiction. *Curriculum Inquiry, 15,* 281–317.

Kluegel, J. R., & Smith, E. R. (1986). *Beliefs about inequality: Americans' views of what is and what ought to be.* New York: Aldine de Gruyter.

Kohn, M. L. (1977). *Reassessment, 1977, class and conformity: A study of values* (2nd ed.). Chicago: University of Chicago Press.

Kohn, M. L. (1983). On the transmission of values in the family: A preliminary formulation. *Research in Sociology of Education and Socialization, 4,* 1–12.

Kohn, M. L., & Schooler, C. (1983). *Class, stratification and psychological functioning: An inquiry into the impact of social stratification.* Norwood, NJ: Ablex.

Kornblum, W. (1984). Lumping the poor: What is the underclass? *Dissent, 31,* 295–302.

Kugelmass, J. S. (1987). *Behavior, bias, and handicaps.* New Brunswick, NJ: Transaction Books.

Kumar, K. (1989). *Social character of learning.* New Delhi, India: Sage.

Laosa, L. M. (1982). School, occupation, culture, and family: The impact of parental schooling on the parent–child relationship. *Journal of Educational Psychology, 74,* 791–827.

Lareau, A. (1987). Social class differences in family–school relationships: The importance of cultural capital. *Sociology of Education, 60,* 73–85.

Lather, P. (1986). Research as praxis. *Harvard Educational Review, 46,* 257–277.

Lather, P. (1992). Critical frames in educational research: Feminist and poststructural perspectives. *Theory into Practice, 31,* 1–13.

Leahy, R. L. (1981). The development of the conception of economic inequality: Discriptions and comparisons of rich and poor people. *Child Development, 52,* 523–532.

Leahy, R. L. (1983). The development of the conception of social class. In R. L. Leahy (Ed.), *The child's construction of social inequality* (pp. 79–107). New York: Academic Press.

LeCompte, M. (1978). Learning to work: The hidden curriculum of the classroom. *Anthropology and Education Quarterly, 9,* 22–37.

Lesko, N. (1988). *Symbolizing society: Stories, rites and structure in a Catholic high school.* New York: Falmer.

Levine, D. U., & Havighurst, R. J. (1977). *Concentrations of poverty and reading achievement in five big cities.* Kansas City, MO: Center for the Study of Metropolitan Problems in Education.

Levine, D. U., & Havighurst, R. J. (1988). *Society and education*. Boston: Allyn & Bacon.

Levine, D. U., Kukuk, C., & Meyer, J. K. (1979). In H. J. Walberg (Ed.), *Educational environments and effects* (pp. 331–352). Berkeley, CA: McCutchan.

Lightfoot, S. L. (1981). Toward conflict and resolution: Relationships between families and schools. *Theory into Practice, 20*, 97–104.

Lightfoot, S. L. (1983). *The good high school: Portraits of character and culture*. New York: Basic Books.

Lightfoot, S. L. (1987). On excellence and goodness. *Harvard Educational Review, 57*, 202–205.

Lindsey, J. D., Daniels, V. I., & Rutledge, D. D. (1986). The learning disabilities and juvenile delinquency link: A major concern for professionals. *The High School Journal, 69*, 126–131.

Livingstone, D. (1983). *Class ideologies and educational futures*. Sussex, UK: Falmer.

Maccoby, E. E. (1986). Social groupings in childhood: Their relationship to prosocial and antisocial behavior in boys and girls. In D. Olweus, J. Block, & M. Radke-Yarrow (Eds.), *Development of antisocial and prosocial behavior: Research, theories, and issues* (pp. 263–284). New York: Academic Press.

Maccoby, E. E., & Martin, J. A. (1983). Socialization in the context of the family: Parent–child interaction. In E. M. Hetherington (Ed.), *Socialization, personality, and social development* (pp. 109–137). New York: Wiley.

MacLeod, J. (1987). *Ain't no makin' it: Leveled aspirations in a low-income neighborhood*. Boulder, CO: Westview.

Mare, R. D. (1981). Change and stability in educational stratification. *American Sociology Review, 46*, 72–87.

Marotto, R. A. (1986). "Posin' to be chosen": An ethnographic study of inschool truancy. In D. M. Fetterman & M. A. Pitman (Eds.), *Educational evaluation: Ethnography in theory, practice, and politics* (pp. 193–211). Beverly Hills: Sage.

Marshall, H. H., & Weinstein, R. S. (1986). Classroom context of student-perceived differential teacher treatment. *Journal of Educational Psychology, 78*, 441–453.

McDill, E. L., Natriello, G., & Pallas, A. M. (1986). A population at risk: Potential consequences of tougher school standards for school dropouts. *American Journal of Education, 94*, 135–181.

McLaren, P. (1986). *Schooling as a ritual performance: Towards a political economy of educational symbols and gestures*. London: Routledge & Kegan Paul.

McLaren, P. L. (1987). On ideology and education: Critical pedagogy and the politics of empowerment. *Social Text, 7*, 153–186.

McLaren, P. (1989). [Review of Nancy Lesko's "Symbolizing society: Stories, rites, and structure in a Catholic high school"]. *Anthropology and Education, 20*, 51–56.

McNamara, D. (1990). Research on teachers' thinking: Its contribution to educating student teachers to think critically. *Journal of Education for Teaching, 16*, 147–160.

McNeil, L. M. (1987). *Contradictions of control: School structure and school knowledge*. New York: Routledge & Kegan Paul.

Mehan, H. (1979). *Learning lessons: Social organization in the classroom*. Cambridge, MA: Harvard University Press.

Mehan, H., Hertweck, A., & Meihls, J. L. (1986). *Handicapping the handicapped: Decision making in students' educational careers*. Stanford, CA: Stanford University Press.

Metz, M. H. (1978). *Classrooms and corridors: The crisis of authority in desegregated secondary schools*. Berkeley: University of California Press.

Mickelson, R. A. (1990). The attitude achievement paradox among black adolescents. *Sociology of Education, 63*, 44–61.

Mitman, A. L., & Lash, A. A. (1988). Students' perceptions of their academic standing and classroom behavior. *The Elementary School Journal, 89*, 55–68.

Moran, M. R. (1984). Excellence at the cost of instructional equity: The potential impact of recommended reforms on low-achieving students. *Focus on Exceptional Children, 16*, 1–12.

Morgan, W. R., Alwin, D. F., & Griffin, L. J. (1979). Social origins, parental values, and the transmission of inequality. *American Journal of Sociology, 85*, 156–166.

Morine-Dershimer, G. (1989). Preservice teachers' conceptions of content and pedagogy: Measuring growth in reflective, pedagogical decision-making. *Journal of Teacher Education, 40*, 46–52.

Moscovici, S., & Paicheler, G. (1978). Social comparison and social recognition: Two complementary processes of identification. In H. Tajfel (Ed.), *Differentiation between social groups* (pp. 251–266). London: Academic Press.

Newmann, F. M. (1981). Reducing student alienation in high schools: Implications of theory. *Harvard Educational Review, 51*, 546–564.

Newmann, F. M., & Kelly, T. E. (1985). In R. Gross & B. Gross (Eds.), *The great school debates* (pp. 222–228). New York: Simon & Schuster.

Newson, J., Newson, E., & Barnes, P. (1977). *Perspectives on school at seven years old*. London: George Allen & Unwin.

Nicholls, J. G. (1989). *The competitive ethos and democratic education*. Cambridge, MA: Harvard University Press.

Nicholls, J. G., Patashnick, M., & Nolen, S. B. (1985). Adolescents' theories of education. *Journal of Educational Psychology, 77*, 683–692.

Nicholls, J. G., & Thorkildsen, T. A. (1989). Intellectual conventions versus matters of substance: Elementary school students as curriculum theorists. *American Educational Research Journal, 26*, 533–544.

Oakes, J. (1985). *Keeping track: How schools structure inequality*. New Haven, CT: Yale University Press.

Oakes, J. (1988). Tracking: Can schools take a different route? *National Education Association, 6*, 41–47.

Ogbu, J. U. (1978). *Minority education and caste: The American system in cross-cultural perspective*. New York: Academic Press.

Ogbu, J. U. (1981). Origins of human competence: A cultural–ecological perspective. *Child Development, 52*, 413–429.

Ogbu, J. U. (1986). Structural constraints in school desegregation. In J. Prager, D. Longshore, & M. Seeman (Eds.), *School desegregation research: New directions in situational analysis* (pp. 21–45). New York: Academic Press.

Olneck, M. R., & Bills, D. B. (1980). What makes Sammy run? An empirical assessment of the Bowles–Gintis correspondence principle. *American Journal of Education, 89,* 27–61.

Olson, C. P. (1983). Inequality remade: The theory of correspondence and the context of French immersion in northern Ontario. *Journal of Education, 165,* 75–98.

Ornstein, A. C. (1978). *Education and social inquiry.* Itasca, IL: Peacock.

Packer, G. (1992). Class interest, liberal style: A social conflict in Massachusetts. *Dissent, 39,* 51–56.

Page, R. N. (1991). *Lower-track classrooms: A curricular and cultural perspective.* New York: Teachers College Press.

Palonsky, S. B. (1987). Political socialization in elementary schools. *The Elementary School Journal, 87,* 493–505.

Parker, I., Gottlieb, J., Gottlieb, B. W., Davis, S., & Kunzweiller, C. (1989). Teacher behavior toward low achievers, average achievers, and mainstreamed minority group learning disabled students. *Learning Disabilities Research, 4,* 101–106.

Payne, C. (1989). Urban teachers and dropout-prone students: The uneasy partners. In L. Weis, E. Farrar, & H. G. Petrie (Eds.), *Dropping out: Issues, dilemmas, and solutions* (pp. 113–128). Albany: State University of New York Press.

Perlmutter, M. (Ed.). (1986). *Cognitive perspective on children's social and behavioral development.* Hillsdale, NJ: Erlbaum.

Perrin, J. E. (1981, August). *Reciprocity of aggression in youthful offenders.* Paper presented at the annual meeting of the American Psychological Association, Los Angeles.

Pink, W. T. (1982). School effects, academic performance, and school crime. *Urban Education, 17,* 51–72.

Poplin, M. S. (1988). The reductionistic fallacy in learning disabilities: Replicating the past by reducing the present. *Journal of Learning Disabilities, 21,* 389–400.

Prawat, R. S., Lanier, P. E., Byers, J. L., & Anderson, A. L. H. (1983). Attitudinal differences between students in general mathematics and algebra classes. *Journal of Educational Research, 76,* 215–220.

Proctor, C. P. (1984). Teacher expectations: A model for school improvement. *The Elementary School Journal, 84,* 469–481.

Pugach, M., & Sapon-Shevin, M. (1987). New agendas for special education policy: What the national reports haven't said. *Exceptional Children, 53,* 295–299.

Ramsay, P. D. K. (1985). Social class and school knowledge: A rejoinder to Jean Anyon. *Curriculum Inquiry, 15,* 215–222.

Rawls, J. (1972). *A theory of justice.* Cambridge, MA: Harvard University Press.

Ray, C. A., & Mickelson, R. A. (1990). Corporate leaders, resistant youth, and school reform in Sunbelt city: The political economy of education. *Social Problems, 37,* 178–190.

Reitman, S. W. (1981). *Education, society, and change.* Boston: Allyn & Bacon.

Reynolds, M. C. (1988). A reaction to the JLD special series on the Regular Education Initiative. *Journal of Learning Disabilities, 21,* 352–356.

Rist, R. C. (1970). Student social class and teacher expectations: The self-fulfilling prophecy in ghetto education. *Harvard Educational Review, 40,* 411–449.

Rist, R. (1978). *The invisible children.* Cambridge, MA: Harvard University Press.

Rist, R., & Harrell, J. (1982). Labeling and the learning disabled child: The social ecology of educational practice. *American Journal of Orthopsychiatry*, 52, 146–160.

Rodman, H., & Voydanoff, P. (1978). Social class and parents' range of aspirations for their children. *Social Problems*, 25, 333–344.

Rohrkemper, M. M. (1984). The influence of teacher socialization style on students social cognition and reported interpersonal classroom behavior. *The Elementary School Journal*, 85, 244–275.

Rosenberg, L. A., Harris, J. C., & Reifler, J. P. (1988). Similarities and differences between parents' and teachers' observations of the behavior of children with learning problems. *Journal of Learning Disabilities*, 21, 189–193.

Rosenholtz, S. J., & Simpson, C. (1984). Classroom organization and student stratification. *The Elementary School Journal*, 85, 21–37.

Rosenthal, R., & Jacobson, L. (1968). *Pygmalion in the classroom: Teacher expectation and pupils' intellectual development*. New York: Holt, Rinehart, & Winston.

Rowan, B., & Miracle, A. W. (1983). Systems of ability grouping and the stratification of achievement in elementary schools. *Sociology of Education*, 56, 133–144.

Rumberger, R. W. (1987). High school dropouts: A review of issues and evidence. *Review of Educational Research*, 57, 101–121.

Rutter, M. (1983). School effects on pupil progress: Research findings and policy implications. *Child Development*, 54, 1–29.

Sabornie, E. J., Marshall, K. J., & Ellis, E. S. (1990). Restructuring of mainstream sociometry with learning disabled and nonhandicapped students. *Exceptional Children*, 56, 314–323.

Sachs, J. J., Iliff, V. W., & Donnelly, R. F. (1987). Oh, O.K., I'm LD! *Journal of Learning Disabilities*, 20, 92–93.

Safran, S. P., & Safran, J. S. (1985). Classroom context and teachers' perceptions of problem behaviors. *Journal of Educational Psychology*, 77, 20–28.

St. John, N. (1972). Mothers and children: Congruence and optimism of school-related attitudes. *Journal of Marriage and the Family*, 34, 422–430.

Salvia, J., & Munson, S. (1985). Attitudes of teachers in regular education toward mainstreaming mildly handicapped students. In C. J. Meisel (Ed.), *Mainstreaming handicapped children: Outcomes, controversies, and new directions* (pp. 111–128). Hillsdale, NJ: Erlbaum.

Saucier, J. F., & Ambert, A. M. (1982). Parental marital status and adolescents' optimism about their future. *Journal of Youth and Adolescence*, 11, 345–354.

Scheck, D. C., & Emerick, R. (1976). The young male adolescent's perception of early child rearing behavior: The differential effects of socioeconomic status and family size. *Sociometry*, 39, 39–52.

Schmuck, P., & Schmuck, R. (1990). Democratic participation in small-town schools. *Educational Researcher*, 19, 14–19.

Schostak, J. F. (1986). *Schooling the violent imagination*. London: Routledge & Kegan Paul.

Schunk, D. H. (1989). Self-efficacy and cognitive achievement: Implications for students with learning problems. *Journal of Learning Disabilities*, 22, 14–22.

Schwartz, G. (1987). *Beyond conformity or rebellion: Youth and authority in America*. Chicago: University of Chicago Press.

Scott-Jones, D. (1984). Family influences on cognitive development and school achievement. In E. W. Gordon (Ed.), *Review of research in education, 11* (pp. 259–304). Washington, DC: American Educational Research Association.

Scrupski, A. (1975). The social system of the school. In N. K. Shimahara & A. Scrupski (Eds.), *Social forces and schooling: An anthropological and sociological perspective* (pp. 114–186). New York: McKay.

Seeman, M. (1959). On the meaning of alienation. *American Sociological Review, 24,* 783–791.

Seginer, R. (1983). Parents' educational expectations and children's academic achievements: A literature review. *Merrill-Palmer Quarterly, 29,* 1–23.

Sexton, P. C. (1961). *Education and income: Inequalities in our public schools.* New York: Viking.

Shapiro, H. S. (1983). Class, ideology, and the basic skills movement: A study in the sociology of educational reform. *Interchange, 14,* 14–24.

Shimahara, N. K. (1983). Polarized socialization in an urban high school. *Anthropology and Education Quarterly, 14,* 109–130.

Shor, I., & Freire, P. (1987). *A pedagogy for liberation: Dialogues on transforming education.* South Hadley, MA: Bergin & Garvey.

Sieber, R. T. (1982). The politics of middle-class success in an inner-city public school. *Journal of Education, 164,* 30–47.

Simmons, R. G., & Rosenberg, M. (1971). Functions of children's perceptions of the stratification system. *American Sociological Review, 36,* 235–249.

Sinclair, R., & Ghory, W. (1987). *Reaching marginal students: A primary concern for school renewal.* Berkeley: McCutchan.

Skrtic, T. (1988). The crisis in special education knowledge. In E. Meyen & T. Skrtic (Eds.), *Exceptional children and and youth: An introduction* (pp. 415–488). Denver, CO: Love.

Sleeter, C. E. (1986). Learning disabilities: The social construction of a special education category. *Exceptional Children, 53,* 46–64.

Sleeter, C. (1987). Literacy, definitions of learning diabilities, and social control. In B. M. Franklin (Ed.), *Learning disability: Dissenting essays* (pp. 67–87). London: Falmer.

Smith, E. R. (1984). Model of social inference processes. *Psychological Review, 9,* 392–413.

Solomon, R. P. (1988). Black cultural forms in schools: A cross national comparison. In L. Weis (Ed.), *Class, race, and gender in American education* (pp. 249–265). Albany: State University of New York Press.

Sroufe, L. A., & Fleeson, J. (1986). Attachment and the construction of relationships. In W. W. Hartup & Z. Rubin (Eds.), *Relationships and development* (pp. 51–71). Hillsdale, NJ: Erlbaum.

Stainback, W., & Stainback, S. (1984). A rationale for the merger of special and regular education. *Exceptional Children, 51,* 102–111.

Steinberg, L. (1987). Single parents, stepparents, and the susceptibility of adolescents to antisocial peer pressure. *Child Development, 58,* 269–275.

Sternberg, R. (1984). What should intelligence test? Implications of a triarchic theory of intelligence for intelligence testing. *Educational Researcher, 13,* 5–15.

Sternberg, R. J., Conway, B. E., Ketron, J. L., & Bernstein, M. (1981). People's conceptions of intelligence. *Journal of Personality and Social Psychology, 41*, 37–55.

Stipek, D. J., Lamb, M. E., & Zigler, E. F. (1981). OPTI: A measure of children's optimism. *Educational and Psychological Motivation, 41*, 131–143.

Strahan, D. (1988). Life on the margins: How academically at-risk early adolescents view themselves and school. *Journal of Early Adolescence, 8*, 373–390.

Strahan, D. (1989). Disconnected and disruptive students: Who they are, why they behave as they do, and what we can do about it. *The Middle School Journal, 21*, 1–5.

Strauss, C., Frame, C., & Forehand, R. (1987). Psychosocial impairment associated with anxiety in children. *Journal of Clinical Child Psychology, 16*, 235–239.

Switzky, H. N., & Schultz, G. F. (1988). Intrinsic motivation and learning performance: Implications for individual educational programming for learners with mild handicaps. *Remedial and Special Education, 9*, 7–14.

Tajfel, H. (1982). Social psychology of intergroup relations. *Annual Review of Psychology, 33*, 1–39.

Thiessen, D. (1987). Curriculum as experienced alternative world views from two students with learning disabilities. In B. M. Franklin (Ed.), *Learning disability: Dissenting essays* (pp. 88–117). London: Falmer.

Thompson, E. P. (1978). Eighteenth-century English society: Class struggle without class. *Social History, 3*, 133–165.

Thompson, J. B. (1987). Language and ideology: A framework for analysis. *The Sociological Review, 35*, 517–536.

Thorne, B. (1986). Girls and boys together; but mostly apart: Gender arrangements in elementary schools. In W. W. Hartup & Z. Rubin (Eds.), *Relationships and development* (pp. 145–159). Hillsdale, NJ: Erlbaum.

Tinney, J. S. (1983). Interconnections. *Interracial Books for Children, 14*, 4–6.

Tochon, F. V. (1990). Heuristic schemata as tools for epistemic analysis of teachers' thinking. *Teaching and Teacher Education, 6*, 183–196.

Toles, T., Schulz, E. M., & Rice, W. K., Jr. (1986). A study of variation in dropout rates attributable to effects of high schools. *Metropolitan Education, 2*, 30–38.

Tomlinson, S. (1982). *A sociology of special education.* London: Routledge & Kegan Paul.

Tyack, D. B. (1974). *The one best system.* Cambridge, MA: Harvard University Press.

United States Bureau of the Census. (1992). *Census of population of Indiana: General population characteristics.* Table 6. Series 1990 CP-1-16. Washington, DC: Gov. Pub.

Vaneck, H. J., & Ames, N. L. (1980). *Who benefits from federal education dollars? The development of ESEA Title I allocation policy.* Cambridge, MA: Abt.

Vanfossen, B. E., Jones, J. D., & Spade, J. Z. (1987). Curriculum tracking and status maintenance. *Sociology of Education, 60*, 104–122.

Varenne, H. (1983). *American school language: Culturally patterned conflicts in a suburban high school.* New York: Irvington.

Varenne, H. (1986). *Symbolizing America.* Lincoln: University of Nebraska Press.

Veldman, D. J., & Sanford, J. P. (1984). The influence of class ability level on student achievement and classroom behavior. *American Educational Research Journal, 21*, 629–644.

Vernberg, E. M., & Medway, F. J. (1981). Teacher and parent causal perceptions of school problems. *American Educational Research Journal, 18,* 29–37.

Wagner, R. K., & Sternberg, R. J. (1984). Alternative conceptions of intelligence and their implications for education. *Review of Educational Research, 54,* 179–223.

Walker, S., & Barton, L. (Eds.). (1983). *Gender, class, and education.* Sussex, UK: Falmer.

Wang, M. C. (1987). Toward achieving excellence for all students: Program design and student outcomes. *Remedial and Special Education, 8,* 25–34.

Wang, M. C., Reynolds, M. C., & Walberg, H. J. (1986). Rethinking special education. *Educational Leadership, 44,* 26–31.

Weiner, B. (1979). A theory of motivation for some classroom experiences. *Journal of Educational Psychology, 71,* 3–25.

Weinstein, R. S. (1983). Student perceptions of schooling. *The Elementary School Journal, 83,* 285–312.

Weis, L. (1988). High school girls in a de-industrializing economy. In L. Weis (Ed.), *Class, race, and gender in American education* (pp. 183–208). Albany: State University of New York Press.

Weis, L. (1990). *Working class without work: High school students in a de-industrializing economy.* New York: Routledge.

Weis, L., Farrar, E., & Petrie, H. G. (1989). *Dropouts from school: Issues, dilemmas, & solutions.* Albany: State University of New York Press.

Wexler, P. (1988). Symbolic economy of identity and denial of labor: Studies in high school number 1. In L. Weis (Ed.), *Class, race, and gender in American education* (pp. 302–315). Albany: State University of New York Press.

Wexler, P. (1992). *Becoming somebody: Toward a social psychology of school.* London: Falmer.

Whitty, G. (1985). *Sociology and school knowledge: Curriculum theory, research, and politics.* London: Methuen.

Williams, R. (1982). *Problems in materialism and culture.* London: Verso Books.

Willis, P. (1977). *Learning to labor: How working class kids get working class jobs.* New York: Columbia University Press.

Wilson, A. B. (1967). Educational consequences of segregation in a California community. In U.S. Commission on Civil Rights, *Racial isolation in the public schools* (pp. 180–181). Washington, DC: U.S. Government Printing Office.

Wilson, W. J. (1987). *The truly disadvantaged: The inner-city, the underclass, and public policy.* Chicago: University of Chicago Press.

Winn, W., & Wilson, A. P. (1983). The affect and effect of ability grouping. *Contemporary Education, 54,* 119–125.

Witt, J. C., Moe, G., Gutkin, T. B., & Andrews, L. (1984). The effect of saying the same thing in different ways: The problem of language and jargon in school-based consultation. *Journal of School Psychology, 22,* 361–367.

Wolman, C., Bruininks, R., & Thurlow, M. L. (1989). Dropouts and dropout programs: Implications for special education. *Remedial Education and Special Education, 10,* 6–20.

Wyche, L. G., Sr. (1989). The tenth annual report to Congress: Taking a significant step in the right direction. *Exceptional Children, 56,* 14–16.

Wynne, E. A., & Walberg, H. J. (1985). The complementary goals of character development and academic excellence. *Education Leadership, 43,* 15–18.

Young, R. (1990). *A critical theory of education: Habermas and our children's future.* New York: Teachers College Press.

Ysseldyke, J. E., Algozzine, B., & Richey, L. (1982). Judgment under uncertainty: How many children are handicapped? *Exceptional Children, 48,* 531–534.

Yussen, S. R., & Kane, P. T. (1983). Children's ideas about intellectual ability. In R. L. Leahy (Ed.), *The child's construction of social inequality* (pp. 109–133). New York: Academic Press.

Zahn-Waxler, C., Radke-Yarrow, M., & King, R. A. (1979). Child rearing and children's prosocial initiations towards victims of distress. *Child Development, 50,* 319–330.

Zeichner, K. (1983). Alternative paradigms of teacher education. *Journal of Teacher Education, 34,* 3–9.

Zill, N., & Schoenborn, C. A. (1990). Developmental, learning, and emotional problems: Health of our nation's children, United States, 1988. *Advance Data, 190,* 1–18.

Index

Ability grouping. *See* Tracking
Achievement behavior, 168–189
  adult support for postschool plans, 185–186
  aspirations and expectations for college, 175–176
  aspirations and expectations for high school completion, 170–175
  dominant-culture messages and, 197–198
  equal opportunity and, 180–182
  friendship and, 165
  perceptions of requirements for college attendance, 176–178
  personal chances to get ahead, 182–185
  post-high school plans, 178–180
Adams, B. D., 125
Adelman, H. S., 129
African-American students
  affect toward school, 71
  college attendance and, 177
  friendship and, 165–166
  perceptions of school, 6
Aggression, 128–129
  image of low-income students and, 132–134, 145
  in intergroup relations, 57–59
  origins of, 128–129
  types and causes of, 129–132
  See also Conduct problems
Alden, L., 157
Alexander, P. A., 7
Algozzine, B., 85
Alpert, G., 69
Alvarado, M., 5
Alwin, D. F., 147
Amato, J., 70
Ambert, A. M., 154
Ames, N. L., 25
Anderson, A. L. H., 69
Andrews, L., 191
Anger, 128–129
  image of low-income students and, 132–134, 145

  of low-income students, 132–134, 144–146, 193, 196
Anyon, J., 2, 16, 17, 27, 40, 104, 109, 190
Apple, M. W., 5, 42, 102, 109
Arnold, J., 44, 128
Aronowitz, S., 1, 4, 102
Attendance problems, 134–135
Attitudinal attributes, of students, 110–111

Bakhtin, M., 4, 7, 67
Balch, R. W., 70, 109, 129
Barnes, P., 167
Baron, S. W., 6
Barton, L., 2
Bastian, A., 11, 27, 168, 202
Bayer, A., 105
Beckerman, T., 41
Beckman, L. J., 11
Becoming Somebody (Wexler), 2
Beery, R. G., 169
Bender, W. N., 103
Berger, J., 126
Berman, E. H., 103
Berndt, T. J., 162, 163
Bernstein, M., 109
Beyer, L., 5
Bichard, S. L., 157
Bills, D. B., 169
Birksted, I. K., 109
Block, J., 145
Bluestone, B., 168
Blumenfeld, P. C., 109
Bourdieu, P., 4, 5, 40, 43, 64, 66, 104, 126, 127, 167, 194
Bowers, C. A., 8
Bowles, S., 1–2, 43, 200
Brady, P. M., 70, 109
Brantlinger, E. A., *xii*, 11, 15, 85, 106, 142, 154, 166, 167, 175
Brantlinger, P. M., 193
Breakwell, G., 42
Brookover, W. G., 109

Brophy, J. E., 3, 10
Bruininks, R., 85
Bugetal, D. B., 147, 167
Bukowski, W. M., 157, 163, 164
Bullough, R. V., Jr., 8, 10, 105
Burr, W. R., 174
Byers, J. L., 69

Cairns, B. D., 58
Cairns, R. B., 58
Calhoun, C. J., 69
Canada, 5
Carlberg, C. P., 104
Carlson, D., 1
Carnoy, M., 104
Carrier, J. G., 85, 145
Carter, J., 85
Casebolt, H., 125
Cashmore, E. E., 6, 69
Cashmore, J., 74, 147, 154
Castlebury, S., 44, 128
Cervantes, L., 128
Chapter I programs, 25, 80
Civil Rights Acts, 41
Clark, C. M., 10
Class conflict, 192–193
Cliques, 43–45, 52–56, 114
Cockburn, A., 154
Cognitive mapping, of social relationships,
  66
Cohen, A. K., 128
Cohen, D., 199
Coleman, J. S., 40–41, 157
College
  adult support for postschool plans, 185–186,
    187–188
  aspirations and expectations for, 175–176
  equal opportunity and, 180–182
  perceptions of requirements for attendance,
    176–178
  in post-high school plans, 178–180
Comer, J. P., 145
Conduct problems, 128–146
  angry image of low-income youth and, 132–
    134, 144–146
  attendance problems and, 134–135
  extent and nature of punishment, 137–141
  interpretations of, 135–137
  nature and extent of trouble-making, 129–
    132
  parental reactions to, 141–144, 153–154

Conflict
  with parents, 149, 153
  social class, in schools, 192–193
  with teachers, 131, 135–137, 172
Conflict theory, schools and, 1–2
Conklin, M. E., 169
Conway, B. E., 109
Cooper, H., 3, 10
Correspondence theory, 1–2, 5, 8–9, 45
Covington, M. V., 121, 169
Cox, D., 124
Critical consciousness, 197–198
Critical self-reflexivity, 8–9
Crowell, R., 82
Curriculum
  depoliticization of, 102–103
  student criticism of, 171

Dahrendorf, R., 51
Daily, A. R., 169
Dale, R., 1
Damon, W., 41
Daniels, V. I., 129
Davis, S., 103
deBettencourt, L. U., 85
Delinquency, 57–59, 128. *See also* Conduct
  problems
Diener, C. I., 194
Discipline. *See* Conduct problems; Punish-
  ment
Displacement theory, 58
Dodge, K., 3
Dominant groups, 48–51
Donnelly, R. F., 85
Douvan, E., 157
Dropouts, 69, 109, 128, 145, 169, 171–174.
  See also Conduct problems
Drummond, H., 145
Dunham, R., 69
Dupont, H., 85
Duran, B. J., 124
Dweck, C. S., 194

East, P. L., 163
Eckert, P., 5
Edelman, M. W., 150
Eder, D., 10, 43, 44, 63, 66, 82, 105, 109, 157
Edgar, E., 104
Edmonds, R., 41, 201
Educational attainment, of parents, 17, 154,
  167, 169

Ehrenreich, B., 150, 188
Eisenhart, M. A., 6
Ekstrom, R., 69
Elder, G. H., 154
Elementary and Secondary Education Act, 25, 80
Elias, M. J., 128, 129, 145
Ellis, E. S., 103
Embourgeoisement, 8
Emerick, R., 154
Emerson, H., 10
England, 5, 6, 42, 45, 70, 126
Enright, R. D., 35
Enright, W. F., 35
Equality of Educational Opportunity (Coleman et al.), 40–41
Equal opportunity, 40–41, 180–182
Erickson, E. L., 82
Erickson, F., 21
Esland, G., 1
Esquivel, G. B., 85
Ethnic identity
  of participants in study, 17
  perceptions of school and, 6–7
  See also African-American students; Race
Everhart, R. B., 101, 102, 104
Evertson, C. E., 105
Ewert, G. D., 1, 9
Expectations
  for college, 175–176
  family background and, 168–169
  for high school completion, 170–175
  post-high school plans, 178–180
Explicit knowledge, perceptions of school and, 7–8
Extracurricular activities, participation in, 124–125

Family, 147–157, 166–167
  aggressive behavior and, 128
  equal opportunity and, 180–182
  expectations and, 168–169
  financial status of, 50, 176–178, 180
  influence of, on school, 194
  intergenerational patterns of poverty, 183–184
  lifestyle of, 147–150
  living arrangements of, 18, 19
  parents as role models in, 149, 150–152
  parents' roles related to schooling, 154–157
  as reason for leaving high school, 172–173

student perception of, 147–150
student relationships with members of, 152–154
  See also Parents
Farber, P., 200
Farrar, E., 6
Faunce, W. A., 109, 126, 169
Fay, B., 1, 2, 5
Fenstermacher, G. D., 10
Ferguson, B., 5
Festinger, L., 66, 71, 116
Fine, M., 6–9, 69, 70, 145, 169, 171
Finn, J. D., 124
Fischer, M., 187
Fleeson, J., 157
Florio-Ruane, S., 10
Forehand, R., 145
Forgas, J. P., 66
Foucault, M., 5, 126
Fox, C. L., 103
Frame, C., 145
Freire, P., 103, 198, 199
Friends, 157–166, 167
  characteristics of, 158–162
  influence of, on educational outcomes, 103–104
  reasons for friendships, 159, 162–166
  student perceptions of attitudes toward school, 74–75
Frieze, I., 168
Fringe groups, in group classification, 52
Fruchter, N., 11, 168
Fuchs, E., 10
Furnham, A., 7, 70

Gamoran, A., 168
Gardner, H., 120
Gartner, A., 106, 109
Garvar-Pinhas, A., 103
Geertz, C., 2–3
Gender
  conduct problems and, 129, 130
  friendship and, 165
  intergroup relations and, 57–58
  of participants in study, 17
  perceptions of school and, 6–7
Gerber, M. M., 85, 109, 129
Ghory, W., 125
Gintis, H., 1–2, 43, 200
Giroux, H. A., 1, 8, 9, 67, 102, 127, 195, 200
Gittell, M., 11

Gjerde, P. F., 145
Gladstone, W. E., 168
Glaser, B., 19–20
Goerts, M., 69
Goffman, E., 55
Goldstein, A., 146
Good, T. L., 3, 10, 41, 109, 169, 194
Goodlad, J. I., 10, 27, 109, 145
Goodman, J., 10
Goodnow, J. J., 74, 147, 154
Gordon, N. J., 3
Gottfredson, L. S., 168, 169
Gottlieb, B. W., 103
Gottlieb, J., 103
Grades
    impact of, on self-concept of students, 114–
        117
    intelligence and, 120–121
Gramsci, A., 8, 42
Granovetter, M., 109
Grant, C. A., 7, 9
Greer, G., 11
Greer, J. V., 85
Griffin, L. J., 147
Gronlund, N. E., 41
Group classification
    dynamism of, 67
    group power and, 64–66
    group relations and, 55–59
    intergroup mobility and, 63–64
    intergroup perceptions and, 54–55
    intragroup divisions and, 62–63
    middle status in, 50–51
    origin and stability of groups, 53–54
    social class self-identification and, 37–38,
        42, 59–62
    special-interest groups in, 53, 61, 62
Group classifications, specific, 45–52
    dominant groups, 48–51
    fringe groups, 52
    nonlabelers, 45–46
    nonmember students, 51–52
    subordinate groups, 48–51
Group relations, 55–59
Gunter, B., 7, 70
Guskin, S. L., 106
Gutkin, T. B., 191
Guttman, J., 128

Habermas, J., 8
Haertel, G. D., 103

Hahn, A., 145
Hall, S., 1, 8
Hallinan, M. T., 43, 70, 105
Hamilton, U. L., 109
Handicapped students, 41. *See also* Special
    education
Hare, V. C., 7
Harel, K. H., 10
Harkness, S., 11, 154
Harrell, J., 70
Harris, B. E., 35
Harris, J. C., 10
Harrison, B., 168
Hartup, W., 3
Haskins, K., 11
Havighurst, R. J., 17, 23, 41
Heavey, C. L., 129
Hebdige, D., 6
Hegemony, 8
Henderson, R. W., 147, 154, 167
Hertweck, A., 106
Hess, L. E., 163
Hess, R. D., 11, 147, 154
Hidden curriculum, 69
High school
    expectations for completing, 170–175
    post-high school plans, 178–180
Hill, R., 174
Hodge, R., 6, 192
Hoelter, J. W., 169
Holland, D. C., 6
Hollingshead, A. B., 43–44
Holm, G., 200
Howe, H., 102
Hoza, B., 157
Humiliation, in school, 139, 193
Hutson, H. M., 25

Ianni, F. A., 69
Ide, J. K., 103
Identity formation. *See* Self-concept, of
    students
Iliff, V. W., 85
Images, of school, 75–77
Implicit knowledge, perceptions of school
    and, 7–8
Intelligence, 109
    of friends, 160
    importance of, 118, 123
    signs of, 117–122
    student perceptions of, 117–124

student self-assessment of, 122–123, 194–195

variations in, 118, 123–124

Intergroup conflict, 57–59, 131, 133

Intergroup mobility, 63–64

Intergroup perceptions, 54–55

Interview methodology, 15–21

  data analysis, 21

  interview procedures, 20

  participants, 15–19

  problems of, 190–192

Intragroup divisions, 62–63

Jackman, M. R., 42

Jackman, R. W., 42

Jackson, B., 6

Jacobson, L., 10

Jefferson, T., 1, 8

Jeffrey, J. R., 41

Jencks, C., 11, 24, 27, 41

Jenkins, R., 7, 9, 70, 104

Johnson, D., 167

Jones, J. D., 82, 105

Kagan, D. M., 10

Kandel, D. B., 162

Kane, P. T., 109

Katz, P. A., 66

Kavale, K., 104

Keddie, N., 69

Kelly, D. H., 70, 109, 129

Kelly, T. E., 27, 202

Kerckhoff, A. C., 169

Ketron, J. L., 109

Kickbusch, K. W., 102, 104

King, R. A., 158

Kluegel, J. R., 36, 41, 187

Knight, R., 147

Kohn, M. L., 2, 8, 11, 43, 142, 147, 154

Kornblum, W., 16, 188

Kress, G., 6, 192

Kugelmass, J. S., 85

Kukuk, C., 41

Kumar, K., 1

Kunzweiler, C., 103

Lamb, M. E., 187

Lanier, P. E., 69

Laosa, L. M., 147, 154, 168

Lareau, A., 75, 166

Lash, A. A., 109

Lather, P., 1, 9

Lazerson, M., 199

Leahy, R. L., 36, 158, 183

Learning disabilities, 86, 129

Learning to Labor (Willis), 5

LeCompte, M., 101

Leitenberg, H., 187

Lerner, R. M., 163

Lesko, N., 7, 45

Levin, H. M., 104

Levine, D. U., 23, 41

Levine-Donnerstein, D., 109, 129

Lightfoot, S. L., 11, 27, 40, 129, 145

Liker, J. K., 154

Lindsey, J. D., 129

Lipsky, D. K., 106, 109

Livingstone, D., 5–6, 8

Maccoby, E. E., 66, 147, 167

MacDonald, M., 1

MacLeod, J., 6, 9, 70, 71, 102, 171

Mainstreaming, 90–91, 103

Manheim, L. A., 35

Manni, J. L., 70

Mare, R. D., 154

Marotto, R. A., 109

Marsden, D., 6

Marshall, H. H., 70

Marshall, K. J., 103

Martin, J. A., 147, 167

McDill, E. L., 109, 169

McLaren, P. L., 5, 6, 8, 103, 200

McMahon, R. J., 157

McNamara, D., 10

McNeil, L. M., 109

Medway, F. J., 11, 129

Mehan, H., 82, 106

Meihls, J. L., 106

Meritocracies, schools as, 1, 199–202

Metz, M. H., 69, 70

Meyer, J. K., 41

Mickelson, R. A., 6–8, 107, 198–199

Miracle, A. W., 105

Mitman, A. L., 109

Moe, G., 191

Moral development, 79

Moran, M. R., 85

Morgan, W. R., 147, 167

Morine-Dershimer, G., 10

Moscovici, S., 41

Motivation
  for achievement behavior, 169
  problems with, 131–132
Munson, S., 10

Natriello, G., 109
Nelson, P., 129
Newcomb, A. F., 157
Newmann, F. M., 27, 129, 146, 201, 202
Newson, E., 167
Newson, J., 167
Nicholls, J. G., 4, 69
Nolen, S. B., 69
Nonlabelers, in group classification, 45–
  46
Nonmember students, in group classifi-
  cation, 51–52
Nye, F. E., 174

Oakes, J., 10, 27, 43, 70, 105, 109, 145, 194,
  200
Ogbu, J. U., 1, 2, 8, 101–102, 104, 109
Olneck, M. R., 169
Olson, C. P., 8, 107, 199, 200
Omelich, C. L., 121
Ornstein, A. C., 41

Packer, G., 8
Page, R. N., 82, 105
Paicheler, G., 41
Pallas, A. M., 109
Palonsky, S. B., 2
Parents
  attitudes toward children finishing school,
    174–175
  conflict with, 149, 153
  educational attainment of, 17, 154, 167, 169
  influence of, on schools, 25–26, 27–28
  occupational status of, 18, 169
  participation in schooling, 154–157, 166–
    167
  perceptions of schooling, 11
  reactions to conduct problems, 141–144,
    153–154
  as role models for children, 149, 150–152,
    175
  role of, related to schooling, 154–157, 166–
    167
  socialization by, 147
  student perceptions of attitudes toward
    school, 74–75, 186–187

support for postschool plans, 185–186, 187–
  188
See also Family
Parker, I., 103
Parkerson, J., 103
Passeron, J. C., 43, 104
Patashnick, M., 69
Patterson, A., 109
Payne, C., 3
Peers. See Friends
Perlmutter, M., 69
Perrin, J. E., 58
Personality
  of friends, 160–161
  of teachers, 99–100
Peterson, P. L., 10
Petrie, H. G., 6
Pink, W. T., 105, 129
Pintrich, P. R., 109
Piven, F. F., 150, 188
Pollack, J., 69
Poplin, M. S., 106
Post-high school plans, 178–180
Poverty
  social class self-identification and, 37–38
  student perceptions of, 35–37
Power, student perception of group, 64–66
Prawat, R. S., 69
Principals, school composition and, 28–29
Proctor, C. P., 10
Public Law 94-142, 41, 85, 156
Pugach, M., 106
Punishment, 129
  amount and types received, 137–138
  for conduct problems, 137–141
  nature of, 138–141
  by teachers, 94, 139–141, 142, 145

Race
  of participants in study, 17
  perceptions of school and, 6–7
  school composition based on, 33–35
  social class influences and, 40–41
Radke-Yarrow, M., 158
Ramsay, P. D. K., 127
Ransom, E., 167
Rawls, J., 189
Ray, C. A., 6
Reifler, J. P., 10
Reiss, I. L., 174
Reitman, S. W., 189, 199

Rejection, of school, 5–6
Reproduction theories, 67–68
Resistance, to school, 5–6
Reynolds, M. C., 106
Rice, W. K., Jr., 187
Richey, L., 85
Rist, R. C., 10, 43, 70, 109
Rock, D., 69
Rodman, H., 147, 154, 168
Rohrkemper, M. M., 3, 169
Role models, parents as, 149, 150–152, 175
Rosenberg, L. A., 10
Rosenberg, M., 42, 187
Rosenberg, P., 6, 69, 70
Rosenholtz, S. J., 42, 70, 126, 154, 169
Rosenthal, R., 10
Rowan, B., 105
Rumberger, R. W., 109, 169
Rutledge, D. D., 129
Rutter, M., 129, 145

Sabornie, E. J., 103
Sachs, J. J., 85
Safran, J. S., 129
Safran, S. P., 129
St. John, N., 154
Salvia, J., 10
Sanford, J. P., 105
Sapon-Shevin, M., 106
Saucier, J. F., 154
Schallert, D. L., 7
Scheck, D. C., 154
Schmelkin, L. P., 103
Schmuck, P., 23
Schmuck, R., 23
Schoenborn, C. A., 109, 129
School
    aggressive behavior and, 128–129
    conflict theory and, 1–2
    impact of, on self-concept of students, 111–114
    influence of family on, 194
    as non-neutral setting, 193
    parental influence on, 25–26, 27–28, 154–157, 166–167
    segregation of, by social class, 29–32
    student affect toward, 70–73
    student evaluations of, 77–80
    student images of, 75–77
    student perceptions of, 6–9, 69–80
School composition
    community class divisions and, 23–26
    nature of high- and low-income schools, 26–29
    race in, 33–35
    social class in, 29–33
    student perceptions of, 29–32
    student preferences for, 33–35
Schooler, C., 8, 43, 142
Schooling in Capitalist America (Bowles and Gintis), 1–2
Schostak, J. F., 146
Schultz, G. F., 194
Schulz, E. M., 187
Schunk, D. H., 145, 194
Schwartz, G., 9, 44, 67, 109
Scott-Jones, D., 154
Scrupski, A., 43
Seeman, M., 194
Seginer, R., 10, 154, 168
Segregation, school and community, 24–26
Self-concept, of students, 109–127
    impact of school on, 111–114
    intelligence in, 117–124
    participation in school activities and, 124–125
    school evaluation role in, 114–117
    social class and, 4, 37–38, 42, 59–62, 193–195
    strengths and weaknesses in, 110–111
Self-reports, problems of, 191
Sexton, P. C., 27
Shapiro, H. S., 1
Shimahara, N. K., 6, 45
Shipman, V., 147
Shor, I., 103
Sieber, R. T., 8, 107, 199, 200
Simmons, R. G., 42, 187
Simpson, C., 42, 70, 126, 154, 169
Sinclair, R., 125
Skrtic, T., 145
Slavings, R. L., 10
Sleeter, C. E., 7, 9, 70, 106
Smith, D. C., 129
Smith, E. R., 36, 41, 69, 187
Snyder, H., 168
Social class
    as basis for punishment received, 139–141, 142, 145
    cliques vs., 44
    community and, 23–26

Social class (*continued*)
  cross-class vs. intraclass violence, 131
  educational attainment and, 154–157
  friendship and, 165–166
  group classifications and, 45–52
  impact of school on perception of, 194–
    195
  increasing segregation and isolation by,
    23–26, 168
  intergroup perceptions and, 54–55
  nature of high- and low-income schools,
    26–29
  perceptions of, 8–9, 35–37, 195–199
  segregation of schools by, 29–32
  self-identification of, 4, 37–38, 42, 59–62,
    193–195
  separation of community by, 12–13
  social cognition approach to studying,
    2–4
  social mobility and, 38–39, 42
  student identification with parents', 43–45,
    52–53
  track level and, 84, 104
  transmission of, in schools, 1–2
  underclass in, 16
  within-class variations in cognitions and,
    6–7
Social cognitions
  school rejection and resistance in, 5–6
  shifts in, 8–9
  in studying social class influences on
    schooling, 2–4
  understanding, 4–5
  within-class variations in, 6–7
  within-subject complexities in, 7–8
Social determinism, 8
Socialization, 147, 169
  school-based ability formation in,
    126
  by schools, 104
  school structure and, 3–4
Social mobility, 19, 45
  equal opportunity and, 180–182
  between groups, 63–64
  intergenerational, 184
  student attitudes toward, 182–185
  student opinions about, 38–39, 42
Social skills, of students, 111
Solomon, R. P., 5
Sorensen, A. B., 43, 70, 105
Spade, J. Z., 105

Special education, 80
  parent involvement and, 156
  student perceptions of, 70, 85–90, 105–
    106
  student self-assessment of education and,
    122
Special-interest groups, 53, 61, 62
Sroufe, L. A., 157
Stainback, S., 106
Stainback, W., 106
Stanford, S., 63, 157
Steinberg, L., 128
Sternberg, R. J., 109
Stipek, D. J., 187
Strahan, D., 125
Strauss, A., 19–20
Strauss, C., 145
Student–teacher ratios, 29
Subject strengths, of students, 110
Subordinate groups, 48–51
Sugai, G., 85
Super, C. M., 11, 154
Switzky, H. N., 194

Tajfel, H., 4, 41
Teachers
  attributes of, 96–101
  conflict with, 131, 135–137, 172
  parental contact with, 157
  perception of students by, 10
  punishment of students by, 94, 139–141,
    142, 145
  student conflict with, 131, 135–137
  student perceptions of, 70, 91–101, 107–
    108
  transfer of, and school composition, 28
Thiessen, D., 85
Thomas, S., 109
Thompson, E. P., 2
Thompson, J. B., 5, 69, 105
Thorkildsen, T. A., 69
Thorne, B., 57
Thornton, H., 85
Thurlow, M. L., 85
Tilley, C., 168
Tinney, J. S., 199
Tochon, F. V., 10
Toles, T., 187
Tomlinson, S., 106
Tracking, 56, 80–84, 104–105
  methods of, 81–82

social class and, 84, 104
  student perceptions of, 70, 82–84, 104, 106
Truancy, 134–135
Tyack, D. B., 200

Underclass, 16
United States Bureau of the Census, 12

Vaneck, H. J., 25
Vanfossen, B. E., 105
Varenne, H., 4, 44–45, 66
Veldman, D. J., 105
Vernberg, E. M., 11, 129
Violence
  of low-income students, 144, 146
  See also Conduct problems
Voydanoff, P., 147, 154, 168

Wagner, R. K., 109
Walberg, H. J., 103, 106, 145
Walker, L. J., 157
Walker, S., 2
Wang, M. C., 106, 109
Wealth
  social class self-identification and, 37–38
  student perceptions of, 35–37
Weffer, R. E., 124
Weiner, B., 169
Weinstein, R. S., 3, 70, 109
Weis, L., 6
Wexler, P., 2, 4, 57

Whitty, G., 69, 192
Williams, R., 2
Willis, P., 4–7, 42, 45, 66, 70, 102, 126, 171,
  200
Wilson, A. B., 41
Wilson, A. P., 109
Wilson, P., 200
Wilson, W. J., 16, 23, 188
Winikur, D. W., 70
Winn, W., 109
Witt, J. C., 191
Wolman, C., 85
Work, post-high school opportunities for, 186,
  188–189
Work habits, of students, 110, 131–132
World War II, class struggle after, 8
Wyche, L. G., Sr., 85
Wynne, E. A., 145

Yoshida, R. K., 85
Young, R., 5, 9
Ysseldyke, J. E., 85
Yussen, S. R., 109

Zahn-Waxler, C., 158
Zane, N., 7, 69
Zeichner, K., 1
Zelditch, M., Jr., 126
Zigler, E. F., 187
Zigmond, N., 85
Zill, N., 109, 129

About the Author

Ellen Brantlinger teaches in the Division of Special Education in the Department of Curriculum and Instruction at Indiana University in Bloomington. In addition to her interest in the social class influences on schooling, she does research in and teaches about education for diverse students in integrated settings and sexuality and family life education for people with disabilities. Prior to university-level teaching, she worked in a deinstitutionalization project and taught secondary social studies and special education in Massachusetts, California, Ohio, and Indiana. She received her undergraduate degree from Antioch College in Yellow Springs, Ohio, and her doctorate from Indiana University.